Laws of the Wild™

Apocalypse Second Edition

Laws of the Wild

Credits

Written by: Thomas M. K. Stratman

Development by: Richard E. Dansky

Editing by: Cynthia Summers, Ken Cliffe, Ed Hall, Cary Goff and Allison Sturms

Previously published material has appeared in: Werewolf: The Apocalypse Second Edition, Masquerade Second Edition, Laws of the Night, Oblivion and Apocalypse

Art Direction by: Lawrence Snelly

Photographs by: Ronni Radner

Models: Mike Chaney, Tim Hargrove, Rob Hatch, Laura Perkinson, Rebecca Schaefer

Cover Design: Jeff Holt and Katie McCaskill

Layout and typesetting by: Katie McCaskill

Help Above and Beyond the Call: The Wonder Interns: Donna, Laurah and Lori

Special Thanks To:

Chad "Gettin' Leid" Brown, for obstinately refusing to do something stupid enough to be mentioned as a Special Thanks.

Ken "Wild Man of Borneo" Cliffe, for letting his hair down on the bus.

Aaron "Pretty in…whatever" Voss, for his radical interpretation of Richard Butler's vocals.

Brian "Gutter" Glass, for being That Guy all the time.

Rob "Material Grrrrrl" Hatch, for, well, you had to be there. You really had to be there.

And Extra-Special Thanks to our playtesters:

The Coterie of the Silent Voice Playtest team: Marc "Spence" Spencer, Tori Mauslein, Dan Hawthorne, David Blackwell, Renee Hawthorne, Glenys McGhee, Dave Cole, Mike Porter, Mike Chambers, Geoff Hinkle, Christa Hinkle, David Hoelscher, Mike Metcalf, Brian Gates, Misty Melton, Sandy Duda, Brian Hare, Carolyn Smith and Tom Stratman

Associated Folks from Colombia, MO: Quimbie Olmstead, James Ernst, Clinton Hayes, Francis J. Saunders, Mark W. Sprinkle and Pamela Jo Lord

The Daring Denizens of Worcester, MA, led by the infamous H. MacKiernan, Stephanie Apprille, Andrew LaPorte, Kathy Journeay, J. Bendonis, Jesse Perry, Christopher Chaney, Christopher Mello, Tara Halwes, Seann Ives, Steve Langer, Jony Balboni, Elizabeth Ditchburn and Kerry Campbell (whew!)

Check out White Wolf online at
http://www.white-wolf.com; alt.games.whitewolf
and rec.games.frp.storyteller

735 PARK NORTH BLVD.
SUITE 128
CLARKSTON, GA 30021
WHITE WOLF USA
GAME STUDIO

PRINTED IN CANADA

Table of Contents

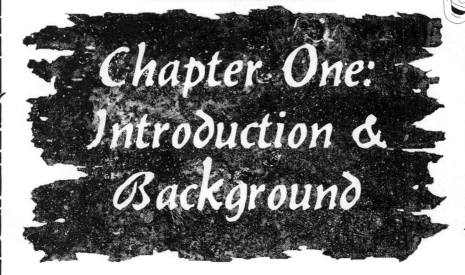

Chapter One: Introduction & Background

What This Book Is

You hold in your hands **Laws of the Wild**, the second edition of live-action **Werewolf** rules for **Mind's Eye Theatre**. In essence, this book is a second edition of **Apocalypse**, with revised and updated rules to make gameplay faster, smoother and more enjoyable for everyone.

The game is still **Apocalypse**. It's just that the rules have changed — for the better.

The Rules of Safety

Behave yourself so that everyone can enjoy this game. **Apocalypse** is to be played in the home, at conventions or at other safe locations. At all times, you should remember that it is a game, only a game, and nothing but a game. If you feel yourself getting too wrapped up in what's going on, take a time-out and step back from gameplay for a moment. It's for your own good.

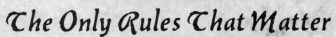
The Only Rules That Matter

Here are the rules of **Mind's Eye Theatre** (**MET**), the only rules that absolutely must always be obeyed. These are common sense rules to keep everyone — other players, yourself, strangers in the area and the police — safe and happy with your game.

These rules are designed to limit the opportunities anyone has to destroy the fun of your game. They're not intended to interfere with gameplay or your enjoyment; they're here to make sure that you play sensibly and safely.

#1 – It's Only a Game

This is by far the most important rule. If a character is killed, if a plot falls apart, if a rival wins the day — it's still only a game. Don't take things too seriously, as that will spoil not only your fun, but also the fun of everyone around you.

Leave the game behind when it ends. Playing **Apocalypse** is a lot of fun; spending time talking about the game is great. However, calling the person who plays the sept alpha at 4:13 A.M. on Sunday to discuss an idea your character has for a new rite is another matter entirely. Make sure to keep a little perspective.

#2 – No Touching

Never actually have physical contact with other players, no matter how careful you are. Accidents happen, and someone will get hurt. Rely on the rules to cover physical logistics.

#3 – No Stunts

Never climb, jump, run, leap or swing from anything during a game. Keep the "action" in your action low-key. If you can imagine you're a werewolf, you can imagine that you're leaping from rooftop to rooftop. Avoid attracting the attention of people who aren't playing, and use your imagination to its fullest.

#4 – No Weapons

Fake or real weapons of any sort are absolutely forbidden. Even obviously silly toy weapons are not allowed. Such props give other people the wrong impression as to what you are doing, and in the dark they could conceivably be mistaken for the real thing. Use item cards to represent weapons instead.

#5 – No Drugs or Drinking

This one is a real no-brainer. Drugs and alcohol do not create peak performance. They reduce your ability to think and react, meaning that, among other things, your roleplaying ability will be impaired. Players impaired by drugs or alcohol are a danger to other players, and to the game as a whole. There's nothing wrong with *playing* a character who's drunk or stoned, but actually bringing such stuff to a game is in bad taste at best and illegal at worst. Don't do it.

#6 - Be Mindful of Others

Remember, not everyone you see, or who sees you, is playing the game. A game can be unnerving or even frightening to passersby. Be considerate of nonplayers in your vicinity, and make sure that if you are in a public area, your gameplay actions are not going to alarm anyone. Trying to explain to a policeman at 3 A.M. that you didn't really kill your friend, your Black Fury just "throated" him, is often an exercise in futility.

#7 - The Rules Are Flexible

Feel free to ignore or adjust any of the rules in this book if it will make your game better. We at White Wolf call this "The Golden Rule." If some rule included in this book (besides the ones listed here) doesn't work for your troupe, change it. Just be consistent and fair. Nobody likes rules that change every week or "no-win" scenarios. If your troupe finds a new way to handle, say, the Umbra, that works better for you than the one in this book, go for it. The idea is to have fun.

#8 - Have Fun

Not "Win." Not "Go out and kill everyone else." Just "Have fun." The object of **Apocalypse** is not to win. In fact, there are no rules for "winning." The goal is to tell great stories, not to achieve superiority over the other players. In **Apocalypse** it's not about how the game ends, it's about the journey and what happens along the way.

What Is Storytelling?

We have been telling each other stories since the earliest days, when cavemen gathered around the fire to act out tales of their hunts. We painted cave walls, pressed reeds into soft clay tablets, inked papyrus and vellum, performed plays, illuminated manuscripts, printed books, filmed movies, scripted radio and television shows, and programmed computers. Now, one of the newest methods of storytelling is actually a return to the oldest form. Live-action roleplaying (LARP), which grew out of the tabletop roleplaying games of the '70s, is just the kind of "participatory" taletelling that we can still recognize among cultures around the globe. It features the same emphasis on character and story that you can find in the myths of our most ancient cultures, and that led to the creation of what we call "storyteller" games. The book you hold in your hands is an attempt to explore those universal tales of the Hero's Journey.

What Is *Mind's Eye Theatre?*

This game is probably different from any game you have played before. In many ways, it is really not a game at all. **Laws of the Wild** is more concerned with stories than with winning, rules, game boards or dice. You will find that this game has more in common with childhood games of adventure than with card games or *Monopoly*-type board games. This book contains all the information necessary to catapult you into worlds of imagination. You create the action, and you choose your own paths. We have a name for this style of game. We call it **Mind's Eye Theatre**.

Playing **Mind's Eye Theatre** is like being in a movie. You and your friends portray the main characters, but the script follows your decisions. The director of this improvisational movie is called the Storyteller; he, along with his assistants, called Narrators, creates the stage and the minor characters with whom you interact during your adventure. Most scenes are played out in real-time, and always in character. You should only break character when there is a rules dispute or a change of scene that requires adjudication from the Storyteller or Narrators.

In **Mind's Eye Theatre**, there are no limits to the worlds you can explore. In **Laws of the Wild**, you will come to discover the threat of the impending Apocalypse that looms over Gaia. You assume the persona of one of Her guardians, and learn what it is to be a werewolf, one of the people called the Garou.

The Character

When you play **Laws of the Wild**, you take on the persona of a Garou, a defender of the world's natural places against the ravages of all who would corrupt, defile and destroy those few that remain. Your character can be anyone from any walk of life. The only limit on your character concept (besides the rules) is your imagination. You create a character, then roleplay her over the course of a story and perhaps a chronicle (a series of connected stories). You decide what your character does and says. You decide what risks to accept or to decline.

During the game, you speak as your character. Unless you're talking to a Narrator or Storyteller, whatever you say is what your character says. Because most of what a **Mind's Eye Theatre** player perceives depends on the characters around him, players must be vivid and expressive. The characters direct the plot, but at the same time the events of the game guide and develop the characters, helping them to achieve the story's goals. To an extent, as a player in a storytelling game, you have a responsibility beyond simply portraying your character. You need to consider the story as a whole and your role in making sure that other players enjoy the game.

Creating a character for **Apocalypse** is easy and only takes a few moments. Only a few things are necessary to define a basic character, and once you've done that, you can play the game. There's another phase to creating a character, though, one that makes playing **Mind's Eye Theatre** all the more rewarding. Your character should be more than just a series of Traits and numbers. Rather, she should be a living, breathing person with a past, motives, drives, likes, dislikes — everything you want to see from a character in a movie or a novel. So it's probably a good idea to take time to figure out *who* your character is as well as what she is *before* you start playing. While certain details and personality traits will come out while you're playing her, you'll want to have the basics in place before you start playing. It's just like an actor asking his director for his character's motivation.

Characters are the heart and soul of a story. Without them, all the patient efforts of the Storyteller would be for naught. Appreciate the Storyteller's efforts by following the rules and taking an active part in the game.

Narrators

In **Apocalypse**, Narrators are the people who help the Storyteller present adventures. Narrators are the impartial judges who describe scenes and events that cannot be staged, adjudicate rules, and occasionally play the roles of antagonists. Generally, enlisting the aid of one Narrator for every 10 players makes for a good ratio. The best number of Narrators for your game usually depends on the gaming experience of the players; the more experienced your players, in all probability, the fewer Narrators they'll need. Narrators usually play characters of their own, as well as helping out in certain situations. That way they can be a part of the action instead of just trying to correct it from the outside.

Storyteller

Every game must have a Storyteller, who serves as the ultimate authority and final judge in any game of **Apocalypse** you play. The Storyteller creates the basic elements of the plot, and makes sure that the story unfolds well — in addition to doing everything the Narrators do. Storytelling is a demanding job, but it is also a very rewarding one, for it is the Storyteller who creates the framework upon which the players build their experiences.

The Storyteller makes certain the story has content, interesting hooks and a narrative flow. This does not mean that a Storyteller should just sit back and dictate the plot — characters who don't have free will are no fun to play. Instead, a Storyteller creates the "framework" elements of the plot, then turns players loose in order to see what happens.

During the game, the Storyteller must be watchful and ready to create new elements to make sure that the story works out well. He is also responsible for safety, ensuring that all of the players have something to do and that everyone is abiding by the rules. Although performing all of these tasks simultaneously can be exhausting, the sense of accomplishment gained from creating a successful story makes the whole process worthwhile.

In the end, the goal of **Apocalypse** is for everyone to have fun.

Props

Props can be anything that the Storyteller approves to help you define your character, including costumes, makeup and jewelry. Have fun and employ any props that you feel are necessary to enhance your character. However, if you have any doubts as to whether a prop (such as anything remotely resembling a weapon) will be allowed in-game, consult your Storyteller and abide by her decision.

Werewolf: The Apocalypse

The basic premise of **Laws of the Wild** is derived from the table-top roleplaying game **Werewolf: The Apocalypse**. It is not necessary to own or know **Werewolf** in order to play **Apocalypse**, but the world of **Werewolf** has many useful source materials that can be adapted easily for games based on **Laws of the Wild**.

Elegantly Simple

This game was designed to be easy to learn and even easier to play. **Apocalypse** is a storytelling game. The rules are aimed at resolving conflicts quickly so that players can stay with the story without ever stepping outside their characters in order to figure out what happens. We have made every effort to create rules that maintain the integrity of the story and the background in which the story is set.

With this book as your guide, you will be able to tell stories about the secret defenders of the Earth. In **Apocalypse**, you take the part of a Garou, a werewolf. Together with your shapeshifter brethren, you must heed Gaia's cry for help and try to defend the remaining wild places of the world. Welcome to **Mind's Eye Theater: Laws of the Wild**.

A World of Darkness

The fictional world of **Laws of the Wild** is, in many ways, just like our world. Children are born, grow up, go to school, follow careers, grow old and die. The sun rises and sets day after day. In the World of Darkness, however, everything is just a little grittier, a little more corrupt and a little more tainted. Gang warfare is rampant. Poor areas are even more impoverished. Even the "nice" places are tainted with a hint of something dark and corrupt. This darkness is expressed in the ambiance of Gothic art, demonstrated by the feelings expressed in the architecture of high cathedral ceilings, gargoyles and towering, grotesque structures that pierce the night sky. It is also expressed in raw rage, random violence and rebellion — basic elements of the Punk movement. Gothic-Punk is a synthesis of both moods, and, in **Laws of the Wild**, it is represented in a very different way than you might expect.

Mystic Modern Primitive

Werewolves in this game are not the same creatures as those who stalk across movie screens, looking for oversexed teenagers to shred. The Garou of **Laws of the Wild** are mythic symbols of ancient times given life in the modern age. What it means to be a Garou, a protector of Gaia, is not easily understood even by the Garou themselves. It is simply what they are. The Garou are neither wolves who turn into humans nor humans who turn into wolves. They are a separate race in and of themselves, with unique customs, ways and perspectives. Unlike the werewolves of the movie screen, the Garou are born either as wolves or as humans, and only learn their full identities when they take on other forms after they mature. The Garou are an ancient species with a lineage that reaches back before history, and they can trace their bloodlines back to the days when humans first stood erect and used fire to drive back the darkness.

This game is about people, all kinds of people, who are doing their best to get through life after the revelation of their true nature. No longer just humans or wolves, they are shapeshifters, a dying Earth's last protectors against the terrible forces that grow stronger in the night.

In the modern world, Garou have to deal with technology and civilization while retaining their mythic roots. In this respect, they have become both modern and primitive, as their mystical nature (especially in the world of rites, spirits and totems) is still the most vital part of who they are.

The Garou are honorable, noble, savage, uncanny, proud, angry, heroic, monstrous, adaptable, wise, mysterious and tenacious. The Garou believe themselves to be the defenders of Gaia, the Earth, although if you ask several Garou who, or what, Gaia is, you'll get several different answers. (It is important to understand that all of these ideas are considered to be correct by one group or another — arguing over what exactly Gaia is has become a favorite pastime of more philosophically minded werewolves.) The Garou defend Gaia from the Wyrm, a very real manifestation of the destructive impulse to consume, taint and destroy. Not only is the Wyrm real, but its servants — evil spirits and humans under its thrall — are powerful and nearly omnipresent, especially in the cities. The war against the Wyrm is a battle that predates the first cities, and one that is slowly being lost. The Garou are losing because most have allowed the Wyrm into their own hearts and minds. In order to win, the Garou must become heroic once again, taking up the mantle of all the qualities they claim to possess. They must defeat the monsters within by exerting self-restraint, virtue, wisdom and genuine courage.

The Silver Record: A History of the Garou

The Garou's most sacred writing, the Silver Record, describes how their race emerged from the raw earth, and how they carved their grand mythic past out of the world primeval. The Record is a collection of Garou glyphs and symbols, each of which marks an important stanza in the epic poem. The Record speaks of the time when the Garou were appointed to be the defenders

of Mother Gaia, who can be seen as the entire Earth, all of existence or both. The Record tells of how the Garou were given the power of changing, the strength of Rage, the insight of Gnosis and the freedom of spirit-walking. These were the birth-gifts given by the Four Winds, the Gifts the Garou were given by Luna, the moon and Gaia's sister.

The Garou's Birth-Gifts

As part of their unique heritage, Garou can control the shapes they wear. A Garou chooses to take a specific form anywhere on a spectrum ranging from human to wolf. Garou may assume the form of a natural wolf (Lupus), a mighty dire wolf form (Hispo), fully human (Homid), bestial human (Glabro), or the most powerful and frightening form (Crinos), the half-wolf/half-man shape. In Crinos, Garou are towering monsters and deadly warriors.

Garou are creatures of Rage and Gnosis. Their Rage, when channeled properly, enables them to move and act with unnatural speed. Their Gnosis allows them to tap into the spiritual wealth of Gaia to use Gifts in Her service. All Garou are beings of two worlds: our Earth and the spirit world, called the Umbra. They can move into this spirit world, where the spiritual is real and our reality is only a shadowy reflection. Entering the Umbra is commonly called "stepping sideways," or "reaching," by more traditional Garou.

The Record also speaks of the Gifts that the moon gave to the Garou. Luna is revered for her mystical knowledge, but is also reviled for the consuming madness that she brings. Luna waxes and wanes, growing full and slipping away to nothingness. The Moon is at the same time the Garou's mentor and their crazy aunt, the teacher of secrets and the giver of madness.

It is said that Luna took the first Garou to her lodge in the sky and taught them secret knowledge. She looked into each Garou's heart and saw what phase the moon was in at the Garou's birth, then provided the Garou with Gifts to fit each one's personality. This tale accounts for what are called auspices, roles in Garou society determined by the phase of moon under which a Garou is born. A Garou's auspice determines not only his role in society, but also some of the secret lore with which he is familiar, and, to an extent, his personality as well.

The Sacred Ways of the Garou

Over the centuries, many spirits have given wisdom and knowledge of special powers to the Garou. These powers and secrets are shared among the other members of a Garou's breed and auspice, and also serve to further define a Garou's purpose and role within a tribe.

The Tribes

Among Garou, the tribe is part heritage and part community. When a Garou is among the members of his tribe, he is not only participating in Garou society, he is also connecting to the wisdom of Garou in the same tribe. The tribe shapes a Garou's political outlook, viewpoints on human society and general perspective.

The Record speaks of the Forgotten Times, when there were no tribes to divide the Garou Nation. During the millennia that followed, packs took to different ideologies and spread out to different breeding areas. Those differences developed into 16 groupings of Garou, called tribes. Of those 16 tribes, 13 remain: the *Black Furies* (all-female alphas who followed their own path along the Mediterranean coasts), the *Bone Gnawers* (scavengers and survivors who seek refuge and anonymity in the streets of the cities), the *Children of Gaia* (who seek peace and reunification of all the Garou), the *Fianna* (bold, brash warrior-poets of Ireland), the *Get of Fenris* (who live for battle and a glorious death, and are usually of Teutonic stock), the *Glass Walkers* (builders and shapers who moved into the cities and learned to use the tools of humanity), the *Red Talons* (predatory wolf-born hunters of humans), the *Shadow Lords* (schemers and politicians who hail from Slavic lands), the *Silent Striders* (secretive soothsayers and wanderers who vanished into Africa, only to re-emerge centuries later), the *Silver Fangs* (rulers and noble warrior-heroes touched by madness), the *Stargazers* (mystical, philosophical Garou who watch the skies for learning), the *Uktena* (cunning shaman-warriors of the American Southwest), and the *Wendigo* (ever-proud "Pure Ones" of Native American stock).

Those Garou without a tribe are called the Ronin, for they have no tutors or masters. These people are usually renunciates, in voluntary or forced exile from their tribes, and they do not seek to help or hinder the Garou. Most Garou perceive Ronin to be at least partially of the Wyrm, and therefore shun them. The Ronin are mysterious, shadowy and distrusted.

Those Who Have Been Lost

Three tribes of the original 16 have been lost: the *Croatan* (the "Pure Ones" who sacrificed themselves to defend the Pure Lands from the Wyrm), the *Bunyip* (who died at the hands of their brothers in Australia), and the *White Howlers* (Pictish Garou who succumbed to the seduction of the Wyrm, and are now known as the *Black Spiral Dancers*).

During prehistory, after humans captured the secret of fire and began hunting other animals for more than just the food they needed, a great Garou council ordained that the Garou must watch over the humans in much the same way a shepherd watches over his flock. Included in this oversight was the culling of human herds to keep their numbers at safe levels. This millennium-long practice, which the Garou called "The Impergium," turned out to have little effect. The humans prospered anyway, building their own civilizations in the Fertile Crescent and the East. Accusations brought by the Shadow Lords and Red Talons against tribes they blamed for allowing this unchecked growth eventually led to the reconsideration of the whole idea — and to war. After every tribe became embroiled in the conflict, a grand council was held and the Impergium was ended, three thousand years after it had begun. The legacy of the Impergium haunts the Garou to this day.

But, for a time, all Garou prospered, and the Wyrm was held at bay.

The Triat

Three powerful spirits that each embody a fundamental force in the universe are collectively referred to as the Triat. They are the Wyld (which is pure creative energy, and chaos), the Weaver (which is stability, order and form) and the Wyrm (which is corruption, decay and oblivion). Together they form the balance of nature. Something went horribly wrong with the balance of the Triat — no one is quite certain how. The Weaver went insane and attempted to encase everything in her webs. In her spinning and weaving, she captured Wyrm, and Wyrm, maddened with pain and rage, now seeks to devour all of Gaia.

The Garou believe that humans are children of mad Weaver, flaunting their technology and cities as they try to impress order upon everything. They also believe that wolves are of the Wyld, as are all natural and untainted places in the wilderness. Consequently, many feel that the metis, the breed that results from two Garou mating, are of the Wyrm. This is hardly the case, although all metis bear some disfigurement, which is considered a mark of corruption (and therefore a mark of the Wyrm) by many Garou.

Avatars of the Wyrm manifest in many forms, while the actual Wyrm resides in a metaphorical Pattern Web. The spirit army of the Wyrm consists of corrupted incarnations of nature, evil animal spirits, tainted elements and so on, all of which represent the Wyrm's corrupting influence and power. Many humans unknowingly serve the Wyrm as well, especially when they do corrupt or destructive things. Moreover, the Wyrm has wrapped its tendrils around many aspects of modern daily life. Soft drinks, the movie industry, comics, politicians — the list goes on and on. Indeed, the Wyrm lies waiting for anyone seeking power in this world.

The Wyrm is quite powerful in these last days. Its spirit armies grow in the dark realm of Malfeas. Its Wyrm-infested human servitors (called fomori) spread out across the planet, and its followers in the major corporations of the world, especially a powerful corporation called Pentex, do the Wyrm's bidding on a global scale.

The Wyrm is an ever-present threat to the Garou, and its Black Spiral Dancers are everywhere. The Wyrm has also revealed ancient evil lore to humans who are Kinfolk of the Garou, preying on the jealousy some feel for their Garou kin. The ritual that these humans learned is capable of changing them into Garou — but only by means of a process utilizing the prepared skins of slain werewolves. These Skindancers, as they are called, are worse than the warped Black Spiral Dancers in many ways, for they appear as normal Garou to all but the most keenly sensitive mystics.

The War for Gaia

The Garou are at war with the Wyrm and the Weaver, taking the front lines in the last defense of Gaia and the Wyld. Many also believe that these are the last days of that war, that the prophecies of the Apocalypse are coming true before their eyes, and that the end of all things, even Gaia, is near. This threat of Armageddon influences all of the Garou's actions. The more unstable Garou tend to fluctuate between the extremes of frenzy, in which they are totally consumed with hatred of the Wyrm, and Harano, in which they are totally overwhelmed by the imbalance of the fight they wage and become utterly depressed. The balance that the Garou strive to attain is somewhere between those extremes.

The Legacy of Lore

The signs of the Apocalypse have been foretold in countless prophecies, and many of these predictions of impending doom have already come true. It is difficult to doubt that these are the last times. Because of the immediacy of the war against the Wyrm, the Garou have had to adapt their ways and traditions to the modern world and the demands of the current crisis. In recent centuries, the Garou had grown standoffish, uniting along tribal lines and ignoring others of their kind. Now all of the tribes have been thrown together by Fate, and they must find ways to interact and function.

The key to this cooperation lies in the Litany, an ancient collection of laws given from the very first Garou onward. The Garou maintain and build upon the Litany to help them combat the Wyrm within, as well as the Wyrm without, through ancient proven practices and wise insights.

Among the proscriptions in the Litany is the restriction that Garou shall not mate with Garou. When two Garou mate, they produce a sterile, disfigured breed of Garou called a metis, although sometimes such a fetus will not even come to term. Mating with another Garou is a taboo similar to incest. Since the presence of a metis is a direct result of a violation of the Litany, metis Garou aren't well-received, especially if their disfigurements are obvious.

Another important idea in the Litany is "the Veil," a custom which dictates that the Garou must forever hide their presence from the mass of humanity and keep their existence and sacred knowledge secret. The Veil is reinforced by the power of the Delirium, a masking effect caused by the Garou's prehistoric participation in the Impergium. This effect is useful in keeping the Veil because as a result of the Delirium humans have a difficult time remembering the presence of a rampaging Garou. When a Garou reveals himself in Crinos form, he triggers an ancient memory in human minds which results in an all-consuming fear. The human mind, overwhelmed, usually responds by rationalizing and blocking out the memory of the Garou.

Finally, many Garou legends and stories are preserved as a means to keep history, illuminate Garou wisdom and serve as object lessons for Garou wanting to become as famous as the heroes of yore. Yet the Wyrm continually captures and devours bits and pieces of the vast legacy of lore that has been left for the Garou. This is part of the Wyrm's ultimate plan to destroy them.

Others Who Dwell in Darkness

The Garou claim the whole Earth as their territory, and can turn up anywhere. They aren't restricted to the cities or banned from them. However, the Garou are not alone in the World of Darkness. They must contend with many other supernatural peoples and entities.

Among the traditional enemies of the Garou are the Kindred, vampires, who are called Leeches by the Garou. Because vampires feed on blood, often employ dark powers and dwell in the Wyrm-infested cities, the Garou believe them to be of the Wyrm. The interaction between Garou and Kindred constantly fluctuates between uneasy peace and all-out war. The Garou tend to watch the vampires of an area and often seek to limit their influence without openly assaulting them, while a city's vampires will pick off the occasional nosy Garou without inciting full-scale battles. In the end, the Garou and the Kindred could easily assure each other's destruction, so they slowly circle each other for now, daring one another to make the first move. Usually, the Gangrel clan of vampires interacts most successfully with the Garou (see p. 245), as the Gangrel are closest to werewolves in temperament.

The Garou also share the World of Darkness with mages, humans who command strange powers and often seek out Garou as sources of lore and mystic energy. Cloaked in mystery and often working as servants of the Weaver, mages are widely distrusted and disliked by the Garou. Only those few mages who speak for Gaia have found some acceptance.

The dark spirits of the dead, called wraiths, are often glimpsed hovering just outside the range of Garou perception, although what they wish of the Garou is still clouded in mystery. They seem to be particularly attracted to huge Garou battles, so much so that they have been called "war crows," as they often hover in the Dark Umbra around a battlefield. Silent Striders in particular find themselves haunted by wraiths, many of whom demand assistance from the Garou.

Many Garou have relations with the faerie folk, the changelings of Earth who, born as humans, have discovered their faerie origins and now lead dual lives. The Fianna in particular have good relations with these enigmatic but powerful and slightly mad creatures.

Other shapeshifters also inhabit the world. In ancient times, the werebears (Gurahl), wererats (Ratkin), wereravens (Corax), werecoyotes (Nuwisha), werecats (Bastet), werelizards (Mokolé), werespiders (Ananasi) and other lycanthropes grew and prospered alongside the Garou. However, in their ignorance, the Garou started a great War of Rage against the other Bête, or shapechangers. Now these other shapeshifters are mostly in hiding. Their numbers are few, and they thirst for revenge. Only the Nuwisha and the Corax have peaceful and regular dealings with the Garou.

There are some humans who take it upon themselves to hunt the Garou. These hunters see werewolves as monsters who wantonly destroy human life. Perhaps such humans are attuned to the racial memories of the times when the Garou used to cull their ancestors from the "herds." Perhaps they are simply reacting to the Delirium in a violent fashion, perhaps they serve the Wyrm, or perhaps they see Garou as some kind of diabolic evil that must be cleansed. Some hunters are undoubtedly thrillseekers and glory hounds, for the Garou are certainly the most dangerous game one can hunt. Whatever their motive, werewolf-hunters are deadly, despite their mortal natures. Some have toughened themselves against the Delirium, and some of them are

Kinfolk to the Garou. Many of them use magical weapons or stolen Garou artifacts. Nearly all use silver in some fashion, for just as the legends say, silver weapons cause Garou horrible agony. A Garou must walk lightly when dealing with hunters; one misstep may rip the Veil to tatters.

Still, despite the presence of many potential foes stalking the streets of the World of Darkness, it is the Garou themselves who are their own worst enemies. This is in part because of the nature of Garou society.

Garou Society

Garou are as much wolf as human, and their society reflects this fact. They have two families: the normal families of their birth and the Garou families of their tribes, breeds, auspices, septs and packs. The bonds of what they are affect duties, romance and friendships. Issues of dominance, station, territory and the pack are strongly influenced by the lupine heritage of the Garou.

The Pack

The pack is more than a family to a Garou. Anyone who is a member of a pack will risk her life for a packmate. A Garou stands by her pack in all things, even when not in complete agreement with her packmates. In fact, many Garou do not totally get along with their packmates, yet internecine squabbles quickly vanish when the pack faces a threat.

Many Garou instinctively know when a member of their pack is in danger. Over time, this mystical bond strengthens so that a pack appears to move and fight as one, its members perfectly integrating themselves in any action. In addition, the adoption of a pack totem, which serves as an almost parental tie to the Garou who choose it, helps the pack fulfill its purpose.

Many packs are formed from groups of Garou that undergo the Rite of Passage together. The Rite of Passage is what marks a Garou's passage from childhood to full adult status. Sometimes, however, a pack loses all of its members except for one or two, and Garou come together to form a new pack and gain a new totem by the Rite of the Totem.

Each packs chooses a name that is appropriate to its ethics, beliefs and quest. For example, a pack called the Messengers of Unity might be interested in increasing cooperation between all Garou, while a pack called the Spectrum Knights might be a group of chivalrous Garou nobility drawn from every aspect of werewolf society.

Most packs are multitribal, and the most successful of these have most, if not all, of the auspices represented. If a pack contains a metis, the group usually defends the metis from discrimination and attacks when no other Garou will. As the individual members of a pack grow more powerful and higher in Rank and station, they tend to live apart from their packmates. However, their mystical bonds keep them in touch with the others; the bond of the pack is not forgotten. The pack is family, after all, and for many Garou a pack is the only family left to them.

Not all Garou live in packs. Some Garou are never accepted into or even try to be included in a pack. Usually a Garou without a pack has some problem associated with him or her. It is up to septs, the guardians of caerns, to see that these "lone wolves" either get accepted into a pack or at least have something to occupy their time. The Wyrm loves an idle Garou, and many of these "lone wolves" become tools of corruption.

The Sept

There are places of power that the Garou recognize as sacred to Gaia all around the world — in secret places in the wilderness, hidden in city alleyways and in national parks, high atop skyscrapers and deep within caves. These spaces are called caerns, for they originally were dedicated to the honored dead of the Garou. Now each serves as a central gathering point for all the Garou in an area. If a moot is to be held, it will be held at a caern. Each Garou-held caern is guarded by a sept, a collection of Garou who take and hold a caern against the Wyrm. Each sept also has traditional offices, which are usually filled by the most capable Garou around — although in these days it is difficult to find a competent Garou for every position.

There are many packs in a sept. Sometimes, members of a single pack come to hold all the key positions in a sept, and these septs are particularly strong — or tyrannically run.

Sept Positions

Not every sept has all the positions mentioned below. In this case, roles are either "doubled up" or simply ignored, to the detriment of the Garou as a whole.

Sept Alpha and Beta

The alpha is the Garou who is ultimately in charge of the sept and its day-to-day operations. Although the sept alpha is an elder, the position is set above all the other elders, indeed, all of the other Garou in the sept. It is a position of much respect and honor, and the sept leader has the right to demand obedience of all who serve the sept. The sept beta is the alpha's second, and speaks as leader when the alpha is not present.

Warder and Guardians

The Warder is the Garou who is in charge of protecting the caern and keeping it safe. Under her are the Guardians, Garou who aid the Warder with caern security. The Warder has final say in matters concerning the safety of the caern. She cannot call war parties, but if one is called, the Warder dictates who must stay and protect the caern. The Warder has the authority to bar others from the caern, and can "close the caern" in times of danger.

Master of the Rite

The Master of the Rite has authority, as seneschal, over all rites at a caern. All Garou must have permission from the Master of the Rite before a rite is performed at the caern's center. Rites may be performed elsewhere in the area surrounding the caern, which is called the bawn, without this permission, as long as the Rite does not draw attention or cause potential harm to the caern. Generally, it is the Master of the Rite who decides who will take the various roles in the Moot Rite.

Master of the Challenge

The Master of the Challenge is more properly a sept title, but since most ritual challenges take place in a caern, the title is considered a caern title. The Master of the Challenge judges the outcomes of challenges in his purview, and makes sure that all challenges are conducted honorably. The decision of the Master of the Challenge can only be overturned by the unanimous vote of the crowd present. The Master of the Challenge should be fluent in Gamecraft and name-calling, as well as physical combat.

Gatekeeper

The Gatekeeper is the opener and closer of the Moon Bridge. She is in charge of all Moon Bridge travel to and from the caern. It is the Gatekeeper who decides whether a Moon Bridge is opened to another caern. While in this office she holds the Pathstone, a fetish that allows the Gatekeeper to remain in constant contact with the caern's totem in order to open bridges.

Keeper of the Land

The Keeper of the Land is in charge of keeping the bawn, the land around the caern, beautiful and clean. This is not a frivolous position. A bawn that is well-maintained in its natural state shows respect for Gaia and the spirits, and therefore affects their reactions to sept members. The Keeper can recruit other Garou to help in his duties, especially if they are responsible for damaging something in the bawn area.

Den Mother or Father

All Garou of Rank are responsible for aiding the education of the cliath (cubs, children, those without Rank) at a caern, but the Den Mother/Father is the final authority on the cliaths' training. She also protects the cubs during wartime, and keeps them from getting into dangerous mischief. This position has much respect attached to it, as a good Den Mother must have wisdom, patience, stamina and resilience. She may assign any member of the sept to teach a particular lesson to a cliath (usually this is also a refresher course for the Garou chosen).

The Sept and Society

The sept is the main focus of all Garou society. Most Garou social dynamics occur at sept level. Many septs are ruled by a council of elders, which includes those sept members who hold positions of authority, as well as councilors from all the tribes represented in the area. Some septs are ruled by a single tribe; some are governed by Garou from a diverse collection of tribes. Justice tends to be a local affair at a sept. There is usually not enough time to send messengers to the nearest Silver Fang sept to ask questions about whether something is legal or not (Moon Bridges being too costly to use frivolously). It falls to the Master of the Challenge and the sept alpha to decide what is to be done about infractions against the Litany or about intersept conflicts.

The Garou, as a nation, are ruled by many powerful tribal septs. The Silver Fangs have always held the most power, though the Shadow Lords seek to upset their position of authority. It is the Children of Gaia who are most instrumental in maintaining the peace and keeping the Garou on an even course because of their willingness to get between two rivals and make them see the common good. Many Ragabash and most of the Silent Striders serve as messengers between caerns and heralds for the great septs. And Philodox judges of respected rank follow complicated Moon Bridge "circuits" to bring Garou justice to even the farthest reaches of the world.

Protectorates, areas which are guarded and watched by the Garou, are defined by the septs. Septs also define hunting areas and settle disputes between packs and individual Garou. Sept elders enforce punishment for judgments against violators of the Litany, and are the ultimate clearinghouse for Renown as they mark the rise and fall of Glory, Honor and Wisdom among the Garou of their sept.

In short, without access to a sept, a Garou has no way to gain Renown. He is therefore in danger of treading on another's territory, and has no legal presence in the protectorate that the sept claims. Many important rites like the Rite of Accord, the Rite of the Totem and the Moot Rite are not generally available to septless Garou, since these rites require the presence of many Garou and a caern at the site. Since many elder Garou are generally members of a given sept, a sept's territory is also a good place to seek a tutor for knowledge or instruction on a rite.

Polite Introductions

It is traditional to announce one's presence in an area by means of howls or direct introductions when a visitor arrives. If the sept is threatened or otherwise in danger, the Warder may ask visitors to join the guardians of the sept, if only temporarily. However, one thing to remember is that every new sept is a different situation with distinct rules.

When a Garou decides to join a sept, she asks the Warder to mention her name at the next moot. Usually the Galliards use this opportunity to tell what stories they know about the petitioning Garou, and the assembled company decides whether or not the petitioner is worthy.

All in all, a sept is a complicated scene, full of action, intrigue, fellowship and danger. **Laws of the Wild** focuses on the sept as the stage on which many of your **Mind's Eye Theatre** stories will be played. This, by nature, requires the creation of Narrator characters to fill in where needed, unless the story hinges on a position being empty.

Moon Bridges

In addition to being a sacred place of Gaia, a caern is also a means of transportation. From a caern, Garou can step into a Moon Bridge, a mystical tunnel through the spirit world, and can travel long distances to another caern in the twinkling of an eye. It is possible for a Garou to travel all the way around the world without ever relying on terrestrial transportation, simply by making use of Moon Bridges.

Lexicon

A different existence calls for a different vocabulary. Below is a list of **Mind's Eye Theatre** and **Apocalypse**-specific terms that define the aspects of Garou life and the **MET** system.

Ability: Your character's skills, knowledges and talents; the things your character knows and can do.

Adren: A pupil or a student who learns from a mentor. Also used as the title of a Garou who is Third Rank.

Airts: The magical paths within the spirit world (e.g., Spirit Tracks, Moon Paths, etc.).

Aisling: A journey into the spirit world.

Anchorhead: A spirit gate between the Near and Deep Umbra.

Anruth: A Garou who travels from caern to caern but is bound to none of them.

Athro: Teacher, mentor; also used as the title of a Garou who is of the Fourth Rank.

Apocalypse: The age of destruction, the final cycle, the everlasting corruption, the end of Gaia — a word used in Garou mythology to describe the time of the final battle with the Wyrm. Many consider the present to be the time of the Apocalypse.

Auspice: The phase of the moon under which a particular Garou is born, commonly thought to determine personality and tendencies. The auspices are: Ragabash (New Moon; Trickster), Theurge (Crescent Moon; Seer), Philodox (Half Moon; Judge), Galliard (Gibbous Moon; Moon Dancer), Ahroun (Full Moon; Warrior).

Ape: A slang term for humans and homid-born Garou.

Bane: Evil spirits that follow the Wyrm. There are many different kinds of Banes: Scrag, Kalus, Psychomachiae and more.

Bawn: A boundary area around a caern.

Blight: Any corrupted area, in either the spirit world or physical reality.

Breed: The ancestry of the Garou, be it lupus (wolf), homid (human) or metis (two Garou).

Brugh: Any sort of mystic place, whether a Garou caern or a Wyrmhole; often a glade or cave located somewhere in the wilderness.

Caern: A sacred place; a meeting spot where Garou can contact the spirit world.

Cadaver: Derogatory slang for a vampire.

Celestine: The greatest of spirits; the closest thing to gods in Garou mythology. Examples are Luna (the moon), Helios (the sun) and Gaia (the Earth/Creation).

Challenge: The system by which conflict between two or more characters is resolved through bidding of Traits and the playing of "Rock-Paper-Scissors."

Charach: A Garou who sleeps with another Garou. Often used as an expletive.

Chiminage: Traditionally, a sept can make a request of any Garou who uses its caern. Chiminage is the technical term for that request.

Cliath: A young Garou, not yet of any standing rank.

Concolation: A great moot, wherein many tribes gather to discuss matters of concern to the Garou Nation.

Concord, The: The agreement all the tribes reached nearly 9,000 years ago, after which the Impergium was ended. The traditions of the Concord are still obeyed today.

Corruption: The act of destroying, devolving or debasing life; also, the almost overwhelming effects of the Wyrm's actions. In the present age, the term often refers specifically to the ecological ruin humans wreak upon the environment.

Crinos: The half-wolf, half-human form of the Garou. Causes the Delirium in humans and is considered a threat to the Veil if witnessed by outsiders.

Deep Umbra: The aspects of the Umbra that lie outside the Membrane. Reality becomes more and more fragmentary the farther one travels from the physical Earth. The Deep Umbra is comparable to deep space in reality.

Delirium: The madness suffered by humans who see Garou in Crinos form.

Domain: A mini-Realm in the Umbra, usually connected to a larger Realm in the Deep Umbra.

Elder: A leader of Garou society. The most well-known and renowned members of a sept are called elders. Also used as the title of a Garou who is of the Fifth Rank.

Feral: Slang term for lupus.

Flock, The: All of humanity, particularly those humans from whom the Garou recruit their Kinfolk.

Fomori: Humans or animals that have turned to the Wyrm and draw power from it. These tainted things are blood-enemies of the Garou.

Fostern: A Garou's pack brothers and sisters; those who are family by choice. Also used as the title of a Garou who is of the First Rank.

Gaffling: A simple spirit servant of a Jaggling, Incarna or Celestine. Gafflings are rarely sentient.

Gaia: The Earth and Her related Realm, in both a physical and spiritual sense. Most often referred to as Mother.

Garou: The term werewolves use for themselves.

Gauntlet: The barrier between the physical world of Earth and the spirit world of the Umbra. It is strongest around places of technology (Weaver), but weakest around caerns (Wyld places).

Hispo: The near-wolf form of the Garou; does not cause Delirium and does not threaten the Veil.

Homid: A Garou of human ancestry. Occasionally used disdainfully by ferals (e.g., "That boy fights like a homid").

Gallain: The Kinfolk of the Garou. Those humans and wolves related to Garou by blood, but not manifesting the recessive gene that creates full Garou. "Breeding true" occurs only 10% of the time with humans and 12% of the time with wolves. Gallain are not prone to the Delirium.

Glabro: The near-man form of the Garou. Does not cause Delirium, nor does it threaten the Veil.

Gremlin: A malevolent spirit.

Harano: Inexplicable gloom. Inexpressible longing for unnameable things. Weeping for that which is not yet lost. Some say it is depression caused by contemplation of Gaia's suffering.

–ikthya: "Of the Wyrm"; a suffix appended to a name.

Impergium: The 3,000 years immediately following the birth of agriculture, during which strict population quotas were maintained on all human villages by Garou "shepherds."

Incarna: A class of spirits; weaker than Celestines, but still greater spirits by any measure.

Jaggling: A spirit servant of an Incarna or Celestine.

Kenning: The empathic calling some Garou perform when howling.

Kinain: The relationship among Garou who are related by blood through an ancestor. This term of endearment and pride is never used when referring to metis.

Leech: see *Cadaver*.

Litany: The code of laws kept by the Garou.

Lupus: A Garou of wolf origin.

Membrane, The: The barrier between the Near and Deep Umbras. To breach it, an Anchorhead must be found.

Metis: The sterile and often deformed offspring of two Garou, generally reviled by Garou society.

Moon Bridge: The gate between two caerns. Moon Bridges most often appear during moots.

Moon-Calf: Idiot, simpleton.

Moot: A sept or tribal conclave that takes place at a caern.

Mule: A slang term for metis.

Near Umbra: The spirit world surrounding the Gaia Realm.

Pack: A small group of Garou bound to each other by ties of friendship and mission as opposed to culture.

Penumbra, The: "Earth's shadow"; the spirit world directly surrounding the physical world; many, but not all terrain features in the Penumbra mimic those of the real world.

Praenomen: The guardian spirit of a pack.

Protectorate: The territory claimed and patrolled by a pack or sept.

–rhya: "Greater in station"; suffix appended to a name.

Reaching: Traveling into the spirit world.

Realms: The worlds of "solid" reality within the Tellurian. Earth is referred to as the Realm.

Renown: The descriptive Traits a character earns from his sept for performing acts of Glory, Wisdom and Honor. Renown is needed at certain minimal levels to secure higher rank in Garou society.

Ronin: A Garou who has chosen or been forced to leave Garou society.

Run: A ritual hunt or revel that takes place at the conclusion of a moot.

Sept: A group of Garou who live near and tend an individual caern.

Sheep: A slang term for humans.

Stepping Sideways: Entering the spirit world. Most elders consider this term flippant and disrespectful.

Tellurian: The whole of reality.

Throat: To best someone in ritual combat. Used as a verb (e.g., "I throated his sorry butt!").

Totem: A spirit joined to a pack or tribe and representative of its inner nature. A tribal totem is an Incarna, while a pack totem is an Incarna avatar (a Jaggling equivalent).

Traits: The adjectives used to define your character.

Triat, The: The Weaver, the Wyld and the Wyrm. The trinity of primal cosmic forces.

Tribe: The larger community of Garou. Tribe members are often bound by similar totems and lifestyles.

Urrah: Garou who live in the city; also, the tainted ones.

Umbra: The spirit world.

Veil, The: The term used to describe the present situation, where the Garou attempt to keep the reality of their existence hidden. Also see *Delirium*.

Ways, The: The traditions of the Garou.

Weaver, The: The manifestation and symbol of order and pattern. Computers, science, logic and mathematics are examples of the Weaver's influence on the material plane.

Wyld, The: The manifestation and symbol of pure change. The chaos of transmutation and elemental forces.

Wyrm, The: The manifestation and symbol of evil, entropy and decay. Vampires are considered manifestations of the Wyrm, as are toxic waste and pollution.

Wyrmhole: A place that has been spiritually defiled by the Wyrm; invariably a location of great corruption.

–yuf: "Honored equal"; a suffix appended to a name.

Chapter Two: Character

All the world is a stage, and all the men and women in it merely players. They have their exits and their entrances; and one man in his time plays many parts.
— William Shakespeare, *As You Like It*

You have come to the place of adventure. Now we need to decide who you are and what part you are to play in the story that is unfolding before you.

Before you can play **Apocalypse**, you must first create a character. Unlike simple make-believe, in **Mind's Eye Theatre** you don't just make up a character as you go along. Instead, you create your character before you start playing, which prevents confusion or arguments down the road.

A character is, quite simply, the person you choose to portray in the game. Your character can continue from one story to the next, or you can play a different character each time. The choice is up to you. One given of the matter, however, is this: The more creative effort you put into your character during the creation stage, the more depth and believability she'll have when the story begins.

This chapter contains all the information you need to create your Garou character. The process is relatively simple and proceeds in a step-by-step fashion.

In the Beginning...

You first need to decide upon your character concept: Who he is at heart, what his upbringing was like, and what his auspice is. Next, develop your character's background and history, which in turn help make up your character's personality. Get a general idea as to which breed and tribe would best suit the personality and background you've developed, and you've already got the framework in place to create a fully fleshed-out character.

Generally, it is assumed that a new character is a young Garou who has recently undergone the *Rite of Passage*, and is now an assimilated member of a pack. Beyond that, your character's background is left open for you to decide.

It is possible that the Storyteller may limit your character creation choices for the purposes of the story she wishes to tell. It is also possible that she will offer you choices not listed here. Many times, a story will have certain roles that need to be filled, and you may be asked to create a character to fill one of those roles.

This game's character creation system is based on a process of selection, allowing you to design your character to your specifications. By choosing Traits (qualities that describe your character) from a series of lists, you build the capabilities of the persona you are going to play. It is best to list all the Traits and qualities you would like your character to have and then eliminate the ones that aren't essential to your concept.

Character Creation Process

- **Step One: Character Concept — Who and what are you?**

Choose Nature and Demeanor

Choose a breed

Choose an auspice

Choose a tribe (the Storyteller has the right to refuse any of your choices)

- **Step Two: Select Attributes — What are your basic capabilities?**

Prioritize Trait Attributes (seven primary, five secondary and three tertiary)

Choose Traits

- **Step Three: Select Advantages — What do you know and what can you do?**

Choose five Abilities

Choose three Basic Gifts (one each from breed, auspice and tribe)

Choose five Backgrounds

Note Renown (by auspice)

- **Step Four: Finishing Touches — Fill in the details.**

Record Rage (determined by auspice)

Record Gnosis (determined by breed)

Record Willpower (determined by tribe)

Choose Negative Traits (if any)

Select Merits and/or Flaws, if desired (see p. 141)

Purchase Influences, if desired

- **Step Five: Spark of Life — Narrative descriptions and other details**

Step One: Character Concept

Before you write anything down on your character sheet, you need to find inspiration for the character you want to play. Once you have the inspiration that you have been looking for, the rest of the character should flow around the structure of that initial inspiration. You should work with your Storyteller throughout the character creation process, which should help make your character eminently suitable for the chronicle in which you will be playing. Remember, your choices should be made to develop a character, not for game mechanic advantage.

Character development begins with defining his personality. This is where you decide who your character is, what his private, innermost self is like, and what sort of face he shows to the world.

Nature and Demeanor

Your character's Nature and Demeanor define the basic tenets of her personality. Nature and Demeanor are, quite simply, the disposition and image of your character. The first step in character creation is selecting appropriate Archetypes for your character's Nature and Demeanor from the list below.

A character's Nature is her true inner self, while her Demeanor is the mask she most often shows to the world. It is not unheard of for a character to have the same Nature and Demeanor; however, it is unlikely. Few people are that honest with other people, or even themselves.

Archetypes
- Alpha — You are a born leader. You pride yourself on knowing what you are doing and what needs to be done next. Getting others to follow you is not a matter of if, it is a matter of when.
- Architect — You believe in creating something of lasting value. You seek to leave a legacy of some kind for those who will come after you, and want to know that what you do will last.
- Avant-Garde — You are only interested in what is new or on the cutting edge. You must be the first to discover or create something that people have never seen before. The thrill of experimentation is a major lure to the Avant-Garde, and you are not afraid to take a few risks if they are necessary.
- Bravo — You're a bully. Fear equals respect in your mind. You reinforce your own self-worth by pumping yourself up and denigrating others, and you take every opportunity to make others "respect" you.
- Bureaucrat — You enjoy the solace and comfort that the System provides for you. You understand that chaos might come at any moment, but know that if the proper procedures are in place and are followed, disaster can be averted.
- Caregiver — You want to protect and help others. You are highly concerned about helping others fight the constant pull of frenzy and Harano. Those who deserve help shall receive whatever aid you can render.
- Competitor — You must be the winner in anything you do. Everything is a contest to you, and as far as you're concerned, if you don't come out on top you've lost.
- Confidant — You are a good listener. You feel honored to be trusted, and strive to earn the respect and confidence of others.

29

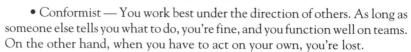

• Conformist — You work best under the direction of others. As long as someone else tells you what to do, you're fine, and you function well on teams. On the other hand, when you have to act on your own, you're lost.

• Conniver — You try to get ahead in the world by taking advantage of others. As far as you are concerned, the rest of the population consists of suckers for you to exploit, authorities to circumvent and rivals to be avoided. You are always trying to get someone else to do your dirty work for you.

• Critic — You find a purpose in life by revealing weaknesses and faults in others. You can find the bad points in any situation or achievement, but as far as you're concerned, you are just pointing out things that need to be fixed.

• Cub — You are naive at times and have an air of innocence about you, but at the same time, you know that you can get what you want if you pout and whine enough.

• Curmudgeon — You are dry and cynical. You find the wry humor in life's little woes. You are the first to see the bad news coming, for you have always put your faith in the ineptitude of others.

• Deviant — You do not quite fit in, but it's not as if you want to. Walking your own path you are happy, but don't expect others to understand or even accept what you're doing.

• Explorer — The excitement of finding new people, places and things fills your existence with the greatest excitement imaginable. It's not what you find that's important, it's the discovery itself that matters.

• Fanatic — You are obsessed with a cause. You alone know the truth, and any contrary viewpoints are automatically wrong. If others disagree with you, it is because they are against you and must be dealt with.

• Gallant — You love all of the social graces and decorum. You strive to be the most genial and ingratiating, and therefore the most worthy person in any group.

• Gambler — You believe life is all about taking chances. You do things, not for the outcome, but for the thrill that the action provides. Whether you win or lose is not necessarily important; you thrive on the high that comes from risking yourself time and time again.

• Jester — You find humor in everything. To you life is one big joke. Someone has got to look on the bright side, and that someone is you.

• Judge — You seek the truth and reconciliation in everything. You have little time for the games of others, and strive to reach the heart of every matter.

• Lone Wolf — You exist on the periphery. You have your own plans and they do not include getting bogged down by others. Having to work with others means you have to rely on them; you prefer to rely on yourself.

• Martyr — You are totally willing to make sacrifices for your beliefs, even unto death. Knowing that someone else is happy makes any misery you put yourself through worthwhile. You do not want any rewards other than recognition for your sacrifices.

• Penitent — You wish to atone for who or what you are, or to make up for something that you've done. You always feel you should have done better.

As far as you're concerned, Gaia is losing because you, personally, are not carrying your own weight. The Apocalypse is coming and it is all your fault.

• Predator — You are the quintessential hunter. The stalking and the chase are all part of your art. The world is full of targets and challengers to be brought down and feasted upon.

• Rebel — You are strong-willed and a real free thinker. If the system needs to come down, you are just the one to start it tumbling. There always seems to be something you are reacting against, though you do not necessarily have a better solution in mind. You just know that things cannot stay the way they are.

• Reluctant Garou — You long for a normal life. The life of adventure and danger isn't for you. Why can't the Apocalypse be kept at bay by someone else? The world survived all these years without you fighting its battles, and you're sure it will continue long after you are gone.

• Reveler — You live to experience life's many pleasures. Your hedonism might be immoral in the eyes of some, but no matter what, your pursuit of new pleasures is your main concern. If it does not hurt innocents, there is nothing wrong with it.

• Showoff — You get your self-worth from others. Be the brightest dresser, the silliest, the boldest, the brashest — that's what you need to feel good about yourself. If others do not pay attention to you, it's because you have not done anything worthy of their attention.

• Survivor — You always pull through. No matter what happens, you intend to survive. You will never say never, even to the Apocalypse. No matter what Fate throws at you, you will fight to the bitter end for just one more minute of existence. Sometimes this means sacrificing things (or people), but that's a price you're willing to pay.

• Traditionalist — You are conservative and bound to tradition. If it worked for the last 15,000 years, it works for you. There are tried and true ways of dealing with things, and you follow them because they work. Why take a chance on something new when the old standbys are still standing by?

• Visionary — You see beyond the boundaries of the conventional. You know there has to be something more to it all, something unimaginably greater than just existence. This is what keeps you going.

Breed

The Garou are the Changing Race, torn between the two worlds of wolves and men. However, the very nature of their existence prevents them from truly having a home with either race. Indeed, they are doubly cursed, for Garou cannot mate with Garou, and thus, the Changing Breed must dwell within, yet never truly be a part of, the worlds of humans and wolves.

It is against the oldest of laws for Garou to mate with one another. The product of a Garou-Garou union is always sterile and usually malformed. Such werewolves are called metis, and are often shunned by their lupus and homid brethren. Therefore, Garou must continually mate (or breed) with those outside their own race.

The Garou keep track of those humans and wolves with whom they breed and their offspring, watching carefully for signs that the recessive gene that controls changing has been passed on or "bred true." The product of a Garou mating with a human or wolf is not always a Garou. Very few children breed true and pure enough to undergo their First Change.

There are three breeds of Garou to choose from: homid (human), lupus (wolf) and metis (offspring of two Garou). A Garou's breed is determined by the breed of his mother. The three breeds are:

• **Homid**: You were raised as a human, by human parents. You may have had dreams of the hunt and running wild as an animal, but you did not know that you were a werewolf until you were nearly an adult and underwent the First Change.

Nickname: Ape

Initial Gnosis: One

Breed Gifts: (choose one) *Jam Technology, Persuasion, Smell of Man*

• **Metis**: Both of your parents are Garou. You are malformed and sterile as a result of their forbidden union. A true pariah, you understand the less glorified aspects of Garou culture more deeply than other breeds do.

Nickname: Mule (and many others)

Initial Gnosis: Two

Breed Gifts: (choose one) *Create Element, Sense Wyrm, Shed*

• **Lupus**: You were raised in the wilds as a wolf, and did not become aware of your true nature until you were nearly fully grown. Human society puzzles you, for you know Gaia's way better than the other breeds do.

Nickname: Feral

Initial Gnosis: Three

Breed Gifts: (choose one) *Catfeet, Heightened Senses, Scent of the True Form.*

Auspice

Your auspice is the phase of the moon under which your character was born. This aspect is held in astrological reverence by most Garou. It does more than predetermine certain aspects of your personality: It also helps to define your role in Garou society.

There are five auspices which a character may be. Each has its own special strengths and weaknesses. Many commonly held ideas about auspices can be dismissed as superstition, yet there is certainly some truth behind them as well.

Some truly exceptional Garou have rebelled against their moon-signs. They have renounced their birth auspices in favor of other ones. These Garou are rare indeed, for one loses everything when one chooses a new auspice. Such a renunciate must start her education over again.

For more on auspices, see also pp. 68-71.

The auspices of the Garou are:

Ragabash

New Moon
The Trickster
Initial Rage: One
Auspice Gifts: (choose one) *Alter Scent, Blur of the Milky Eye, Open Seal, Scent of Running Water*
Beginning Renown: Three Renown Traits in any combination

Theurge

Crescent Moon
The Seer
Initial Rage: One
Auspice Gifts: (choose one) *Mother's Touch, Name the Spirit, Sense Wyrm, Spirit Speech, Sight from Beyond*
Beginning Renown: Two Wisdom Traits, One Glory or Honor Trait

Philodox

Half Moon
The Judge
Initial Rage: Two
Auspice Gifts: (choose one) *Resist Pain, Scent of the True Form, Strength of Purpose, Truth of Gaia*
Beginning Renown: Two Honor Traits, One Wisdom Trait

Galliard

Gibbous Moon
The Moon Dancer
Initial Rage: Two
Auspice Gifts: (choose one) *Beast Speech, Call of the Wyld, Mindspeak*
Beginning Renown: One Glory Trait, Two Wisdom or Honor Traits

Ahroun

Full Moon
The Warrior
Initial Rage: Three
Auspice Gifts: (choose one) *Inspiration, The Falling Touch, Razor Claws*
Beginning Renown: Two Glory Traits, One Honor Trait

Tribe

A tribe is a character's family of sorts. It is his lineage and heritage, at once genetic, cultural and social. Your tribe says a great deal about who and what you are. Each tribe has its own beliefs, pursuits, strengths and weaknesses. There is a great variety of tribes; 13 in all still fight the Wyrm.

For more information on the tribes, see also pp. 72-92

The tribes of the Garou are:

• **Black Furies:** Composed almost entirely of women, the Furies serve the Wyld and avenge the losses of the Garou.

Initial Willpower: One

Backgrounds: No restrictions.

Tribe Gifts: (choose one) *Heightened Senses, Sense of the Prey, Sense Wyrm*

• **Bone Gnawers:** These Garou live on the city streets. They're usually well-informed, if somewhat smelly.

Initial Willpower: Two

Backgrounds: May not buy *Past Life* or *Pure Breed*, or begin the game with *Finances* Influence; must spend two Traits on Kinfolk.

Tribe Gifts: (choose one) *Odious Aroma, Scent of Sweet Honey*

• **Children of Gaia:** The most moderate of all the tribes, the Children are mediators of the Garou and defenders of humanity.

Initial Willpower: Two

Backgrounds: No restrictions.

Tribe Gifts: (choose one) *Calm, Mother's Touch, Resist Pain*

• **Fianna:** Each member of this tribe is Celtic in descent and fiercely proud of her heritage.

Initial Willpower: Two

Backgrounds: No restrictions.

Tribe Gifts: (chose one) *Persuasion, Resist Toxin*

• **Get of Fenris:** Savage and bloodthirsty, the Get are largely of Nordic descent.

Initial Willpower: One

Backgrounds: May not begin the game with more than three Influences.

Tribe Gifts: (choose one) *Razor Claws, Resist Pain, Snarl of the Predator*

• **Glass Walkers:** They live in skyscrapers and throughout the cities of the world. The Glass Walkers are the Garou best adapted to the modern era.

Initial Willpower: Two

Backgrounds: May not buy *Past Life* or *Pure Breed*; also start with an additional Influence

Tribe Gifts: (choose one) *Control Simple Machine, Cybersenses, Persuasion*

• **Red Talons:** The Red Talons are composed entirely of lupus Garou, and are almost always extremists.

Initial Willpower: Two

Backgrounds: May not begin the game with Influences.

Tribe Gifts: (choose one) *Beastmind, Scent of Running Water, Sense of the Prey*

• **Shadow Lords:** Domineering and demanding, the Shadow Lords covet the leadership position held by the Silver Fangs.

Initial Willpower: Two

Backgrounds: May not begin the game with more than three levels of Influences.

Tribe Gifts: (choose one) *Aura of Confidence, Clap of Thunder, Disfigurement, Fatal Flaw*

• **Silent Striders**: They live their lives traveling, and know many secrets of both the mortal and spirit worlds.

Initial Willpower: Two

Backgrounds: May not buy *Past Life* or Influences that are not accessible worldwide (Storyteller approval).

Tribe Gifts: (choose one) *Messenger's Fortitude, Sense Wyrm, Speed of Thought*

• **Silver Fangs**: The most noble of all tribes, the Silver Fangs rule the Garou and many notable human organizations.

Initial Willpower: Two

Backgrounds: Must spend at least three Background Traits on *Pure Breed*.

Tribe Gifts: (choose one) *Lambent Flame, Paralyzing Stare, Sense Wyrm*

• **Stargazers**: They search throughout the world for enlightenment and truth.

Initial Willpower: Three

Backgrounds: May not begin the game with fetishes or Influences.

Tribe Gifts: (choose one) *Catfeet, Sense Wyrm, Surface Attunement*

• **Uktena**: Holding Native Americans as their Kinfolk, the Uktena are cunning and mysterious, and noted for their hidden knowledge.

Initial Willpower: Two

Background: No restrictions.

Tribe Gifts: (choose one) *Blur of the Milky Eye, Sense Magic, Spirit of the Fish*

• **Wendigo**: Warriors of the Pure Ones, the Wendigo are still fiercely independent and somewhat extremist in their beliefs.

Initial Willpower: Two

Backgrounds: May not begin the game with Influences.

Tribe Gifts: (choose one) *Call the Breeze, Camouflage, Cutting Wind, Speak with the Wind Spirits*

Step Two: Attributes

Attributes are everything a character naturally is. Are you strong? Are you brave? Are you persuasive? Questions such as these are answered by the way you distribute your Attributes.

There are three categories of Attributes: Physical, Social and Mental. You must prioritize the three categories, placing them in order of importance to your character. These choices may well be influenced by your auspice, for most auspices tend toward one Attribute category more than the others. For example, an Ahroun usually sets his Physical Traits primary and his Social Traits tertiary, while a Ragabash is likely to make Social Traits most important.

Attribute Traits reflect how competent your character is at different kinds of actions. The more Traits you have in one Attribute category, the more skillfully your character can perform actions involving that category and the higher you can bid on relevant tests.

Attribute Categories

Physical Attributes describe the abilities of the body, such as strength, dexterity and endurance.

Social Attributes describe a character's appearance and charisma and ability to influence others.

Mental Attributes describe a character's mental capacity. They include things such as awareness of one's surroundings, resolve, memory, self-control and concentration.

Traits are adjectives that describe your character's strengths and weaknesses, defining your character just as a character in a novel is defined. In your primary (strongest) Attribute category, choose seven Traits. In your secondary category, choose five. In your tertiary (weakest) category, choose three. You can take the same Trait more than once to illustrate that the character is particularly gifted in a certain area (a character who is a pickpocket might well have the Trait: *Dexterous* three times).

Physical Traits

Athletic: You have conditioned your body to respond well, especially in competitive events.

Uses: Sports, duels, running, acrobatics and grappling.

Brawny: Bulky, muscular strength.

Uses: Punching, kicking or grappling in combat when your goal is to inflict damage. Power lifting. All feats of strength.

Brutal: You are capable of taking nearly any action in order to survive.

Uses: Fighting an obviously superior enemy.

Dexterous: General adroitness and skill involving the use of one's hands.

Uses: Weapon-oriented combat (*Melee* or *Firearms*). Picking pockets. Punching.

Enduring: A persistent sturdiness against physical opposition.

Uses: When your survival is at stake, this is a good Trait to risk as a second, or successive, bid.

Energetic: A powerful force of spirit. A strong internal drive propels you, and you can draw on a deep reservoir of enthusiasm and zeal in physically stressful situations.

Uses: Combat.

Ferocious: Possession of brutal intensity and extreme physical determination.

Uses: Any time that you intend to do serious harm. When in frenzy.

Graceful: Control and balance in the motion and use of the entire body.

Uses: Combat defense. Whenever you might lose your balance (stepping on a banana peel, fighting on four-inch-wide rafters).

Lithe: Characterized by flexibility and suppleness.

Uses: Acrobatics, gymnastics, dodging and dancing.

Nimble: Light and skillful; able to make agile movements.

Uses: Dodging, jumping, rolling and acrobatics. Hand-to-hand combat.

Quick: Speedy, with good reaction time.

Uses: Defending against a surprise attack. Running, dodging and attacking.

Resilient: Characterized by strength of health; able to recover quickly from bodily harm.

Uses: Resisting adverse environments. Defending against damage in an attack.

Robust: Resistant to physical harm and damage.

Uses: Defending against damage in an attack. Endurance-related actions that could take place over a period of time.

Rugged: Hardy, rough and robustly healthy. Able to shrug off wounds and pain to continue struggling.

Uses: When resisting damage. Any challenge that you enter while injured.

Stalwart: Physically strong and uncompromising against opposition.

Uses: Resisting damage, or when standing your ground against overwhelming odds or a superior foe.

Steady: More than simply physically dependable: controlled, unfaltering and balanced. You have firm mastery over your efforts.

Uses: Weapon attacks. Fighting in exotic locations. Piloting oil tankers.

Tenacious: Physically determined through force of will. You often prolong physical confrontations, even when it might not be wise to do so.

Uses: Second or subsequent Physical Challenge.

Tireless: You have a runner's stamina. You are less taxed by physical efforts than ordinary people are.

Uses: Any endurance-related challenge, second or subsequent Physical Challenge with the same foe or foes.

Tough: A harsh, aggressive attitude and a reluctance ever to submit.

Uses: Whenever you are wounded or winded.

Vigorous: A combination of energy, power, intensity and resistance to harm.

Uses: Combat and athletic challenges when you are on the defensive.

Wiry: Tight, streamlined, muscular strength.

Uses: Punching, kicking or grappling in combat. Acrobatic movements. Endurance lifting.

Negative Physical Traits

Note: For more information on Negative Traits, see pp. 55 and 160-161.

Clumsy: Lacking physical coordination, balance and grace. You are prone to stumbling and dropping objects.

Cowardly: In threatening situations, saving your own neck is all that is important. You might even flee when you have the upper hand, just out of habit.

Decrepit: You move and act as if you are old and infirm. You recover from physical damage slowly, are unable to apply full muscular strength and tire easily.

Delicate: Frail and weak in structure, you are easily damaged by physical harm.

Docile: The opposite of the *Ferocious* and *Tenacious* Traits; you lack physical persistence and tend to submit rather than fight long battles.

Flabby: Your muscles are underdeveloped. You cannot apply your strength well against resistance.

Lame: You are disabled in one or more limbs. The handicap can be as obvious as a missing leg or as subtle as a dysfunctional arm.

Lethargic: Slow and drowsy. You suffer from a serious lack of energy or motivation.

Puny: You are weak and inferior in strength. This could mean diminutive size.

Sickly: Weak and feeble. Your body responds to physical stress as if it were in the throes of a debilitating illness.

Social Traits

Alluring: An attractive and appealing presence that inspires desire in others.

Uses: Seduction. Convincing others.

Beguiling: The skill of deception and illusion. You can twist the perceptions of others and lead them to believe what suits you.

Uses: Tricking others. Lying under duress.

Charismatic: The talent of inspiration and motivation, the sign of a strong leader.

Uses: In a situation involving leadership or the achievement of leadership.

Charming: Your speech and actions make you appear attractive and appealing to others.

Uses: Convincing. Persuading.

Commanding: Impressive delivery of orders and suggestions. This implies skill in the control and direction of others.

Uses: When you are seen as a leader. Direct confrontations.

Compassionate: Having deep feelings of care or pity for others.

Uses: Defending the weak or downtrodden. Defeating major obstacles while pursuing an altruistic end.

Dignified: Something about your posture and body carriage appears honorable and aesthetically pleasing. You carry yourself well.

Uses: Leadership situations. Might be important in impressing some tribes for advancement.

Diplomatic: Tactful, careful and thoughtful in speech and deed. Few are displeased with what you say or do.

Uses: Very important in intrigue. Leadership situations.

Elegant: Refined and tasteful. Even though you do not need money to be elegant, you exude an air of richness and high society.

Uses: High society. At moots with Silver Fangs.

Eloquent: The ability to speak in an interesting and convincing manner.

Uses: Convincing others. Swaying emotions. Public speaking. Storytelling.

Empathetic: Able to identify and understand the emotions and moods of people with whom you come in contact.

Uses: Gauging the feelings of others.

Expressive: Able to articulate thoughts in interesting, significant, meaningful ways.

Uses: Producing art, acting, performing. Any social situation in which you want someone to understand your meaning.

Friendly: Able to fit in with everyone you meet. Even after a short conversation, most find it difficult to dislike you.

Uses: Convincing others.

Genial: Cordial, kindly, warm and pleasant. You are pleasing to be around.

Uses: Mingling at parties. Generally used in a second or later Social Challenge with someone.

Gorgeous: Beautiful or handsome. You were born with a face and body that is good-looking to most people you meet.

Uses: Modeling, posing and flirting.

Ingratiating: Able to gain the favor of people who know you.

Uses: Dealing with elders in a social situation.

Intimidating: A frightening or awesome presence that causes others to feel timid. This Trait is particularly useful when attempting to cow opponents.

Uses: Inspiring common fear. Ordering others.

Magnetic: People feel drawn to you; those around you are interested in your speech and actions.

Uses: Seduction. Intimation. Leadership.

Persuasive: Able to pose believable, convincing and correct arguments and requests. Very useful when someone else is undecided on an issue.

Uses: Cajoling or convincing others.

Seductive: Able to entice and tempt. You can use your good looks and your body to get what you want from others.

Uses: Subterfuge and subversion.

Witty: Cleverly humorous. Jokes and jests come easily to you, and you are perceived as a funny person when you want to be.

Uses: At parties. Entertaining someone. Goading or insulting someone.

Negative Social Traits

Bestial: Your body looks decidedly inhuman (or subhuman). Perhaps you are skeletal, or have glowing orange eyes, or maybe your teeth are just a little too long.

Callous: You are unfeeling, uncaring and insensitive to the suffering of others. Your heart is a frozen stone.

Condescending: Whether you mean it or not, others perceive in you a contempt that is impossible to hide.

Dull: Those with whom you speak usually find you boring and uninteresting. Conversing with you is a chore. You do not present yourself well to others.

Naive: You lack the air of worldliness, sophistication or maturity that most carry.

Obnoxious: You are annoying or unappealing in speech, action or appearance.

Repugnant: Your appearance disgusts everyone around you. Needless to say, you make a terrible first impression with strangers.

Shy: You are timid, bashful, reserved and socially hesitant.

Tactless: You are unable to do or say things that others find appropriate to the social situation.

Untrustworthy: You are rumored or perceived to be untrustworthy and unreliable (whether you are or not).

Mental Traits

Alert: Mentally prepared for danger and able to react quickly when it occurs.
Uses: Preventing surprise attacks.

Attentive: You pay attention to everyday occurrences around you. When something extraordinary happens, you are usually ready for it.
Uses: Preventing surprise attacks.

Calm: Able to withstand an extraordinary level of disturbance without becoming agitated or upset. A wellspring of self-control.
Uses: Resisting commands that provoke violence. Whenever a mental attack might upset you. Used primarily for defense.

Clever: Quick-witted resourcefulness. You think well on your feet.
Uses: Using mental-related Gifts, riddle contests. Good for a Ragabash.

Creative: Your ideas are original and imaginative. This implies an ability to produce unusual solutions to your difficulties. You can create artistic pieces. A requirement for any true artist.
Uses: Defending against aura readings. Creating anything.

Cunning: Crafty and sly. Possessing a great deal of ingenuity.
Uses: Tricking others.

Dedicated: You give yourself over totally to your beliefs. When one of your causes is at stake, you stop at nothing to succeed.
Uses: Useful in any Mental Challenge when your beliefs are at stake.

Determined: When it comes to mental endeavors, you are fully committed. Nothing can divert your intentions to succeed once you have made up your mind.
Uses: Facedowns. Useful in a normal Mental Challenge.

Discerning: Discriminating, able to pick out details, subtleties and idiosyncrasies. You have clarity of vision.
Uses: Researching or when perception-based Gifts are being used.

Disciplined: Your mind is structured and controlled. This rigidity gives you an edge in battles of will.
Uses: Facedowns. Asserting your will. Concentration.

Insightful: The power of looking at a situation and gaining an understanding of it.
Uses: *Investigation* (but not defending against it). Using *Heightened Senses*.

Intuitive: Knowledge and understanding somehow come to you without conscious reasoning, as if by instinct.

Uses: Reading auras. Seeing through Disciplines or Gifts meant to cloud your mind.

Knowledgeable: You have copious and detailed information about a wide variety of topics. This represents "book learning."

Uses: Remembering information your character might know.

Observant: Depth of vision. The power to look at something and notice the important aspects of it.

Uses: *Heightened Senses*. Picking up on subtleties that others might overlook.

Patient: Tolerant, persevering and steadfast. You can wait out extended delays with composure.

Uses: Facedowns or other mental battles after another Trait has been bid.

Rational: You believe in logic, reason, sanity and sobriety. Your ability to reduce concepts to a mathematical level helps you analyze the world.

Uses: Defending against emotion-oriented mental attacks. Not used as an initial bid.

Reflective: Meditative self-recollection and deep thought. The Trait of the serious thinker, *Reflective* enables you to consider all aspects of a conundrum.

Uses: *Meditation*. Remembering information. Defending against most mental attacks.

Shrewd: Astute and artful. Able to keep your wits about you and accomplish mental feats with efficiency and finesse.

Uses: Defending against mental attacks. Plotting tactics or playing politics.

Vigilant: Alert and watchful. You have the disposition of a guard dog; your eye misses little.

Uses: Defending against *Investigation*. More appropriate for mental defense than for attack.

Wily: Sly and full of guile. You can trick and deceive others easily.

Uses: Tricking others. Lying under duress. Confusing mental situations.

Wise: An overall understanding of the workings of the world.

Uses: Giving advice. Dispensing snippets of Zen.

Negative Mental Traits

Forgetful: You have trouble remembering even important things.

Gullible: Easily deceived, duped or fooled.

Ignorant: Uneducated or misinformed. Never seeming to know anything.

Impatient: Restless, anxious and generally intolerant of delays. You want everything to go your way immediately.

Oblivious: Unaware and unmindful. You would be lucky if you noticed an airplane flying through your living room.

Predictable: Because you lack originality or intelligence, even strangers can easily figure out what you intend to do next. Not a very good Trait for chess players.

Shortsighted: Lacking foresight. You rarely look beyond the superficial; details of perception are usually lost on you.

Submissive: No backbone; you relent and surrender at any cost rather than stand up for yourself.

Violent: An extreme lack of self-control. You fly into rages at the slightest provocation, and your temper is always close to the surface. This is a Mental Trait because it represents mental instability.

Witless: Lacking the ability to process information quickly. Foolish and slow to act when threatened.

Step Three: Advantages

Advantages are Traits that separate one character from another. They allow a player to take actions that would otherwise be impossible. There are four categories of advantages: Abilities, Gifts, Backgrounds and Renown.

Choosing Abilities

Abilities represent the skills you've developed and the training you've had up to this point in your life. They summarize the "mundane" things you know and can do. Many Abilities allow you to perform specific tasks that are only possible through training, while others enhance your performance of everyday tasks and functions. Some specialized tasks are possible only with training: hacking computers, solving enigmas or reading Old English texts. Obviously, some Abilities do not translate well or do not apply to **Laws of the Wild**. Others have been incorporated into the Attributes and can be performed by executing challenges.

If your character is defeated in a challenge, you may choose to sacrifice a level in an appropriate Ability to call for a retest. While any Traits risked are still lost, it is still possible to win the challenge. An Ability lost in this manner is recovered at the beginning of the next session.

Choose five Abilities from the list below. You can take the same Ability more than once to illustrate a higher degree of skill in that particular field.

The use of Abilities is often accompanied by a challenge of one sort or another. Some of these will be performed with a Storyteller who will not only assign the relative difficulty of the challenge (measured by a number of Traits), but will actually perform the test with you. This sort of test is called a Static Challenge.

As a rule, one or no Traits are risked for trivial uses, two to four are at stake in novel, unusual or challenging projects, and five or more are risked by attempting taxing, groundbreaking or unlikely feats. More details concerning difficulty and factors that influence it are included with each Ability.

Other Abilities, such as *Subterfuge* or *Melee*, can be used directly against another player and rarely need the assistance of a Storyteller to use.

Abilities

Animal Ken

This is the ability to understand the actions of animals. Characters with this Ability can not only predict the actions of animals, but can calm or enrage them. Given time you may train an animal to perform simple tasks — fetching, guarding, attacking, and so on. When a command is given, the animal must make a Mental Challenge to understand and carry out the order. In order to give a successful command, you must bid between one and three Traits, depending on the difficulty of the task. You may also attempt to calm an injured, attacking or frightened animal by defeating it in a Social Challenge.

Brawl

You know how to fight bare-handed. This includes punching, kicking, grappling, throttling, throwing, gouging, clawing and biting. *Brawl* serves as a catchall term for any form of unarmed combat.

Bureaucracy

Bureaucracy, a.k.a. the System, is theoretically an organization for getting things done more efficiently. *Bureaucracy* can allow you to obtain appropriate licenses, use contractual agreements to your advantage, and recover, alter or destroy files. *Bureaucracy* often requires a Static Mental or Social Challenge, depending on the type of roleplaying performed, or as a Storyteller sees fit. Difficulty depends on such factors as security, accessibility, nature and cooperativeness of the target or information.

Lupus characters may not start the game with this Ability.

Computer

A character with this Ability has learned many of the secrets of this world where data pulses and flows through silicon circuitry and fiber-optic lines. Systems can be infiltrated, data swapped, business and science secrets can be stolen, and records can be accessed. A Mental Challenge is required to accomplish these and other similar acts. Difficulty is based on system security and accessibility, equipment, time and rarity of information, as assigned by a Storyteller. Failure can lead to investigation by natural and sometimes supernatural agencies that operate in the computer sphere. In a world where the operation of basic word processing software is still a mystery to many adults, even a modicum of knowledge of how to use a computer can be a very powerful thing.

Lupus characters may not start the game with this Ability.

Drive

In much of the world, the majority of adults have at least some familiarity with automobiles, allowing them to handle one with reasonable ease in normal situations. Thus you do not need this Ability just to be able to drive a car. Instead, one who has this Ability is an adept driver capable of tailing (and losing tails), avoiding collisions and using his vehicle as a weapon. These actions often require a Physical or Mental Challenge. Factors influencing difficulty could include the type of vehicle, road conditions and the sort of stunt desired.

Lupus characters may not start the game with this Ability.

Enigmas

This Ability concerns solving mysteries and puzzles. In essence, it is a measurement of your problem-solving skills and how well you combine scattered details into a coherent solution. *Enigmas* comes in handy when solving mazes, answering riddles and the like. This Ability is used with Mental Challenges in order to see if you figure out a problem set before you. The Storyteller may require a variable number of Traits to be risked, depending on the relative difficulty and the character's familiarity with the enigma in question.

Finance

You can manage money, and even have some limited resources to draw on. This ability allows you to follow money trails, perform and verify accounting, and understand such concepts as investment and buyouts. These actions are a function of a Mental Challenge, the difficulty of which depends on any precautions taken by the subject, the amount of money in question and the availability of information. Storytellers should set reasonable totals for monies that can be gained through the use of this Ability each session.

Lupus characters may not start the game with this Ability.

Firearms

This Ability covers both how well you can shoot and your skill at maintaining, repairing and possibly making minor alterations to firearms. The most common use of this Ability is in combat, but a Storyteller can also allow you to attempt a Mental Challenge in order to perform other functions. Those with the *Firearms* Ability may choose to use Mental Traits instead of Physical Traits during a challenge in which a firearm is involved.

Lupus characters may not start the game with this Ability.

Investigation

You know how to locate evidence and perform basic analysis. With sufficient expertise, you can conduct a proper criminal investigation, deduce a criminal's *modus operandi* and reconstruct a crime scene. By succeeding at a Mental Challenge, you can tell if a person is carrying a concealed weapon or the like. When dealing with plots, you may also request a Mental Challenge against a Storyteller to see if any clues have been overlooked, piece together clues, or uncover information through formal investigation. Hunters often employ this Ability to track down Garou.

Law

This is the measure of how well you understand the legal system in which you are entangled. In the world of humans, you can use the *Law* Ability to write up binding contracts, defend clients and know the rights of yourself and others. The difficulty of the Mental Challenges necessary to accomplish these tasks depends on factors like the precedents for and severity of the crime, not to mention legal complexity of the subject or legal action desired. Alternatively, this could be an understanding of "wolf politics" for a lupus character or of Garou law for a metis character.

Leadership

This is a function of confidence, bearing and a profound understanding of what motivates others. It is more than barking orders. It measures how well you can get others to obey your decisions. It also covers how willingly people accede to your wishes, as reluctant followers are worth far less than willing ones. To use this ability they must first be under your command or in some way your subordinates, like an alpha to a packmate. You may use this Ability to cause others to perform reasonable tasks for you. These requests may not endanger the subjects or violate the subjects' Natures or Demeanors. *Leadership* works with a Social Challenge.

Linguistics

This is your ability to define what language is being spoken or is written. Its more common use is to represent tutelage in one or more languages other than your native tongue. The language(s) learned can be anything from ancient hieroglyphics to common national languages to complex dialects. In the case of languages known, they must be specified when the *Linguistics* Ability is chosen — each new Trait allows a character a new language. This skill allows you and anyone who also knows the language to speak privately. Furthermore, you can translate data for yourself or others, though a Static Mental Challenge may be required to do so. *Linguistics* also allows for identifying accents, reading lips, picking up slang and a certain amount of linguistic mimicry.

Medicine

This Ability represents your skill at treating the injuries, diseases and various ailments of living creatures. Narrators can allow a living being under the treatment with someone with the *Medicine* Ability to recover a single Health Level per night with time and a Mental Challenge. The difficulty of the challenge is influenced by the severity and nature of the damage, equipment at your disposal and any assistance or distractions. Other uses of this Ability include forensic information, diagnosis and pharmaceutical knowledge. Of course, knowledge of healing also implies a knowledge of what is harmful to the human form as well.

Meditation

This is the ability to focus and center one's thoughts, calming the emotions, controlling the mind and relaxing the body. Garou may use this Ability to channel and renew their Gnosis. For every 10 minutes spent in meditation, the Garou may convert one Mental or Meditation Trait into a Gnosis Trait. To meditate, one does not necessarily need to be in the lotus position. This is a very personal Ability, and one for which you develop your own technique.

Melee

You are skilled at a broad range of armed combat skills. You are proficient in the use of a variety of weapons, from broken bottles to swords. The *Melee* Ability comes with knowledge of proper care for your weapon as well. A character without this Ability may not use any of the advantages of Abilities in armed combat, including retests.

Occult

There are many supernatural secrets in the World of Darkness, and with the *Occult* Ability, some of them are yours. *Occult* implies a general knowledge of things such as *voudoun*, curses and fortunetelling, as well as information more specific to the supernatural beings that inhabit the world. Examples of applications include identifying the use and nature of visible magicks, rites and rituals, understanding basic fundamentals of the occult, and having knowledge of cults, tomes and artifacts. Most uses of the *Occult* Ability involve a Mental Challenge. The difficulty of this challenge can be subject to many factors, such as obscurity, amount of existing data and the character's individual scope of understanding (Garou know more about their own rites, for example).

Performance

This covers the entire gamut of live artistic expression, including singing, acting, dancing, playing musical instruments and similar skills. A particular specialty should be declared when the skill is taken. It grants you the gift to make your own original creations and/or express these creations to your peers, in a chosen medium. The genius of your creativity or the power with which you convey it is determined by a Static Social Challenge. Some particularly sensitive types, such as Galliards and Toreador vampires, can even become entranced by the use of this skill — after first being defeated in a Social Challenge. In addition to actual performing ability, this Ability also measures how well you know the society surrounding your particular art form and how you fit in with that crowd. Advanced levels of *Performance* usually involve some form of specialization. This Ability can also be used to critique the works of others.

Primal Urge

This describes your native instincts and connection to your ancestral past. It measures your ability to function not only as a wolf, but as a half-wolf. Those Garou skilled in this Ability are very attuned to the bestial part of their inner nature, and can retest perception-related challenges. *Primal Urge* reduces a Garou's time to change forms or pass through the Gauntlet.

Homid characters may not start the game with this Ability, except with Storyteller permission.

Repair

You possess a working understanding of what makes things tick. This Ability covers everything from advanced electronics to shoring up a sagging beam, assuming, of course, that you have the time, tools and parts. You can fix or slightly alter most of the trappings of modern society. This also allows you to excel at sabotage, should you choose to do so. Using this Ability usually calls for a Static Mental Challenge, the difficulty of which depends on such factors as the subject of your attention's complexity, the tools and parts available, the extent of the damage and the time spent on the repairs.

Lupus characters may not start the game with this Ability.

Science

You have a degree of factual and practical expertise in a single field of the hard sciences. This Ability measures not only theoretical knowledge but also how well you can put it to practical use. This knowledge allows you to identify properties of your field, perform experiments, fabricate items, bring about results and access information a player could not normally utilize. A Static Mental Challenge is necessary for all but the most trivial uses of this skill. The difficulty of the Challenge depends on resources available (equipment, data and so forth), complexity of the task and time. A field of study must be chosen when the *Science* Ability is taken. A few examples include physics, biology, electronics and chemistry. Other fields can be allowed at the Storyteller's discretion.

Lupus characters may not start the game with this Ability.

Scrounge

Scrounge allows you to produce items through connections, wits and ingenuity. Many individuals who lack the wealth to purchase the things they desire or need develop this Ability instead. Materials acquired with *Scrounge* aren't always brand new or exactly right and often require some time to obtain, but this Ability sometimes works where *Finance* and outright theft fail. A Static Mental or Social Challenge is necessary to use Scrounge. Some factors that influence the difficulty of the challenge include rarity and value of the item sought, and local supply and demand.

Security

You have a degree of experience in and knowledge of the variety of ways in which people defend and protect things. Not only can you counter existing security, such as locks, alarms and guards, but you can also determine the best way to secure items and areas. Other uses include breaking and entering, infiltration, safecracking and hot-wiring. Almost all applications of the *Security* Ability require a Static Mental Challenge. Difficulty depends on the complexity and the thoroughness of the defenses, the intruder's equipment and the time available.

Lupus characters may not start the game with this Ability.

Streetwise

With this Ability, you have a feel for the street. You know how to uncover its secrets, how to survive out there and how to utilize the network of personalities it houses. You can get information on events on the street, deal with gangs and the homeless, and survive without an apparent income. Some uses of *Streetwise* require a Social Challenge, the difficulty of which is influenced by such things as composition of the local street community and the current environment of the street.

Subterfuge

This is the art of deception and intrigue that relies on a social backdrop to work. When participating in a social setting or conversation with a subject, you can attempt to draw information out of him through trickery and careful probing. Information, such as one's name, nationality, Negative Traits, friends and enemies can be revealed by a successful use of *Subterfuge*.

The first requirement of gleaning information in this way involves getting your target to say something dealing with the desired knowledge, such as entering a conversation about foreign culture when you are really itching to find out where he comes from. If you can accomplish this, you may then propose your true question and initiate a Social Challenge. If you win, then your target must forfeit the information (hopefully by roleplaying his *faux pas*). To use the Ability again, you must once again lure the target into a conversation. *Subterfuge* can be used to suss out a character's Negative Traits, but may not reveal more than one Negative Trait per session. Furthermore, it may be used to defend from others with *Subterfuge*.

The *Subterfuge* Ability may also be used to conceal information or lie without detection.

Survival

You have the knowledge and training to find food, water and shelter in a variety of wilderness settings. Each successful Static Mental or Physical Challenge allows you to provide the basic necessities for yourself or another living creature for one day. This Ability can also be used to track down someone in a wilderness setting. The nature and difficulty of the challenge is usually set by a Storyteller. Important factors in a *Survival* Challenge are the abundance or scarcity of resources, time of year, equipment and type of wilderness.

Gifts

See above for Beginning Gifts; choose one from each list (for a total of three Gifts). See also Gifts on pp. 92-125.

Note that the listed Gifts are simply the Basic ones. There are more powerful Intermediate and Advanced Gifts, although these are possessed only by more knowledgeable Garou.

Backgrounds

Each character has background details that make her unique. They represent special advantages the character possesses by virtue of birth, hard work or plain luck. They help define the character and set her apart as an individual. Background Traits should be chosen to flesh out the player's concept of her character, rather than to bolster a character's power and effectiveness. Most Backgrounds may be lost or added to during the course of play. Backgrounds do not generally increase through experience, so players are not charged experience when they gain new Background Traits through successful play.

At this stage, select your five Background Traits. Members of certain tribes are excluded from selecting certain Background Traits, and members of other tribes are required to take others. Players can select the same Background more than once to illustrate a stronger level of that Background, though Pure Breed and Past Life may never rise above five Traits.

Pure Breed

The Garou hold their dead heroes and mystics in high regard. To actually share the same blood as one of these Renowned Garou bestows a great honor, as well as a great responsibility. With this Background, all other Garou automatically sense your noble lineage. A character with Pure Breed gains a retest on Social Challenges against Garou, one for each level of the Background she possesses. In exchange, those "of the blood" are expected to live up to the standards of their famous ancestors.

Past Life

A Garou with Past Life can call upon the knowledge of his dead ancestors in times of need. You may try to use an Ability you do not have or have already expended once per session for each level of Past Life you possess. To do so, you must win or tie a Simple Test — a basic contest of Rock-Paper-Scissors.

Fetish

Many cultures have a tradition of passing on physical items as heirlooms or concrete examples of tradition. Among the Garou, this custom is especially important because the relics of their past are often items of mystical power. A Garou who carries one of these items may draw upon its powers. If you are chosen to carry a fetish, you have received a great honor and should take your responsibility very seriously. The Storyteller assigns a fetish appropriate to the level of Background taken; picking your own fetish is not allowed.

Rites

You have been introduced to the mysteries of the rites and celebrations of the Garou race. You know the traditions and order of these rites, and can identify them by drawing upon your knowledge of them (the player must win or tie a Static Mental Challenge to do so). Furthermore, you may have been taught how to perform a few of these rites.

One Trait: Has knowledge of Basic Rites and can perform one Basic Rite.

Two Traits: Has knowledge of Basic Rites and can perform two Basic Rites.

Three Traits: Has knowledge of Basic and Intermediate Rites, and can perform three Basic Rites.

Four Traits: Has knowledge of Basic and Intermediate Rites, and can perform four Basic Rites

Five Traits: Has knowledge of Basic, Intermediate and Advanced Rites, and can perform five Basic Rites and one Intermediate Rite.

Individual rites may be learned by any Garou who can find a willing teacher and is willing to pay the appropriate experience cost. Teachers often ask would-be students for hefty favors or require difficult quests before passing on their guarded knowledge. But in these last days, the truly wise realize the importance of making sure the ancient rites are remembered and passed on.

Note: What this Background purchases is an exceptional ability in ritual, even for one of the Garou. This Background supercedes normal Rank restrictions on Rites.

Kinfolk

You are in contact with certain humans or wolves who, while descended from the Garou, did not receive the "changing gene," and so for all practical purposes are normal members of their respective species. They are immune to Delirium, however, and know your origin; they are willing to help you however they can, though most are not in positions of power. Networks of Kinfolk can be invaluable for Garou who wish to deal with the human world, but who cannot risk frenzy.

For each level of this Background, you may call upon a Kinfolk with a specific Ability, Numina or Influence that is desired. A Simple Test must be won for each level of special talent needed. Each Trait of this Background may be utilized only once per session; a character with five levels of Kinfolk may only test five times to find a Kinfolk with *Medical* Ability, as each success equals one level of *Medical* Ability present. Storytellers may require more than one success for each level of particularly rare Abilities, Numina or Influence sought, and may decide that multiple Kinfolk are available for more common Abilities; three Kinfolk with one level in *Melee* rather than one Kinfolk with three levels.

Once a Kinfolk has been accessed, he may be found again only if you win the same number of tests. Otherwise, that particular individual is not available or has moved away the next time you call. Kinfolk can only become permanent fixtures in a game if you have enough Experience to buy them as a Kinfolk Influence, the number of Influences required to do so being determined by the Storyteller.

Kinfolk Modifiers

- Metis may not begin the game with this Background.
- Black Fury Kinfolk with Abilities above three are always females.
- Bone Gnawer Kinfolk all have at least one *Street* Influence if homid.
- Children of Gaia Kinfolk all have the extra Trait *Compassionate*.
- Fianna Kinfolk all have one Trait of Performance if homid. Lupine kinfolk all have the extra Trait *Robust*.
- Get of Fenris Kinfolk all have at least one Trait in fighting-related Abilities.
- Glass Walker Kinfolk are all homid, except for those that are in zoos or are pets, which may have only fighting-related Abilities. All homids gain one Trait in business-related skills automatically. If abused in a business deal, these Kinfolk become enemies of the Garou.
- Red Talons may have only lupine Kinfolk, but may call upon five per Trait of Background.
- Shadow Lord Kinfolk will betray the Garou if the Shadow Lord gives them the opportunity, but will do anything commanded by a Shadow Lord as long as the werewolf is watching.
- Silent Strider Kinfolk can never be called on twice, but will always help to their fullest.
- Silver Fang Kinfolk all gain one Trait in society-, money- and politics-related Abilities automatically.
- Stargazer Kinfolk all gain one Trait in mystical-related Abilities.
- Uktena Kinfolk all gain one Trait in *Occult*-related Abilities. When the Background is played, the Narrator secretly makes a Simple Test against the Kinfolk's Trait of Ability. A loss means the Kinfolk is Wyrm-tainted and will betray the Uktena if given a chance.
- Wendigo Kinfolk may not have Influences in non-Native American society, but gain one Trait in *Survival* Abilities.

Totem

Either you or your pack has a totem spirit that watches over you. When a pack is formed, its members often choose a totem spirit to adopt them. This spirit is then summoned by all the members of the pack, and is created using the total score of the pack's Totem Background. Costs to build the spirit are as follows:

One Trait — Provides three Traits to divide among the totem's Willpower, Rage and Gnosis (minimum of one each).

One Trait — Provides 10 Traits of Power.

One Trait — The totem can speak aloud (you do not require the Gift: *Spirit Speech* to converse with it).

One Trait — The totem can locate and appear in the presence of any pack member.

Two Traits — The totem spends the majority of its time with the pack, and is ready to help out.

Two Traits — The totem has a degree of respect among fellow spirits (may retest a single Social Challenge with another spirit per session).

Two Traits — Provides one Charm.

Three Traits — Grants extra pack member the ability to use the totem's powers in a turn.

Four Traits — Totem's mystical connection to the pack members is so strong that they effectively have the Gift: *Mind Speak* with one another (at Storyteller's discretion).

Five Traits — Totem can contact and interact with the physical world for brief periods of time when the need is great.

Five Traits — Totem is feared by agents of the Wyrm (allows pack members to incite fox frenzy on Wyrm creatures, as per Charm: *Incite Frenzy*; cost is three Gnosis; Mental Challenge versus target's Willpower).

For more information on building a totem spirit, see pp. 225-230.

Renown

A Garou's renown defines the Rank and therefore the station of an individual within Garou society. **Apocalypse** characters usually begin at Rank 2, or fostern. Fostern are Garou who have undergone their *Rite of Passage* and proven themselves to their fellow Garou. They have been accepted into the pack, and are treated as adults.

Renown is divided into three categories: Wisdom, Glory and Honor. A beginning player chooses Renown Traits just as he would choose Traits for any other attribute. However, the type of Renown Traits that a player can choose depends on the character's auspice.

See the "Auspice" section above, for beginning Renown. Also, see pp. 138-139, 172-177 and 210-214 for details of gaining Renown.

Renown Traits

Wisdom: *Crafty, Inspired, Inventive, Pragmatic, Profound, Respected, Revered, Sacred, Scholarly, Spiritual, Venerable, Wise*

Glory: *Bold, Brash, Brave, Courageous, Daring, Exalted, Feared, Fearless, Glorious, Imposing, Impressive, Spirited, Superb*

Honor: *Admirable, Commendable, Dutiful, Eminent, Esteemed, Fair, Honorable, Impartial, Just, Noble, Objective, Proud, Reputable, Trusted, Virtuous*

Rage, Gnosis and Willpower

The following Traits allow the Garou to perform miraculous feats beyond human capacity. These Traits are not represented as adjectives. Instead, they are a pool from which the character may draw. These Traits can be represented by cards, which are torn up when the Trait is used, or players can simply record these Traits on their character sheets.

A character's auspice determines her starting Rage Traits, her breed determines her starting Gnosis Traits, and her tribe determines her initial Willpower.

A character has both a Permanent and a temporary rating for each of these Traits. The Permanent rating (the circles on the character sheet) is what you buy at character creation and with Experience; this number represent's the Garou's maximum number of Traits of this type. Temporary ratings (the boxes) can go up and down during gameplay as characters use and regain Rage, Gnosis and Willpower. However, a character's temporary rating in any of these Traits can never exceed her Permanent rating.

Rage

Rage is the all-consuming passion inherent in every Garou. It is also the psychic energy used to change form, powering the transformation from breed form into other shapes. Rage is a tool of destruction, of anger and violence. It can be a dark impulse pushing a Garou to acts of senseless bloodshed and murder. When used constructively against the forces of the Wyrm, this violence can be a useful thing, destroying the enemies of Gaia and protecting the world from destruction and the coming Apocalypse. But Rage must be tempered, because if it overwhelms the wielder, he becomes nothing more than a mindless instrument of destruction, and a perfect tool of the Wyrm.

Using Rage

Rage can be used in many ways, depending on a character's needs. Several examples of how Rage can be used in the course of a story are listed below.

• **Changing Forms**: Changing forms is easier with the use of Rage. By expending a Rage Trait, you are able to change into another form immediately. Otherwise, changing into another form takes one full action per form shifted (so going from Homid to Crinos normally requires two actions). You may, however, take your natural form automatically without spending Rage.

• **Extra Action**: Rage can give a character the ability to perform extra feats during a challenge. This means that a character can challenge several players to different tests at the same time with no penalty. The number of players challenged is determined by the number of Rage Traits spent, but may add up to no more than one-third of the character's total Physical Attributes.

• **Extra Attacks**: A werewolf can also use Rage to attack with greater frequency and ferocity. A Garou who has just won a Physical Challenge in combat can immediately risk a Rage Trait and make a second challenge to attempt to inflict a second wound on a foe. This followup challenge occurs before a new challenge can begin. Furthermore, the Garou who risked the Rage Trait cannot be wounded as a result of this second test, unless his opponent has also risked Rage (or used the vampiric Discipline: *Celerity*).

• **Remaining Active**: When a character becomes Incapacitated from losing a challenge, she may use a Rage Trait to recover one Health Level so as to continue fighting. Doing this to negate an aggravated wound results in a battle scar unless the player wins a Simple Test.

Once a character loses or uses all of his Rage, he is no longer able to change forms. Garou without Rage Traits are considered to have "lost the wolf within," and revert to natural form, whether that be Lupus, Homid or Metis.

If a Garou's Rage is ever higher than his Willpower, he automatically gains Negative Traits which can be bid against him in *any* challenge:

One Rage over: *Bestial*

Two Rage over: *Shortsighted*

Three Rage over: *Clumsy* (Blind with rage)

Regaining Rage

There are multiple ways a Garou can regain Rage, most of which are fairly simple to simulate in a game of **Apocalypse**. They include:

• **The Moon**: When a Garou first sees the moon at night, something deep in her soul surges. The character regains one Rage Trait, or all spent Rage if the moon is in her auspice. (**Storyteller note**: If your game runs once per month, one particular auspice might have an unfair advantage if every session happens during its phase of the moon. It sometimes behooves Storytellers to "improve" nature a little bit in situations like this.)

• **Confrontation**: At the beginning of any new conflict (not necessarily physical combat) in which a challenge is involved, the character regains a Rage Trait. Only one Rage Trait is regained during the confrontation, regardless of the number of challenges.

• **Wounds**: The first time a Garou is wounded in an evening, she regains a Rage Trait. This happens only once per day.

• **Humiliation**: The character may regain a Rage Trait during a particularly humiliating situation. The award of this Trait is strictly at Narrator discretion.

Gnosis

Gnosis is the power of Gaia within a Garou. It is Her presence made real and tangible, and a Garou gains Gnosis as part of his connection with Her. A character's beginning Gnosis is determined by his breed, because it is his birth that establishes his initial connection to Gaia. He may gain extra Gnosis Traits by spending experience and becoming more spiritually aware in a roleplaying sense. Characters can accomplish this either through meditation or through the guidance of another.

Gnosis Traits are used with Gifts and in rites. One Gnosis Trait can be spent to step sideways into the Umbra immediately.

Garou have both Gnosis Traits and a Gnosis Pool. The Gnosis Pool determines how many Gnosis Traits they can store within them, and is the maximum number of Gnosis Traits a Garou can possess. Gnosis Traits can be bid and spent in Static Challenges, just like other Traits.

Garou can regain their spent Gnosis Traits in the following ways:

• **Meditation**: A Garou may spend a Mental Trait and get a Gnosis Trait if she spends 10 minutes meditating alone. Of course, the Mental Trait spent must be a relevant one. (You must have the *Meditation* Ability to regain Gnosis in this manner.)

• **Fetish**: A Garou may gain Gnosis from a fetish, such as the *Tear of Renewal*.

• **Spirits**: A Garou may gain Gnosis through the "death" of an Engling spirit. After either summoning the Engling or running across it in the Umbra, the Garou must convince the spirit to give itself up for the Garou's benefit. If it agrees, the Engling makes a gift of itself to the Garou, and, in death, recharges all the Gnosis Pools of the Garou involved. The Spirit Keeper (see p. 187) has the option of complicating this process.

• **Rites**: A Garou may gain Gnosis through the *Rite of the Cup* (see pp. 131-132), although this Gnosis is actually shared, and must come from another Garou or from a spirit, as opposed to directly from Gaia.

Gnosis in the Umbra

In the Umbra, a Gnosis Trait may be spent to change the reality of the Umbra in some fashion. For example, a Garou may use a Gnosis Trait to step through an Umbral wall, hide her Umbral form briefly or provide some light in darkness.

You may not spend Gnosis and Rage in the same challenge (or in place of one another) unless the system description specifically says otherwise.

Willpower

Willpower measures the capability of a character to overcome the urges and desires that tempt her and her inner strength of purpose. In times of catastrophe, ordinary people have been known to perform extraordinary feats, such as lifting an automobile off a pinned pedestrian or running through a burning building to save a trapped child. A Garou can even fight death if she truly has the will to live. Willpower gives a character the extra strength necessary to overcome obstacles and succeed where others would give up and fail.

Each character begins the game with a number of Willpower Traits. For Garou, the number of Traits depends on the character's tribe. Willpower Traits can be used for almost anything that the player deems important. A few examples of how Willpower can be used by Garou are provided below. With Willpower, you can:

• Negate the effects of frenzy (by using a Willpower Trait, the character gains a new tolerance of a situation that would ordinarily throw her into frenzy).

• Gain automatic success in any Simple Test or Static Challenge.

• Replenish all lost Traits in any one category: Physical, Social or Mental.

• Ignore the side effects of wounds, such as Incapacitation, for one challenge.

• Negate the effects of any one Mental or Social Challenge.

Once a Willpower Trait has been used, it is gone until the end of the story. It is possible that a Narrator may choose to give a character Willpower during the course of a story as a reward for extraordinary roleplaying. Such a reward should be given for portraying the character's Nature or Derangement appropriately, or for any other exceptional reasons that the Narrator deems suitable.

Final Touches

Your character should now have her basics more or less ready to go. In the final stages of character creation, you have the opportunity to improve certain statistics and add more Abilities, Backgrounds, Merits and/or Flaws and Influences. You also need to add her personal details and develop more of your character's history. Still, at this point the hard part is over; what's left is icing on the cake.

Physical Negative Traits: *Clumsy, Cowardly, Decrepit, Delicate, Docile, Flabby, Lame, Lethargic, Puny, Sickly*

Social Negative Traits: *Callous, Condescending, Dull, Naive, Obnoxious, Paranoid, Repugnant, Shy, Tactless, Untrustworthy*

Mental Negative Traits: *Forgetful, Gullible, Ignorant, Impatient, Oblivious, Predictable, Shortsighted, Submissive, Witless*

For descriptions of these Negative Traits, see pp. 37-42.

Negative Traits and Flaws

The number of Traits and Abilities your character has can be increased by one for each Negative Trait that you add to the three Attribute categories (maximum of five), or each point of Flaws you take on (up to a maximum of seven at character creation)

See also "Flaws," pp. 141-153.

With one Negative Trait, you can:

• Take one additional Trait.

• Take an additional Ability.

• Take an additional Background.

• Take one Trait of Merits.

• Buy an Influence Trait.

With two Negative Traits, you can:
• Take an additional Rage Trait.
• Take an additional Gnosis Trait.
With three Negative Traits, you can:
• Take an additional Basic Gift from your breed, auspice or tribe.
• Take an additional Willpower Trait.

Influence

At this stage, you can, if you wish, buy Influence Traits for your character. Each Influence Trait costs a Trait. Whether that Trait is gained from taking Negative Traits or Flaws is up to you.

A Garou with Influence Traits has gained a certain degree of control in aspects of normal human society. While many Garou shun taking such an active role in human affairs, others see it as the only way to keep accurate tabs on certain organizations and groups. Most forms of influence in this game reflect contacts and allies not of Kinfolk stock. (See also "Kinfolk" Background, pp. 49-50.)

One area of Influence may be chosen for every Trait invested in Influences. Note that Influence does not give you full knowledge of a particular area (Abilities handle that), but it does give you sway over a certain area of human society.

Some uses of Influence may not actually cost anything to employ, but instead require that you possess a certain level of the Influence in question. In these cases, it is likely that a Narrator may require a challenge of some sort to represent the uncertainty or added difficulty involved when exercising Influence.

To use Influence actively, you should explain to a Narrator what sort of effect you wish to create. She decides the number of Traits needed, which can be subject to sudden change depending upon circumstance, the time involved (both real and in-game) and any tests required. In certain cases, the Storyteller may decide that two or more types of Influence are necessary to accomplish a goal. This adds an element of realism, and encourages characters to diversify their interests more widely than they might have otherwise in order to obtain the Influences they need.

A character with Influence is usually given Influence Cards to represent the areas of control that he has. Influence Cards used during a game are returned at the beginning of the next session. Influence may be loaned or traded to others. To do this, the card is given to another player and is not returned to its owner until after it is spent or voluntarily returned, or one month passes. In order for a trade of Influences to occur, the Influence Card in question must be signed over by the owner and the new owner's name is written on the card as well. Traits permanently signed away in this fashion are gone, though one can receive as well as give Influence.

Sometimes characters may wish to try to counteract the Influence of other characters. In such cases, it generally costs one Trait per Trait being countered. The character willing to expend the most Influence Traits (assuming she has them to spend) achieves her goal; all Traits used in this sort of conflict are considered expended.

In practice, the use of Influence is never instantaneous and rarely expedient. While a character may be able to, say, condemn any building in the city, it will not be torn down that night. For sake of game flow, a Storyteller may allow trivial uses of Influence to only take half an hour to occur. Major manipulations, on the other hand, can become the center of ongoing plots that require several sessions to bring to fruition.

The guidelines below by no means limit the number of Influence Traits that can be spent at one time or the degree of change a character may bring about. They are merely an advisory measure to help Storytellers adjudicate the costs of certain actions. The highest number listed on each Influence is just a recommended maximum effect to allow in game play. Higher ratings are only useful to speed up a process (double Trait cost to halve the time needed). Garou characters may not possess more than their total Attribute Traits (Physical, Social and Mental) in Influences at any one time — there's only so much you can keep a handle on.

Actions followed by an asterisk (*) below indicate that their effects can generally be accomplished without expending an Influence Trait; simply having the Traits is enough "pull."

Possible areas of Influence include the following:

Bureaucracy

The organizational aspects of local, state or even federal government fall within the character's sphere of control. She can bend and twist as she sees fit the tangle of rules and regulations that seem necessary to run our society. The character may have contacts or allies among government clerks, supervisors, utility workers, road crews, surveyors and numerous other civil servants.

Cost	Desired Effect
1	Trace utility bills*
2	Fake a birth certificate or driver's license; Disconnect a residence's utilities; Close a small road or park; Get public aid ($250)
3	Fake a death certificate, passport or green card; Close a public school for a single day; Turn a single utility on a block on or off; Shut down a minor business on a violation
4	Initiate a phone tap; Initiate a department-wide investigation; Fake land deeds
5	Start, stop or alter a city-wide program or policy; Shut down a big business on a violation; Rezone areas; Obliterate records of a person on a city and county level
6	Arrange a fixed audit of a person or business

Church

Not even churches are without politics and intrigue upon which an opportunistic person may capitalize. *Church* Influence usually applies only to mainstream faiths. Sometimes other practices fall under the *Occult* Influence. Contacts and allies affected by *Church* Influence include: ministers, bishops, priests, activists, evangelists, witch-hunters, nuns and various church attendees and assistants.

Cost	Desired Effect
1	Identify most secular members of a given faith in the local area; Pass as a member of the clergy;* Peruse general church records (baptism, marriage, burial, etc.)
2	Identify higher church members; Track regular members; Suspend lay members
3	Open or close a single church; Find the average church-associated hunter; Dip into the collection plate ($250); Gain access to private information and archives of a church
4	Discredit or suspend high-level members; Manipulate regional branches
5	Organize major protests; Access ancient church lore and knowledge
6	Borrow or access church relics or sacred items
7	Use the resources of a diocese

Finance

The world teems with the trappings of affluence and stories of the rich and famous. Those with the *Finance* Influence speak the language of money and know where to find capital. They have a degree of access to banks, megacorporations and the truly wealthy citizens of the world. Such characters also have a wide variety of servants to draw on, such as CEOs, bankers, corporate yes-men, financiers, bank tellers, stock brokers and loan agents.

Cost	Desired Effect
1	Earn money; Learn about major transactions and financial events; Raise capital ($1,000); Learn about general economic trends;* Learn real motivations for many financial actions of others
2	Trace an unsecured small account; Raise capital to purchase a small business (single small store)
3	Purchase a large business (a few small branches or a single large store or service)
4	Manipulate local banking (delay deposits, some credit rating alterations); Ruin a small business
5	Control an aspect of city-wide banking (shut off ATMs, arrange a bank "holiday"); Ruin a large business; Purchase a major company
6	Spark an economic trend; Instigate widespread layoffs

Health

In our modern world, a myriad of organizations and resources exist to deal with every mortal ache and ill, at least in theory. The network of health agencies, hospitals, asylums and medical groups is subject to exploitation by someone with *Health* Influence. Nurses, doctors, specialists, lab workers, therapists, counselors and pharmacists are just a few of the workers within the health field.

Cost	Desired Effect
1	Access a person's health records;* Fake vaccination records and the like; Use public functions of health centers at your leisure
2	Access to some medical research records; Have minor lab work done; Get a copy of coroner's report
3	Instigate minor quarantines; Corrupt results of tests or inspections; Alter medical records
4	Acquire a body; Completely rewrite medical records; Abuse grants for personal use ($250); Have minor medical research performed on a subject; Institute large-scale quarantines; Shut down businesses for "health code violations"
5	Have special research projects performed; Have people institutionalized or released

High Society

A clique of people exists, who, by virtue of birth, possessions, talent or quirks of fate, hold themselves above the great unwashed masses. *High Society* allows the character to direct and use the energies and actions of this exceptional mass of talents. Among the ranks of the elite, one can find dilettantes, the old rich, movie and rock stars, artists of all sorts, wannabes, fashion models and trend-setters.

Cost	Desired Effect
1	Learn what is trendy;* Obtain "hard to get" tickets for shows; Learn about concerts, shows or plays well before they are announced to the public*
2	Track most celebrities and luminaries; Be a local voice in the entertainment field; "Borrow" $1,000 as idle cash from rich friends
3	Crush promising careers; Hobnob well above your station*
4	Gain minor celebrity status
5	Get a brief appearance on a talk show that's not about to be canceled; Ruin a new club, gallery, festival or other high society gathering

Industry

The dark world of the Gothic-Punk milieu is built by pumping and grinding machinery and the toil of countless laborers. A character with the *Industry* Influence has her fingers in this pie. Industry is composed of union workers, foremen, engineers, contractors, construction workers and manual laborers.

Cost	Desired Effect
1	Learn about industrial projects and movements*
2	Have minor projects performed; Dip into union funds or embezzle petty cash ($500); Arrange small accidents or sabotage
3	Organize minor strikes; Appropriate machinery for a short time
4	Close down a small plant; Revitalize a small plant
5	Manipulate large local industry
6	Cut off production of a single resource in a small region

Legal

There are those who quietly tip the scales, even in the hallowed halls of justice, and the courts, law schools, law firms and justice bureaus within them. Inhabiting these halls are lawyers, judges, bailiffs, clerks, district attorneys and ambulance chasers.

Cost	Desired Effect
1	Get free representation for minor cases
2	Avoid bail for some charges; Have minor charges dropped
3	Manipulate legal procedures (minor wills and contracts, court dates); Access public or court funds ($250); Get representation in most court cases
4	Issue subpoenas; Tie up court cases; Have most legal charges dropped; Cancel or arrange parole
5	Close down all but the most serious investigations; Have deportation proceedings held against someone

Media

The media serves as the eyes and ears of the world. While few in this day and age believe that the news is not corrupted, many would be surprised at who closes these eyes and covers these ears from time to time. The media entity is composed of station directors, editors, reporters, anchors, camera people, photographers and radio personalities.

Cost	Desired Effect
1	Learn about breaking stories early;* Submit small articles (within reason)
2	Suppress (but not stop) small articles or reports; Get hold of investigative reporting information
3	Initiate news investigations and reports; Get project funding and waste it ($250); Access media production resources; Ground stories and projects
4	Broadcast fake stories (local only)

Occult

Most people are curious about the supernatural world and the various groups and beliefs that make up the occult subculture, but few consider it anything but a hoax, a diversion or a curiosity. This could not be further from the truth. Occult Influence, more than any other, hits the Garou close to home and could very well bring humanity to its senses about just who and what shares this world with them. The occult community contains cult leaders, alternative religious groups, charlatans, would-be occultists and New Agers.

Cost	Desired Effect
1	Contact and make use of common occult groups and their practices; Know some of the more visible occult figures*
2	Know and contact some of the more obscure occult figures;* Access resources for most rituals and rites
3	Know the general vicinity of certain supernatural entities (Kindred, Garou, mages, mummies, wraiths, etc.) and possibly contact them; Access vital or very rare material components; Milk impressionable wannabes for bucks ($250); Access occult tomes and writings; Research a Basic Ritual
4	Research an Intermediate Ritual
5	Access minor magic items; Unearth an Advanced Ritual
6	Research a new or unheard-of ritual or rite from tomes or mentors

Police

"To protect and serve" is a popular motto among the chosen enforcers of the law. But these days, everyone can have reason to doubt the law's ability to enact justice. Perhaps they should wonder whom the law defends, whom it serves, and why. The *Police* Influence encompasses the likes of beat cops, desk jockeys, prison guards, special divisions (such as SWAT and homicide), detectives and various clerical positions.

Cost	Desired Effect
1	Learn police procedures;* Hear police information and rumors; Avoid traffic tickets
2	Have license plates checked; Avoid minor violations (first conviction); Get "inside information"
3	Get copies of an investigation report; Have police hassle, detain or harass someone; Find bureau secrets
4	Access confiscated weapons or contraband; Have some serious charges dropped; Start an investigation; Get money, either from the evidence room or as an appropriation ($1,000)
5	Institute major investigations; Arrange setups; Instigate bureau investigations; Have officers fired
6	Paralyze departments for a time; Close down a major investigation

Politics

Nothing ever gets done for straightforward reasons any more. It's all who knows who and what favors can get paid off in the process. In other words, it's politics as usual, and there's a whole class of people who thrive in this world of favors and policy flacks. Some of these individuals include statesmen, pollsters, activists, party members, lobbyists, candidates and politicians themselves.

Cost	Desired Effect
1	Minor lobbying; Identify real platforms of politicians and parties;* Be in the know*
2	Meet small-time politicians; Have a forewarning of processes, laws and the like; Use a slush fund or fund raiser ($1,000)

3	Sway or alter political projects (local parks, renovations, small construction)
4	Enact minor legislation; Dash careers of minor politicians
5	Get your candidate in a minor office; Enact encompassing legislation
6	Block the passage of major bills; Suspend major laws temporarily; Use state bureaus or subcommittees
7	Usurp county-wide politics; Subvert statewide powers, at least to a moderate degree
8	Call out a local division of the National Guard; Declare a state of emergency in a region

Street

Disenchanted, disenfranchised and ignored by their "betters," a whole collective of humanity has made its own culture and lifestyle to deal with the harsh lot life has dealt them. In the dark alleys and slums reside gang members, the homeless, street performers, petty criminals, prostitutes and the forgotten.

Cost	Desired Effect
1	Have an ear open for the word on the street; Identify most gangs and know their turfs and habits
2	Live mostly without fear on the underside of society; Keep a contact or two in most aspects of street life; Access small-time contraband
3	Get regular insight into other areas of Influence; Arrange some services from street people or gangs; Get pistols or uncommon melee weapons
4	Mobilize groups of homeless; Panhandle or hold a "collection" ($250); Get hold of a shotgun, rifle or submachine gun; Hold respect among gangs and have a say in almost all aspects of their operations
5	Control a single medium-sized gang; Arrange impressive protests by street people

Transportation

The world is in constant motion, its prosperity relying heavily on the fact that people and productions fly, float or roll to and from every corner of the planet. Without the means to perform this monumental task, our "small" world would quickly become a daunting orb with large, isolated stretches. The forces that keep this circulation in motion include cab and bus drivers, pilots, air traffic controllers, travel firms, sea captains, conductors, border guards and untold others.

Cost	Desired Effect
1	A wizard at what goes where, when and why; Can travel locally quickly and freely*
2	Can track an unwary target if he uses public transportation; Arrange passage safe (or at least concealed) from mundane threats (robbery, terrorism, etc.)
3	Seriously hamper an individual's ability to travel; Avoid most supernatural dangers when traveling (such as hunters and vampires)
4	Temporarily shut down one form of transportation (bus lines, ships, planes, trains, etc.); Route money your way ($500)

5	Reroute major modes of travel; Smuggle with impunity
6	Extend control to nearby areas
7	Isolate small or remote regions for a short period

Underworld

Even in the most cosmopolitan of ages, society has found certain needs and services too questionable to accept. In every age, some organized effort has stepped in to provide for this demand, regardless of the risks. Among this often ruthless and dangerous crowd are the likes of hitmen, Mafia, Yakuza, bookies, fences and launderers.

Cost	Desired Effect
1	Locate minor contraband (knives, smalltime drugs, petty gambling, scalped tickets)
2	Obtain pistols, serious drugs, stolen cars; Hire muscle to rough up someone; Fence minor loot; Prove that crime pays (and score $1,000)
3	Obtain a rifle, shotgun or submachine gun; Arrange a minor "hit"; Know someone in "the Family"
4	White collar crime connections
5	Arrange gangland assassinations; Hire a demolition man or firebug; Supply local drug needs

University

In an age when the quest for learning and knowledge begins in schools, colleges and universities, information becomes currency. *University* Influence represents a certain degree of control and perhaps involvement in these institutions. In this sphere of Influence, one finds the teachers, professors, deans, students of all ages and levels, Greek orders and many young and impressionable minds.

Cost	Desired Effect
1	Know layout and policy of local schools;* Access to low-level university resources; Get records up to the high school level
2	Know a contact or two with useful knowledge or skills; Minor access to facilities; Fake high school records; Obtain college records
3	Faculty favors; Cancel a class; Fix grades; Discredit a student
4	Organize student protests and rallies; Discredit faculty members; Acquire money through a grant ($1,000)
5	Falsify an undergraduate degree
6	Arrange major projects; Alter curriculum institution-wide; Free run of facilities

Spark of Life

These are the little peccadilloes and personality details that you can add to your character to make him seem more like flesh and blood and less like just a collection of Traits. These features could be anything, such as a habit of giggling when under stress, an interest in collecting stamps, an aversion to apologizing, "lucky" socks with pigs on them — anything that adds an extra splash of life to your character.

Fleshing it Out

Background

Now is when you fill in all the little details, such as where your character came from and what he does on a regular basis. By casting yourself in the role of your character, you should try to find the answers to the following questions:

What was your childhood like? Did you have any sort of formal schooling after the Change? If you are a lupus, how well did you adjust to what you are, and how do you perceive the world of humans?

You should also give some reasons for your character to be a part of the pack. Always consult your Storyteller before you get your heart set on anything; she might already be planning a story about how your pack forms.

Motivations

What do you want to do, and why? Is there more to your life as a Garou than merely fighting the Wyrm? If not, should there be?

The Garou see the world they know drawing to a close, but that doesn't absolve them of the responsibilities of having lives once they're off the front lines. Many have goals both inside and outside their packs. Most Garou have their own views of the world and opinions on how to affect it. Many are eager to earn the respect of their fellows.

Appearance

What do you look like when you're in Homid form? How do you dress? How do you carry yourself?

Many of these details can be gleaned from your background, but even more should be added here. You should ultimately select an appearance (and costume) that reflects and represents every aspect of your character. Obviously this is not intended to be taken literally, but a Bone Gnawer should definitely have a different wardrobe selection than, say, a Glass Walker.

Equipment

If you already have a fetish (from your Background Traits), then that's something you automatically have. However, your character might have other odds and ends that she carries around. Any selections must be approved by the Storyteller, and don't be surprised if you can't have everything you want. Some of it might not be appropriate to the nature or scope of the story — not everyone can have a satchel full of antipersonnel weapons.

Breeds

A Garou's breed determines part of her basic personality, and often colors her perceptions and beliefs about the world. There are three breeds: homid, metis and lupus. A werewolf's breed is determined by that of her mother, except for the obvious exception (metis).

Homid

The most common breed, homid Garou are born to a human or homid mother and suffer from her lack of connection to Gaia. Because humanity has separated itself from the Wyld and become more focused on the trials and tribulations of civilization, members of the homid breed are disassociated from their wild inner selves.

This is why so many homids are lost cubs, who do not know their true heritage. Many times a homid child will have his First Change in a strange place without the aid of other Garou, and the shock can drive an unprepared new Garou into Lunacy. These Lunatics are often prey for the Wyrm if they are not found and adopted into a tribe or pack.

Yet homids are the most adaptable breed. Many Garou believe that homids will be the last to fall before the Apocalypse is over.

Natural Form: Homid
Beginning Gifts: *Jam Technology, Persuasion, Smell of Man*
Initial Gnosis: One

Lupus

These are Garou whose mother is either a wolf or a lupus Garou. This breed is the least represented among the Garou. This is, in part, because of the nearly genocidal killing of wolves throughout North America and Europe. Wolves once had the largest natural range of any terrestrial mammal except man. Currently, the only significant populations in North America are in Canada, Alaska and northern Minnesota.

Part of playing a lupus character is understanding lupine nature. You must keep in mind some of the facts about wolves that make them different from homid or metis Garou.

Wolves are nocturnal or crepuscular (meaning that they come out at twilight), although diurnal (or daytime) activity is not uncommon, especially during cool weather and in winter. Lupus Garou are often night creatures, tending to be sluggish and sleepy during the day. They are almost entirely carnivorous. Some lupus Garou have adapted enough to eat foods other than meat, but they usually like their meat bloody, warm and freshly killed.

Lupus do not understand many human concepts at first. The concept of time is difficult for them, as are using money and operating technology (they refer to such as "Weaver-tech"). Human laws, bureaucracy and computers are totally alien to lupus Garou.

Furthermore, lupus do not communicate as humans do. In fact, they have to learn human tongues by painstakingly taking Homid form and trying to form strange words. Howling, posturing and marking territory with their scent glands are the ways they normally get a point across.

Lupus characters howl during courtship and mating, as a warning, as part of worshipping the moon and in celebration. In addition to howling, wolves bark, growl and whine. Barking is associated with surprise and warning. Growling occurs during challenges, and is associated with threatening behavior or asserting one's rights. Whines are associated with greetings, hungry cubs, playtime and other signs of anxiety, curiosity or inquiry. These are intimate noises that lupus Garou make to other wolves and to each other.

Lupus posture to show dominance; the most common pose is to place one's paw on another lupus as that lupus rolls over to accept dominance. Lupus also mark possessions and territories with their scent glands, which, in Crinos form, are located on the wrists and the neck.

The dominant members of a lupus pack are the alpha male and alpha female. In a lupus pack, only the alpha pair breeds with wolves, and this pair also suppresses breeding by all other pack members. However, all pack members help care for pups and feed them as well. Unlike packs composed of homid and metis Garou, many lupus packs have Kinfolk wolves as members.

Lupus Garou respect other Garou more when they take Lupus form to communicate. They generally have a hard time considering their actions in terms of future results or as a result of past actions. They live in the present for the most part, and often take the most logical, most commonsensical course of action, rather than involve themselves in complicated schemes. They do not often make elaborate plans; instinct usually guides them.

Lupus believe that Gaia watches over them and will provide for them. They are perhaps the most spiritual of the breeds. They are known to respect Theurges of all breeds more than they do the other auspices, and they show respect for all spirits encountered in the Umbra.

Natural Form: Lupus

Beginning Gifts: *Heightened Senses, Catfeet, Scent of the True Form*

Initial Gnosis: Three

Restrictions: A lupus cannot begin the game with certain Backgrounds or Abilities, as described previously.

Metis

When a Garou mates with another Garou, the result is a metis. This mating is proscribed by the Litany, and is considered a perversion among the Garou. In these last days, when so many Garou are dying and not many are born among the lupus or homids, it is very tempting for some of the remaining Garou to consider producing another Garou this way. Still, the fact that metis are born disfigured is proof enough for most Garou that such offspring are somehow tainted by the Wyrm.

Despite their stigma, metis usually grow up fully aware of their Garou heritage, and have the unmistakable proof (natural Crinos form) that they are Garou from the day they are born. This head start in the world of the Garou is a powerful thing, because metis do not have to go through the traumatic First Change as homids or lupus do, and they are often taught Beginning Gifts even before they show signs of changing. Metis sometimes take their first trips into the Umbra as children, as it is a simple thing for them to step sideways even before they first learn to walk. It is a good thing that a metis has Garou parents; not many human parents could handle a toddler whose natural form is a growling Crinos. Garou mothers usually assume Crinos form in order to give birth to metis, but the births are always difficult and dangerous.

Metis are considered the cursed of Gaia because of the sin that caused their births. They are, by nature, infertile, and they all have at least one disfigurement. This disfigurement is always detrimental.

Natural Form: Crinos. Unlike homid or lupus breeds, metis always regenerate their damage in Crinos, but they also always take damage from silver because of their natural form. They are truly an amalgam of human and wolf, and there is no true "natural" form for them to assume.

Beginning Gifts: *Sense Wyrm, Create Element, Shed*
Initial Gnosis: Two

Metis Disfigurements

All metis characters have some sort of disfigurement. You must choose one from the list below, or make up your own and have it approved by a Narrator. All mandatory Negative Traits that come from a disfigurement do not count toward the normal bonuses gained by Negative Traits. In other words, you cannot gain extra Traits simply by choosing to play a metis, but you can add additional Negative Traits to a metis character.

Bad Hearing: You must take the Negative Trait: *Oblivious*, and you lose all ties related to hearing. You must roleplay your disability. This can actually be useful as you can encourage other Garou to repeat themselves. Of course, many Garou have frenzied for simpler reasons — like just being forced to endure the company of a metis for too long.

Chitinous Skin: You have developed a hard chitinous surface on your skin that cracks and sheds constantly. You gain one Health Level against hand-held weapons, but not bullets. Take all the disadvantages of *Hairless* on this list and the Negative Trait: *Decrepit*.

Cleft Lip: You have a cleft lip. Speaking is difficult for you, but at least you can snarl. You are down one Trait and lose all ties on Social Challenges related to your speech or appearance. You should roleplay this disability; it's hard to understand you when you get excited.

Hairless: Your body hair is mangy, patchy or totally nonexistent. When in Homid form you have the Negative Trait: *Sickly*. When in Lupus form you must take the Negative Trait: *Repugnant* instead. Furthermore, you are one Trait down in any challenge when the temperature outside drops below 50 degrees (10 Celsius).

Human Face: You retain a human face in all your forms, and therefore must take the Negative Trait: *Repugnant*. You also do not gain any Trait bonuses for perception while in Lupus or Crinos forms. This mutation is disgusting to Garou, who will be horrified at the sight of you, and might well assume you to be a fomor or Black Spiral Dancer.

Hunchback: You cannot take any of the following Social Traits: *Elegant, Beguiling, Gorgeous* or *Seductive*, nor may you have the Physical Traits: *Graceful, Lithe* or *Nimble*. You must take the Negative Trait: *Repugnant* as well as either *Lame* or *Clumsy*.

Madness: You are slightly mad. You must either win a Static Mental Test or spend a Willpower Trait whenever you find yourself in a stressful situation. Otherwise, you will have a temporary Derangement imposed on you by a Narrator. This problem can cause many Garou to distrust you.

Malformed Limb: You cannot take the Physical Trait: *Dexterous*, and you must take the Negative Trait: *Lame*. Your movement rate is halved, and you lose all Dexterity-related ties except in combat.

Musk: You smell. Most humans attribute it to bad perfume, but it sets animals on edge and causes lupus Garou to avoid you. You are easily tracked by your smell, and you must take the Negative Trait: *Obnoxious*. You must bid two Traits to initiate a Social Challenge, and even so you still lose all ties to Garou, anyone using *Heightened Senses* or animals.

No Claws: You have no claws, and you do not do aggravated damage when you strike with your paws. Curiously enough, your bite doesn't cause aggravated damage, either. You may never acquire a Gift that allows extra damage to be done by either tooth or claw.

Auspice

The Touch of Luna

It is often difficult to explain the nature of auspice to those who don't have Garou blood coursing through their veins. Some, in their ignorance, assume it merely to be some form of garbled astrology. Others, who have some understanding of such things, dislike the destiny of purpose they think auspice represents. Many young Garou who are disdainful of anything that hints at constraint make similar mistakes. One's auspice is not a predestined and inflexible path that a Garou is forced to follow. Instead, it is a silvery beacon that serves to illuminate her path through life. The influence of an auspice comes as much from within as it does from without.

Auspice also serves as an important focus of Garou social life. The Garou as a whole lack the vast diversity of potential interaction that their human counterparts enjoy. Therefore, it is not uncommon for Garou of a like auspice to gather together for fellowship. These meetings are informal and not at all closed to other Garou. The "Society" section provides more details on these meetings.

In addition to the phase of the moon, many mark a difference between waxing auspices and waning auspices. When waxing, the moon provides a more positive, aggressive and direct auspice. When waning, the moon inspires a more negative, introspective and indirect auspice. Thus, a waxing Galliard may be a great public performer, while a waning Galliard may only create songs for herself and dwell on things in private.

It should be noted that the brighter, more clearly seen planets (Mars, Venus, Mercury and Jupiter) are sometimes also visible in the night sky on the day a Garou is born, as well as whether those planets are rising or falling in the sky. Saturn is ignored, as it is referred to as the "Star of the Wyrm."

Ragabash

Nickname: Trickster, New Moon

Although annoying, the Trickster strives to bring and understand wisdom through the folly of self-importance and humility. The Ragabash keeps others on their toes by pulling pranks that highlight the "personality traps" over which others would otherwise trip.

Mischief may be expected from the Ragabash, but it is not often appreciated. They are tolerated but not trusted. The major strength of a New Moon is the flexibility that comes with her nonstructured behavior.

Ragabash are regarded as necessary nuisances, and given much more of a free rein to bend the Litany and traditions. Elders tend to not notice tricksters working their pranks, but remember that Ragabash are still bound to the sacred laws. A New Moon that pranks to be mean rather than to aid Luna in teaching others to understand her wisdom had best watch his back. Most Garou are not known for their sense of humor.

The Coyote totem has been known to consort with Ragabash, and these Garou are fond of playing jokes on everyone they meet — mages, vampires and especially faeries.

Beginning Gifts: *Alter Scent, Blur of the Milky Eye, Open Seal, Scent of Running Water*

Stereotype: A Ragabash is regarded as a shifty, untrustworthy prankster who must be watched every minute. In reality, however, only those Garou with no sense of humor have reason to fear.

Initial Rage: One

Quote: "You are the fastest runner, so you take the bag. You've proved your speed in front of everyone by racing to be the first to every kill. That is why I wanted to teach you my secret way to hunt my favorite food. Now you squat down here in this prickly bush and hold the bag low, and I'll chase the snipe this way. What does snipe taste like? Umm, it tastes a bit like crow. Now you stay put. I'll be back."

Theurge

Nickname: Seer, Crescent Moon

Theurges explore the paths of the spirit, and are the auspice most familiar with the Umbra. They serve as healers, prophets, exorcists, diviners, spiritual counselors, purifiers, artificers and summoners. Like the human shamans of native cultures, Theurge Garou stand aloof and mysterious.

Because they are allied with the spirit world, Theurges often have conversations with people who aren't "there," and they develop complicated superstitions. Some of these superstitions are Bans laid on them by spirits. (See pp. 199-200.)

Beginning Gifts: *Mother's Touch, Name the Spirit, Sense Wyrm, Sight from Beyond, Spirit Speech*

Stereotype: Although Theurges are powerful in the spirit world, more physically oriented Garou often see Theurges as strange, unearthly and weak in combat. This is not the case; many Theurges learn the martial arts in order to be able to intimidate and/or do battle with spirits. Still, it is not a coincidence that many of the Theurges of a sept tend to gather together in medicine circles, for only a Theurge can truly understand another.

Initial Rage: One

Quote: "Sit by me, and tell me what you see in the smoke from the firepit. You say you see nothing? Well, *they* see you. I have spoken with the spirits of your ancestors in the smoke, and I see them follow you to the place of the Weaver. They know much, but you must hear their wisdom for yourself. Listen to the smoke, not the fire, unless you are afraid of being burned."

Philodox

Nickname: Keeper of the Ways, Half Moon

Much about the Garou is a matter of balance; balance between wolf and man, between spirit and flesh, and between creation and destruction. Born when Luna's face sits on the threshold between light and darkness, Philodox are the physical incarnation of balance, and they are renowned among the Garou for their unbiased outlook. Indeed, the words of Philodox are often taken to heart by even the most radical Garou factions. Philodox value this honor, and strive to maintain their image as fair and impartial judges in the eyes of other Garou. The Philodox who does otherwise may be ostracized by other Half Moons.

A Philodox is often the mediator and peacemaker in packs. The older and wiser are called upon as judges and arbitrators on a wide variety of matters. Few would argue their inestimable value to the already fractious Garou.

Beginning Gifts: *Resist Pain, Scent of the True Form, Strength of Purpose, Truth of Gaia*

Stereotype: The Philodox are often seen as mediators of others' conflicts. They are typically perceived as being the most honorable of all the Garou. Though Philodox cannot help but see the world in terms of balance, they are loath to express their views unless others ask them to. This reluctance to become involved often makes them seem unconcerned to other auspices. Sometimes, by "playing the devil's advocate," they actually hinder split-second decisions that are necessary.

Initial Rage: Two

Quote: "What you are shouting is not The Way. Stop baring your teeth at each other long enough to talk to me. We are going to resolve this problem now so that it does not continue to distract us from our quest. Now, you go first and do not even think about lying, because you know that I'll catch you."

Galliard

Nickname: Moon Dancer, Gibbous Moon

The Garou born under this phase of the moon are imbued with the spark of creation. The greatest poems, songs and tales of the Garou have sprung from their fertile minds. Their thoughts are like quicksilver, racing and fluid, dashing headlong into places where few other Garou give a passing glance. The Moon Dancers lead septs in their howls during moots. Their energetic and inspirational performances infect an entire sept, filling the Garou with a sense of belonging and tradition. This is an important role in a time when so many Garou are losing their sense of direction and purpose.

Passion is the Galliard's strength and most dangerous ally. They feel the passions of life, the ongoing joys of nature, and the pull of carnage that ignites the shadowy parts of the soul. Luna races in their veins, and it is only this dance of life and death that matters.

Beginning Gifts: *Beast Speech, Call of the Wyld, Mindspeak*

Stereotype: The Galliard are seen as having little sense of restraint and no sense of self-control. On the other hand, they possess a great capacity to understand others and guide them.

Initial Rage: Two

Quote: "Why are you not dancing with the rest of us? It is the time of the Revel. I know you miss your packmate, but he died such a glorious death. To die in order to save so many — this was a deed of great Honor, and I shall sing it into the Silver Record. Hurry up! The Hunt is about to begin, and I know how much you love the Chase. It is a glorious night, and it is wonderful to be alive!"

Ahroun

Nickname: Warrior, Full Moon

Ahroun are the teeth and claws of the moon's rage, the fury of the wounded earth itself. If Ahroun live long enough to temper their anger with wisdom, they become the most dangerous creatures alive. But in youth they tend to live for the thrill of battle and life-and-death action. These warriors are known for their temper, their embracing of death as part of the Ahroun's due and their fanatical belief in the war leader's code — "First one into battle, last one standing."

Beginning Gifts: *The Falling Touch, Inspiration, Razor Claws,*

Stereotype: The Ahroun are all that is mighty, proud and foolish in Garou. They make better wartime leaders but sometimes stumble in peacetime situations; there is often too much beast in Ahroun for them to appreciate the worth of things besides battle.

Initial Rage: Three

Quote: "Beat the drums and howl your challenges! Tonight we kill Wyrmspawn. Who charges with me? We shall rip flesh tonight! And brave Garou heroes shall join with Gaia as we water Her fields with our blood. Such a good day to die. Such a good time to be alive!"

Tribes

There are 13 Garou tribes available to characters. These tribes organize the remaining Garou who fight against the Wyrm. Originally all tribes were one. Strife and personality conflict drove wedges into this Pangaea tribe, and as the separate groups moved out across the globe and later mixed with the indigenous cultures, many (nearly irreconcilable) differences were formed. During that time, most tribes were very regional, each controlling and living in a certain portion of the world. However, in recent centuries, as human civilization became more widespread and transportation grew more efficient, the restrictions of geography began to matter less and less. Nonetheless, the Garou still take pride in their origins. A Garou's tribe is the extended family, the heritage, that gives him purpose and prevents him from becoming a lone marauder.

Black Furies

The Black Furies are the sacred protectors of the Wyld, defenders of women and punishers of men. They believe that Luna, in the guise of the Greek goddess Artemis, created the tribe from she-wolves to guard the holy sites and things of Gaia. Like Artemis, the Black Furies uphold their duties with grim determination.

Other tribes see the all-female tribe as suffering from a major gender bias. The Furies either give away or kill any males born to them, except the rare male metis who is kept as an example. Black Furies believe that women naturally have a better understanding of Gaia than any male could ever hope to achieve. Furies search the world for lost sacred places and missing artifacts, worship the virgin huntress, Artemis, as their Goddess, and protect women, Wyld and Nature. They see themselves as aspects of the Goddess incarnate and, in her name, Rage against those who would defile that which they protect.

Black Furies retain strong connections to ancient mysticism and the Wyld. They place such a high value on honor that even their hated rivals concede that the tribe can always be trusted.

Totem: Pegasus

Initial Willpower: One

Tribe Advantage: Artemis

Black Furies can recover one Willpower Trait per day spent at a site holy to Gaia. They may also trade Willpower with other Black Furies (and sometimes with other worshippers of Artemis).

Tribe Drawback: Distrust of Men

Black Furies have a long-lived anger against men, who have forced women to bear the brunt of their desires and whims. Furies lose all ties against frenzy when a stressful situation involves a male.

Backgrounds: No restrictions.

Tribe Gifts: *Heightened Senses, Sense of the Prey, Sense Wyrm*

Wolf Form: Black Furies tend to be dark, predominately black, with white, silver or gray highlights or streaks. They are inevitably broad-shouldered and graceful.

Organization: The Black Furies are run by two major bodies called Calyxes. The Outer Calyx is made up of 13 Ranked Black Furies from all over the world, chosen by lot. The Inner Calyx consists of five Furies chosen directly by Artemis Herself. The Outer Calyx coordinates Fury actions all over the world and provides regional administrators. The Inner Calyx's five positions correspond to the five auspices. Its members act as a council to decide policy, interpret tradition and create laws for the tribe. Those whom Artemis calls for the Inner Calyx are of all Ranks and abilities, not just elders of the tribe, and this fact has caused some discord within the Outer Calyx, members of which believe they should be in line for service eventually.

Habitat: Wherever there is wilderness left in the world, the Black Furies will be present. Wherever there are ancient artifacts that might fall into the talons of the Wyrm, the Black Furies will be ready to fight. Wherever there are women in danger, the Black Furies will come to their aid.

Protectorate: Black Furies see themselves as protectors of the Wyld, which embodies the source of mystery and the force of nature. They tend the wild places that are left in the World of Darkness, and have charged themselves with the recovery, protection and conservation of ancient, semimythical places and things. They see themselves as protectors of women and unspoiled places, and they go to great lengths to uphold their duty to them.

Outlook: The Black Furies primarily ally themselves with the Children of Gaia and the Silent Striders, as these combinations usually work well together. The Furies respect the Stargazers, Wendigo and Red Talons, but can't seem to get along with them. They dislike the Fianna, the Glass Walkers and the Bone Gnawers, but do not usually raise claws against them. They dearly hate the Get of Fenris and the Shadow Lords, and sorely resent the position of dominance that the Silver Fangs hold, although the Furies follow the wisdom of their leaders and generally attack these politically powerful Garou only when they have permission. The stereotype of all Black Furies as "hard cases" or inveterate man-haters is misleading, but there aren't too many weak or empty-headed Furies out there.

Quote: *"My sisters and I do not have time to explain the situation to a fostern on testosterone overload. The item is Gaia's, and a minion of the Wyrm has it. We are going to take it back. Now you can either shut up and follow orders, or get the hell out of the way."*

Bone Gnawers

These misfits have been the scavengers of the Garou since the time before the tribes. The Bone Gnawers survive by using their canny ability to sniff out food and sneak about unseen. It's possible that they were originally of jackal stock. Their legends say that they were the "runts" of litters back in the old days. Today they tend to play the role of convenient scapegoats, although the Children of Gaia often stick up for them in septs. A few Bone Gnawers have gained enough Renown to form their own septs, but this is rare. They often discover or build caerns in cities' secret places, which they take for their own.

Because they are allied with all the dogs in a city (through a complex system of communication called the "Barking Chain"), and because they know many secrets about the sewers and tunnels underneath a city, the Bone Gnawers are pretty much in the know about what goes on in any metropolitan area. This is as much a survival tactic as it is a strategic activity; they need to know when it's time to abandon a sinking ship if things go wrong.

Totem: Rat

Initial Willpower: Two

Tribe Advantage: Rumors

Bone Gnawers always have at least an inkling of what is going on in the city in which they live. As a result, they can gain an instant Influence Trait in any area for the purposes of gathering information. This can be done once per Trait of Rank per session. Their Influences cannot be people per se. These Influences demonstrate the tribe's knack for "just knowing where to look," and cannot be used for anything other than information-gathering.

Tribe Drawback: Social Outcasts

Bone Gnawers are often regarded as filthy and déclassé because of their lifestyles and habits. A Bone Gnawer's Rank is therefore treated as one less by the other tribes. This does not actually affect a Gnawer's Rank, but does apply in moots and social interaction, and may be a handicap when it comes to holding positions in the Garou Nation.

Backgrounds: May not buy *Past Life* or *Pure Breed*, or begin the game with *Finances* Influence; must spend two Traits on *Kinfolk*.

Tribe Gifts: *Odious Aroma, Scent of Sweet Honey*

Wolf Form: Bone Gnawers look much like mangy street dogs. They often pass for such in open view of humans, although this has its own dangers; many Bone Gnawers have been caught by Animal Control units and taken to city pounds, where they orchestrate stealthy and ingenious breakouts. Their coats are a mishmash of clashing colors, and they are smaller than other Garou when in lupus form.

Organization: Bone Gnawers live together in family groups that are usually the result of choice, not breeding. Because they are generally despised by the rest of the Garou for their apparent breeding (they're mongrels), and because of their smell, they tend to flock together and even form septs all their own. They are ruled by Mothers and Fathers, respected elders who gain Renown among them by providing food (Honor), collecting interesting things (Glory), and staying alive (Wisdom).

Because of their similar social status and home environments, the Bone Gnawers and Nosferatu vampires often have positive relations. Indeed, it is believed by some that they often work together to achieve common goals, although the details of such arrangements are carefully guarded secrets.

Habitat: Bone Gnawers live wherever the homeless do. Some of them move out to the country to join their hillfolk cousins, but for the most part, they live and thrive in the city.

Protectorate: Bone Gnawers look after the people they live around — the homeless, dispossessed, insane and drug-afflicted flotsam of the cities. Although they have rules against interfering in the lives of their charges, such rules are usually honored more in the breach than in the observance.

Outlook: Bone Gnawers like anyone who will give them half a shred of respect, but they can sense whenever someone is attempting to take advantage of them. They are very practical and tend to ignore the more high-minded tribes, even making fun of them from time to time. They don't care much about prophecies or even the Wyrm; they're usually too busy surviving on a day-to-day basis.

Quote: *"Whoa, nice suit, monkeyboy. Shame if we got crud all over it down here, yep. Mind your step; but don't worry if you step on something that squishes. It's probably just a rat."*

Children of Gaia

In the sea of violence and anger that consumes the Garou race, there is an island of reason and restraint. These gentle and empathic souls are the Children of Gaia, so named because of their self-professed claim that all tribal differences are false barriers.

Children of Gaia believe, unlike the majority of Garou, that humans can be taught the error of their ways. They argue that by persecuting the blind, naked humans, Garou have only isolated these errant children from their place in Gaia's scheme. Caught as they were between the ravages of the Impergium and the dangers of the untamed wilderness, it is no wonder that the poor apes sought shelter in the dark shadows of the Wyrm.

The Children of Gaia propose that cooperation and education are the best tools the Garou have to rectify the mistakes of the past and hopefully to prevent what appears to be a darkening future. The Children only hope that it's not too late, for humans as well as Garou.

Other Garou tribes grant the Children of Gaia grudging respect. Children are known as honorable peacemakers, if a little soft in the head. When cornered or defending what they see as a noble or just cause, the Children of Gaia can be a terrifyingly lethal force.

Totem: Unicorn

Initial Willpower: Two

Tribe Advantage: Diplomacy

The Children of Gaia are steadfast proponents of peaceful negotiation and discourse. To represent this, Children of Gaia begin with the additional Social Traits: *Diplomatic* x 2, which cannot be lost. (This Advantage can allow Children of Gaia to go over Trait maximums).

Tribe Drawback: Weak Veil

Children of Gaia do not cause a Delirium reaction, and therefore must exercise great care not to break the Veil. Many Children see this as a mixed blessing, since it allows them more opportunities to interact freely with humans, but one never knows when or how it will cause problems.

Backgrounds: No restrictions.

Tribe Gifts: *Calm, Mother's Touch, Resist Pain*

Wolf Form: Children of Gaia resemble the magnificent wolves found in generations of mystic-themed art. Clean-limbed and powerful, they seem to radiate a sense of calm and balance rather than feral coldness. Their fur tends toward shades of brown and gray, and is often spotted or stripped with white.

Organization: The Children of Gaia respect the experience and knowledge of others. However, they also appreciate the energy and originality of the young. Anyone may speak at a meeting of the Children, and everyone is expected to hear what others have to say.

Habitat: The Children of Gaia have no apparent preference when it comes to territory, and do not shun areas frequented by humans as some tribes do. On the contrary, they actively look for opportunities to interact with human society, to understand humans better and hopefully to communicate with them as well. Children of Gaia can be found among ecological movements and activist groups where they believe their message will be heard and spread.

Protectorate: The Children of Gaia become involved with any segment of humanity in which they believe they can institute peaceful change. Some say the recycling movement and current attitudes of ecological awareness owe a great deal to the efforts of the Children.

Quote: *"How sad it is to see someone who has put his wounded pride above Gaia's wounds. Do you think you are the only one to have these troubles, to have these doubts in your heart? We all have been there, young one. We are all of the same spirit, and we can all help each other to learn and prevent the tragic end pride holds for us."*

Fianna

Known among Garou throughout Ireland, Britain and Europe as bards, storytellers and great warriors, the Fianna have earned their reputation through the centuries by mastering both sword and song. Although the Fianna of today make their homes in many parts of the world, their Celtic homelands are still dear to them.

The bards of the Fianna are considered by all tribes to be the most gifted, even by other Gibbous Moons. Taught the glory of song from birth, their memories stretch back to the point where they mix with those of the first Pangaean tribe. Fianna Ahroun are also taught the glory of battle, and prove difficult adversaries against even the most ferocious Get of Fenris.

Of all the tribes, the Fianna seem to be the most tolerant and to hold fewer prejudices than any other tribe, excepting the Children of Gaia. They do have long-standing rivalries with both the Get of Fenris and the Shadow Lords, though, and go to great lengths to show up or embarrass members of those tribes. For the most part, the Fianna are content with a good song and a pint of stout, but they are quick- tempered and dangerous when angered.

In recent years, there has been a division of loyalties among the Fianna over "the Troubles" of Northern Ireland. This internecine conflict has been the greatest threat to Fianna security ever known. Fianna without direct ties to the conflict have tried to moderate the fighting, but to little avail.

Totem: Stag

Initial Willpower: Two

Tribe Advantage: Heirloom

The Fianna are extremely close knit and strongly family-oriented. As a result, all Fianna begin with heirlooms that are the equivalent of a three-Trait fetish in total value. You can spend additional Background Traits if you would like these heirlooms to be even more powerful; however, you can never have a fetish with more than five Traits. Losing such an heirloom causes a loss of two Honor Renown, and no more Renown can be earned until the Fianna asks for forgiveness and receives it from his family elder.

Tribe Drawback: Low Self-Control

The Fianna are creatures of passion. They ride the emotional roller coaster of life's joys, angers, loves and sorrows. Therefore, any attempt to emotionally influence a Fianna will succeed on a win or tie, unless he can overbid. If a Fianna spends a Willpower Trait to avoid frenzy or in order to exert emotional control, the situation still renders him one Trait down in any challenges during the rest of the scene.

Backgrounds: No restrictions.

Tribe Gifts: *Persuasion, Resist Toxin*

Wolf Form: In Lupus form, the Fianna appear as huge blood-red or black wolves with green to greenish-gray eyes. They look very much like the dire wolves or wolfhounds of Ireland.

Organization: Family is very important and blood is everything to this tribe. Fianna and their Kinfolk meet once every lunar month to settle disputes and rejoice in their Celtic heritage, spinning tales of their deeds and bringing greater glory to themselves and the tribe. The governing body that oversees this tribe, the Council of Song, is a group of elder Garou. Members are elected by the tribe, and each member comes from a different auspice. Their responsibility is to decide all matters concerning the tribe, including inter-tribal politics, as well as affairs pertaining to other facets of society, both human and Garou. The councilors are well-respected among the Fianna, and their word is considered law.

Habitat: The Fianna may be found in all environments, although they prefer rural areas. The elders and their kin prefer the quiet life of farming, while the youth are apt to live in cities among humans, whose ways they follow.

Protectorate: These Garou hold close ties to the traditional Celtic way of life, and protect the Irish and British with a fierce passion. As a result of their migrations in recent decades, they have also assumed the responsibility of protecting singers and entertainers of all types.

Outlook: Fianna believe that all the world is their stage (or pub), and believe in enjoying life to the fullest. They tend to ignore their serious cousins in the other tribes, or at least to discount their gloomier predictions.

Quote: *"So I told Seamus that no one was leaving the table until he and James settled their differences without bloodshed, and I had the barmaid bring 'em a few dozen rounds. Then, I locked the bathroom door — believe me, they settled things right quick."*

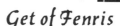

Get of Fenris

Renowned for their physical prowess, fierce tempers, violence and remorseless codes of honor, the Get of Fenris have earned the reputation of being the quintessential warlords of the Garou. As a rule, they are savage and merciless, neither asking quarter of their foes, nor offering them any. They have a powerful code of honor, but it is not clearly understood by other tribes because it is a personal code of heroism, not an abstract social ethic. The Get value strength as the greatest virtue and self-sacrifice as the greatest gift.

Originally from Scandinavia, the Get migrated with the Vikings as they traded and plundered across Europe. They believe in the superiority of their rigorous lifestyle, and most of this tribe still have distinctly Scandinavian heritage. The Get see the other tribes' policy of less-than-total warfare against the forces of the Wyrm as a sign of weakness. The Get, therefore, tend to "protect" these meek tribes by taking and holding places and items of power which need to be protected by the strong arm of the Get.

Members of the Get constantly push their philosophies at moots, and show little restraint when their ideas aren't immediately adopted. The Get believe that those who do not rush into battle are weak and deserve what happens to them. The battlefield is home for the Get of Fenris, and they do not fear death.

When the Get are not in battle, they are planning strategies or telling tales of glory around the fire. They are long-standing enemies of the Wendigo and the Uktena, whose weakness, they believe, caused the death of the Croatan.

Totem: Fenris Wolf

Initial Willpower: One

Tribe Advantage: Warrior's Heart

The Get of Fenris are some of the toughest warriors of all the tribes. Many joke that this is because of their battle-hardened hides, but they are really among the best because of their battle-tested souls. Because of the effects of the Get of Fenris bloodline and their rigorous lifestyle, each Get gains one additional Health Level.

Tribe Drawback: Blind Commitment

The Get of Fenris' desire to destroy the Wyrm, or die trying, has created such hatred that Get tend to be intolerant of anything they perceive as "weakening Gaia's defenses." Players with Get characters should choose something that is not inherently Wyrm-tainted (i.e., cowardice, compromise, peaceniks, high-end Weaver-tech) as an object of blind hatred. When the object of this contempt is near, the Garou must win or tie a Simple Test or do whatever he can to rid himself of the annoyance (one Willpower negates this as if it were a frenzy situation).

Backgrounds: May not begin the game with more than three Influences.

Tribe Gifts: *Razor Claws, Resist Pain, Snarl of the Predator*

Wolf Form: Get of Fenris resemble huge northern gray wolves, broad-shouldered and muscular, with huge jaws. Although some black and brown patches have become common due to their crossbreeding with cultures other than Nordic, most still exhibit uniform coloration.

Organization: This tribe meets regularly on every full moon. These meetings are very strict, with an air of military discipline about them. Ahrouns are given the greatest respect among the Get, as they are the tribe's fiercest warriors. However, each of the auspices has a role in battle. Even a Get of Fenris Ragabash can be a fierce opponent. During these moots, the Get plot war strategies and recount deeds of great glory. They also settle any major disputes within the tribe by combat.

Habitat: The Get tend to live in rural areas, making their homes among the same families they have bred with for years. Some of the younger Get have followed the humans and their ways in a disturbing manner, joining with racist groups and bringing shame to their tribe.

Protectorate: Members of this tribe see themselves as Gaia's claws, often culling "worthless" humans in Her name. Any manifestation of the Wyrm is fair game, and any place that they think is not guarded strongly enough is subject to Get protection. Tribe members will attack other tribes' caerns if they think sites need to be secured against corruption.

Outlook: The Get are a fatalistic lot, determined to crush the Wyrm in their jaws as they die. Life is battle, and war is glory. They were put here to fight, and that is what they shall do. Mercy is for the weak, and those who are not strong enough to stand by their side will receive no pity from Gaia.

Quote: *"Is this all the fight you've got in you? You fight like an old woman! How do you expect to kill even one Black Spiral Dancer if you can't handle a few miserable fomori? Retreat to the caern, and have that Child of Gaia patch you up. I'll get rid of the rest of these Wyrmlings. (muttered) Wimp."*

Glass Walkers

The Glass Walkers thrive in the cities of the world. They see the city as just another part of Gaia. They know that cities have a spirit and life all their own, and they seek to explore the diversity that these "new wildernesses" provide.

The Glass Walkers originated in Mesopotamia, where they split from the first Garou tribe and came to live in the cities. They became enforcers and mercenaries for merchants in the Middle Ages and allied with guilds. They were at the forefront of technological change during the Renaissance and later in the Industrial Revolution, learning that everything has spirits, even great steam engines and assembly lines.

The Glass Walkers developed Mafia ties as a result of their enforcer past, and in the '20s, Glass Walker gangs provided muscle for many Mob actions. With the advent of computers, the Glass Walkers learned about new kinds of spirits: Net-Spiders and computer spirits. Befriending these spirits, they found themselves in control of powers that could alter and gather information from computers all over the world, and they discovered an entirely new world called the CyberRealm. The Glass Walkers believe it is their duty to guide the cities and technology of the world to a path allied with Gaia, and that Gaia is indeed part of the city itself.

Totem: Cockroach

This might seem an odd choice at first, but Cockroach is incredibly adaptable, resilient and is nearly impossible to wipe out. Some Glass Walkers hold Spider in high regard as well.

Initial Willpower: Two

Tribe Advantage: Weaver's Children

Glass Walkers begin the game with one additional Influence Trait. Furthermore, a Glass Walker can purchase more Influence during character creation at the rate of one for one. Once play begins, Glass Walkers can purchase Influence with Experience (other Garou can gain Influence only through roleplaying). One Trait of Influence can be purchased for three Experience Traits, subject to Storyteller approval, of course.

Tribe Drawback: Weaver Affinity

Glass Walkers regain Gnosis only in cities. Caerns are the exception to this rule. Walkers' Weaver ties lead Wyld-minded Garou to distrust them.

Backgrounds: Glass Walkers cannot buy *Past Life* or *Pure Breed*, but they start with an additional Influence.

Tribe Gifts: *Control Simple Machine, Cybersenses, Persuasion*

Wolf Form: They appear as small- to medium-sized wolves, with mottled patterns. Many of the cubs of this tribe indulge in "Urban Primitivism", clipping and dyeing their fur, piercing their bodies, submitting to silver brandings, getting strange tattoos and generally altering their bodies in odd ways.

Organization: The Glass Walkers are generally organized in a very human way. They tend to think of themselves as a corporation, with directors, middle managers and employees. Their caerns are usually located within cities, often in places that shock and alarm other Garou (such as the tops of skyscrapers or in the middle of abandoned factories).

Many of the old-guard Glass Walkers are still very much allied with the Mafia, and tend to rule their septs like Mafia families. Many young Glass Walkers live under very loose structures. These are the hackers and computer Theurges who care more for knowledge and skill than they do for Renown. Some Glass Walker packs merge with other Glass Walker packs, forming large, roaming Urban Primitive tribes.

The Glass Walkers and the Bone Gnawers fight occasionally. But, because they both live in cities, they are usually on friendly terms, or at least are allies against a common enemy.

Many Glass Walkers have positive relations with Ventrue and Toreador vampires, much to the consternation of most other Garou. These civilized Kindred see the Glass Walkers as perhaps the last hope of making peace with the Garou, although competition in financial spheres has caused conflict in the past.

Habitat: The Glass Walkers live in cities, period. Some Glass Walkers seek to beautify their cities by planting hardy trees and creating arboretums, but this is as close to the wild as the Glass Walkers want to get.

Protectorate: The Glass Walkers watch over cities, particularly their movers and shakers: corporate figures, underworld denizens, research scientists, nightclub managers and high-ranking government officials (particularly elected ones). Young Glass Walkers consider it their duty to watch over the worldwide computer net that stretches across the entire globe.

Outlook: Glass Walkers see themselves as the next stage in Garou evolution. They believe that Gaia is leading them to be the rulers of a new world where the Weaver has woven her webs all over the Earth. They believe that they can help humanity and the Garou survive the coming Apocalypse by providing them with technology and spiritual wisdom. Glass Walkers are therefore somewhat arrogant, but almost as subtle and crafty as their Shadow Lord cousins. Indeed, conflicts between Glass Walkers and Shadow Lords are like great chess games using the other Garou as pieces.

Their irreverence for tradition has earned the Walkers many enemies among the tribes. The Silver Fangs are especially worried about the Glass Walkers' weakening physical form and lack of connection to the Wyld. They are severely distrusted by the Red Talons, Black Furies and the Get of Fenris, many of whom have decided that they are of the Wyrm. The Bone Gnawers like the Walkers, but don't get too involved in their plots, if for no other reason than survival.

Quote: *"How can the city be unnatural? It is real. It lives, breathes and moves constantly. There are predators and prey in the city, as in your highly touted wilderness. There are powerful caerns of Gaia in the middle of this Weaverland, as you call it. Urban spirits hold the same energies as rural spirits, and already know the ancient pacts. It's evolution. Get with the program, or don't let Darwin's door hit you on the butt on your way out."*

Red Talons

The Red Talons are perhaps more intolerant of humans than any other tribe. They would enjoy nothing more than seeing the entire race utterly destroyed so that the blood of the slain can cleanse and feed the planet. The Red Talons were the tribe most opposed to ending the Impergium, and still attempt to convince other tribes to reinstate it. They believe humanity as a whole is of the Wyrm, and as such must be removed from the Earth. Only then will the Garou be able to defeat the Wyrm completely.

The Red Talons are comprised entirely of lupus stock, and although they tolerate the other breeds, they disdain being in their presence, considering them weak but necessary in the war against the Wyrm. The Red Talons are the least understood of all the tribes. They are the most wolflike and take great pleasure in performing rituals that the other tribes could never fathom. They also keep to themselves as much as possible, and fighting between tribe members is very rare.

Humans are not the only creatures they despise. Vampires are near the top of the Talons' list. The Red Talons believe that Kindred are no more than dead humans with too much power, a blasphemous manifestation of the Wyrm whose only gift should be destruction. Young members of this tribe have become more tolerant toward humans, and believe that some of them may be worth saving. Only the traditional Garou respect for the right of the young to walk their own path has kept the elder Talons from slaying these upstarts outright.

Totem: Griffin

Initial Willpower: Two

Tribe Advantage: Gaia's Fury

Red Talons gain an additional Rage Trait during character generation and always have a maximum Rage of one higher than the other tribes.

Tribe Drawback: Wyld Affinity

A Red Talon is completely at home in the wild. Unfortunately, he cannot find peace in cities; as a result, a Red Talon cannot regain Gnosis in any urban environment.

Backgrounds: Red Talons may not buy Influences.

Beginning Gifts: *Beastmind, Scent of Running Water, Sense of the Prey*

Wolf Form: A big ruddy or brown wolf with noticeably large jaws. All Red Talons have at least one spot where a shock of flaming red hair grows. When they appear in Homid form, which is rare, they are rough and crude-looking, and often slouch or hunch over.

Organization: As this tribe is very close to its lupine roots, any group is led by an alpha. The strong lead and the weak follow.

Habitat: The Red Talons are found in the wilds, far removed from human settlements of any kind.

Protectorate: The Talons protect the wolves of the world from destruction at the hands of humans. They have sworn to destroy any who bring harm to their lupine Kinfolk.

Outlook: The other tribes proved themselves weak by allowing the humans to reign as they do. Bringing an end to the Impergium was a mistake. Now the Red Talons must suffer under the talons of the Wyrm and its host, humans.

Quote: *"Not expect understanding. They enter hunting ground, they died. Why you care? Only humans, of no use to Gaia."*

Shadow Lords

Wolves are creatures of dominance and submission, mastery and servitude. The Shadow Lords take this quite literally and strive to master all they survey. The Shadow Lords, who settled years ago in the Balkan region, have since expanded throughout the world toward their self-proclaimed "manifest destiny."

Shadow Lords see the Garou as the ultimate life form on the planet. Therefore, Garou are the obvious rulers. Furthermore, as far as they're concerned, there is no tribe greater than the Shadow Lords. With that in mind, it doesn't take a genius to figure out the tribe's agenda.

In the end, the only thing the Shadow Lords respect from Garou of other tribes is power. Even so, they are always ready to displace their rivals at the slightest sign of weakness.

The dark strengths of the Shadow Lords are possibly their greatest weaknesses. Their boundless pride (perhaps better called arrogance) is easily warped by the Wyrm. Under the Wyrm's maddening tutelage, a Shadow Lord's pride can blossom into full-blown megalomania.

Totem: Grandfather Thunder

Initial Willpower: Two

Tribe Advantage: Social Outmaneuver

By spending one Gnosis Trait, a Shadow Lord can double her Social Traits up to a maximum addition of six Traits. These Social Traits may be used for bidding in a single Social Challenge. This includes resolving ties or crushing an opponent in an overbid. For some reason, this advantage fails when used against Garou of equal or higher *Pure Breed*.

Tribe Drawback: Unworthy

Because of the unforgiving nature of their tribe, Shadow Lords suffer double Renown loss for any failing or transgression on their part (if caught).

Backgrounds: Shadow Lords may not begin the game with more than three Influences.

Beginning Gifts: *Aura of Confidence, Clap of Thunder, Disfigurement, Fatal Flaw*

Wolf Form: Resembling wolfish pit bulls, Shadow Lords are short, stocky and well-muscled. Most have dark fur.

Organization: The Shadow Lords boast of a chain of command that would make any corporate division proud. No member is ignorant of his position, power or, most importantly, responsibilities. At the lower end, eager young pups stand ready fill to any vacancy that opens in the tribe's ranks, including vacancies that they sometimes create. Those already in positions of power are constantly on guard against capable upstarts. All in all, the Shadow Lord drive for dominance creates a constant current of change and uncertainty, as those in power inevitably miss a step and are brought down. The Shadow Lords believe in the right to rule through outmaneuvering, outgunning, overpowering, backstabbing and/or assassination — and the right to keep a position in the same ways.

Habitat: The Shadow Lords are highly adaptable. They are better than most Garou at keeping pace with the modern world, although not as much as the Glass Walkers or Bone Gnawers. Their areas of influence include lawyers, businessmen, crime lords and politicians, and go just about anywhere they can exert control over others.

Protectorate: The Shadow Lords respect only power, and those few humans they deal with must either appreciate power or wield it. Many of the Shadowlord's well-established Kinfolk occupy complementary positions of power. As one would expect, vampires and Shadow Lords often find themselves at odds with each other, as they are two species of predator competing for the same niche in the food chain.

Outlook: A Shadow Lord character has to realize that while it is perfectly clear she is the obvious choice as leader, others may not see things that way. Some Garou perceive an ambitious Shadow Lord as a wannabe tyrant (the nerve!). Nonetheless, if not chosen outright as the pack's leader, the character must achieve that position by some other means. Some choose to lead from behind the scenes, manipulating others in a puppet show. Others stage coups or humiliate and discredit current leaders. Regardless of the means she uses, the end will justify her actions — at least to her.

Quote: *"Of course you know. I know you know. He knows you know. You know he knows you know. I know he knows you know, and you know it. We are a very knowledgeable group."*

Silent Strider

As their name suggests, these enigmatic Garou skirt the boundaries of Garou society. Originally from the wastes of the Sahara, the Silent Striders were driven out by others in ancient times, and since then have never found a place they can truly call home. They are respected for their wisdom (by the other tribes), but their solitary and secretive natures concerning their beliefs and rites make it difficult for other Garou to accept them.

The Silent Striders are the ultimate messengers and couriers (among Garou). Striders cross regions other Garou would avoid, and they travel with an alacrity rivaling that of human contraptions. The benefits of their nomadic lifestyle are not without a price, however: Few Silent Striders form lasting friendships with those outside their tribe.

Totem: Owl

Initial Willpower: Two

Tribe Advantage: The Omen of Doom

Once per session, a Silent Strider can "back up" one action (*I had a bad feeling about doing that*), somehow manage to have a common item in his possession at the right moment (*I just had a feeling we might need a bag of salt today*) or restart a challenge sequence that he did not initiate (*O.K., this time I do not walk down the alley, and into the ambush. I stop and tell everyone I have a bad feeling about it*). In other words, a Silent Strider gets little "spooky" feelings after something bad happens in-game and can back up the scene one step to avoid taking an action, or to have remembered to pick up something that becomes instrumental to the success of the scene (Storyteller discretion). An important use of this capacity allows a Silent Strider to negate a combat situation that he did not initiate *before it starts* in order to prevent it or make it come out differently. If the Strider initiated the challenge, he can only back up events to right after the initial challenge, because of a hunch he had about the first outcome. No information is retained about "events that did not happen" thanks to the use of this Advantage.

Note: This power can be either unwieldy or potentially or extremely powerful. Narrators should keep an eye out for characters abusing The Omen of Doom and penalize them appropriately (say, by making them "forget" important items, giving them false hunches, and so on). The Strider tribal advantage should be used no more than once per session, if that often.

Tribe Drawback: Haunted

Because of their ancient interactions with the dead of Egypt, Striders must (once per lunar cycle) succeed in a Simple Test or attract the attention of wraiths. The Silent Strider can see and hear this wraith, which bothers and harasses the Garou until he either helps the wraith with one of her Fetters (an item or person that connects her to this world) or he leaves and remains outside the area of the wraith's haunting (usually about 50 miles) for an entire lunar cycle.

For more information on wraiths, see **Mind's Eye Theatre: Oblivion**. Otherwise, use this sample Gaffling Spirit:

Willpower 5, **Rage** 4, **Gnosis** 3, **Power** 15

Charms: *Airt Sense, Sap Will, Suggestion*

Silent Striders will never reveal a haunting to other Garou.

Backgrounds: Silent Striders may not buy *Past Life* or Influences that are not accessible worldwide (Storyteller approval required).

Beginning Gifts: *Sense Wyrm, Speed of Thought, Messenger's Fortitude*

Wolf Form: Silent Striders come in all shades of gray, and are long and lean, resembling the jackals of Egyptian art. They seem always to have inscrutable expressions and regal countenances.

Organization: Among the Striders, a well-defined structure would be impractical, if not completely useless. Instead, they defer to those with the most experience in the matter at hand.

Habitat: The Silent Striders claim no land as their own, and can be found in almost any corner of the world. They remain in one place only as long as is necessary and then leave, sometimes never to return.

Protectorate: Silent Striders are the advance scouts for the Garou. They sometimes protect humans whom they meet in their travels, but leave the protection of the race as a whole to other tribes. They respect those who share their lifestyle, such as Gypsies, circus performers and the few nomadic peoples left in the world.

Outlook: Silent Striders have an economy of behavior that suits their nomadic existence. They act and speak on what is pertinent, and have little use for what they consider frivolous. They always seem prepared for any situation, and are rarely taken by surprise. Their directness of action leaves them little time or opportunity to make friends; perhaps they prefer it that way.

Quote: *"Yes, the tribes have been informed. Now if you'll excuse me, I have urgent business elsewhere. Goodbye."*

Silver Fangs

It is said that all Garou were Silver Fangs in the beginning. If one were to take the single best quality from each of the tribes and bring them together in a Garou, that Garou would be a Silver Fang. While many would contest this, none can deny that the Silver Fangs, more so than any other tribe, have been the rallying point, the leaders and court of last resort for the Garou race. The palpable charisma and confidence they exude has made them obvious leaders among Garou.

These noble Garou are known for their physical beauty, courage, wisdom and honor. They tend to have many Social Traits and a wide variety of Abilities. Sadly, in recent generations many members of this tribe suffer from odd quirks — absent-mindedness, mild hallucinations, somnambulism — nothing overtly dangerous, but noticeable nevertheless. The noble history of the tribe lays a heavy burden on the shoulders of its members, as many doddering old fools are too proud to ask for help. Still, those who mock the Silver Fangs never do so to their faces.

Though the Silver Fangs espouse the superiority of the Garou, they consider mediation, not slaughter, to be their sacred duty. When their ire is raised, however, the Silver Fangs shed blood as eagerly as any Get of Fenris. Silver Fang characters should lead by example. By best exemplifying the most noble Garou Traits — wisdom, courage and honor — they inspire those around them to act likewise. Remember, the Silver Fangs know more about what it is to be heroic than most of the tribes.

Totem: Falcon

Initial Willpower: Two

Tribe Advantage: First Tribe

Because of the tribal role as traditional leaders and commanders of the Garou for at least the last 15,000 years, a Silver Fang may call for one free retest in all Social Challenges.

Tribe Drawback: Touch of Greatness

The bane of the Silver Fangs, a byproduct of centuries of breeding (and inbreeding) with royalty, manifests itself as odd quirks. All Silver Fangs must begin the game with a Quirk, chosen at character creation. This Quirk can be any of the following, but others can be taken at Storyteller discretion. These Quirks serve as Negative Traits.

Background: Silver Fangs must spend at least three Traits in *Pure Breed*.

Beginning Gifts: *Lambent Flame, Paralyzing Stare, Sense Wyrm*

Wolf Form: Fangs appear as stunningly beautiful pure-white or silver wolves, with long jaws, graceful builds and green or blue eyes. They usually wear some form of jewelry, even in wolf form.

Organization: Silver Fangs honor their aristocratic heritage in their tribe organization. Those with the best lineage and those who have been in power longest are invariably heeded over others. While no one argues with giving an elder her due, many young with new ideas have been drowned out by the rhetoric of the old guard.

Silver Fang Quirks

- Absent-Minded — In highly stressful and traumatic situations, you forget details unless you succeed in a Simple Test. (*Forgetful*)

- Rationality — You compulsively analyze everything and block out as many emotions as possible. (*Callous*)

- Mood Swings — Your energy changes without regard to situation. You begin each story feeling geared up (*Impatient*), normal (*Calm*) or lethargic (*Submissive*). You can change this by either spending a Willpower point or changing your present situation (going into another story line, for example). Starting mood is determined at Narrator discretion.

- Fixation — You tend to get excited, latch onto someone or something new and spend too much time involved with them or it (such as wanting to play a live-action game every week and getting pissed when you have to miss a session). (*Gullible*)

- Apprehension — If you spend any time around someone or something, you begin to consider how things can go horribly wrong. You wonder if your friend really likes you, if your boss is bad-mouthing you behind your back or if your pack really listens to you. In other words, you expect others to let you down, so you often act like they already have. (*Condescending*)

- Anxiety — You worry too much about everything, even things you really can do nothing about. (*Naive*)

- Jealousy — You cannot help wanting the best and the most. Those that have it better than you did not earn it, as you did. (*Tactless*)

- Arrogant — You *have* to be right. When you are proven wrong, you reinterpret your original observation to have been right all along, or maybe others just misunderstood you. (*Ignorant*)

- Hot-Headed — When you have been wronged, you get seriously angry. You will not forget the Veil, but you will not voluntarily spend Willpower to prevent frenzy when angered. (*Violent*)

- Unstable Personality — Every time you enter a new story line, you pick up a different Quirk. Pick one item (randomly) from this list.

Habitat: The Silver Fangs have a deep love for the unspoiled wilderness of whatever land they dwell in. In medieval times, they held fiefs with large tracts of wilderness set aside for their personal enjoyment. They prefer lands of majesty: coastal cliffs, mountains, grand prairies, deep forest glens. They protect their lands from harm with a passion rivaling that of any vampiric Jyhad.

Protectorate: The Silver Fangs are expected to persevere where all others would fail. As a result, they have developed a sort of *noblesse oblige* attitude that many Garou find condescending. However, you haven't seen determination until you've seen a Silver Fang wading through a swarm of lesser minions to face an enemy leader. Think of Lancelot with fur and claws.

Quote: *"You obviously have very little of the Progenitor Wolf within you to call for a Moon Bridge to escape. I have sworn to protect this caern, and as long as I stand, nobody leaves. This caern will not fall, and no Black Spiral Dancer is going to limp away to report its location. Everybody clear on that?"*

Stargazers

The Stargazers are perhaps the most contemplative of the Garou tribes. During the Impergium, the first Stargazer, Klaital, was among the Garou who believed the inhumane treatment of humans would prove to be a costly error, and he sought an end to their persecution. Failing, he fell into Harano and went off to die. Instead, he ended up on a spirit-quest that led to enlightenment. Klaital's message is still followed by Garou who seek inner peace. The Stargazer ranks are swelled by tribal renunciates, the newly recruited and a number of lost cubs.

The Stargazers, despite their peaceful natures, can be as fierce in times of war as any other Garou. Unseen and quiet in the shadows, they protect humanity from the hideous minions of the Wyrm. This has brought them great animosity from some members of other tribes, but their wisdom is widely respected among the Garou. Despite this, the Stargazers are considered untrustworthy by many Garou.

The Stargazers live a Spartan life, shunning civilization completely. They do not seek material wealth of any kind, considering it a burden to spiritual enlightenment. They seek only truth. Due to their spiritual nature, they have strained relations with the Glass Walkers and Bone Gnawers, who have a taste for material things.

Totem: Chimera

Initial Willpower: Three

Tribe Advantage: Inner Peace

A Stargazer begins the game with *Meditation* Ability x 2 and *Enigma* Ability.

Tribe Drawback: Obsessive Mind Games

Stargazers are always trying to solve enigmas or define enigmas to solve. They are (when stumped) slightly unfocused on situations at hand. If a challenge involving the *Enigma* Ability is lost by a Stargazer, he will be down three Traits on all challenges for the rest of the session.

Backgrounds: Stargazers may not begin the game with Fetishes or Influences.

Beginning Gifts: *Catfeet, Sense Wyrm, Surface Attunement*

Wolf Form: This varies from lighter hues through striped gray to completely black. Most are lean, and nearly all radiate a perceptible aura of serenity.

Organization: Stargazers have no council or elders to whom they must answer. Instead, each Stargazer seeks her own path in the world. When they require wisdom, members seek audience with the aged of their tribe

Habitat: The Stargazers are wanderers, traveling the world and calling no place home. They journey from caern to caern, seeking wisdom and enlightenment during their travels. They breed with humans who have also cast away the evils of society: explorers, hermits and rustics who live far removed from the world of men.

Protectorate: Stargazers feel a special bond with the loners and seekers of human society. They protect them quietly and, if they are worthy, teach them of their insights.

Outlook: The Stargazers feel that they must guide their fellow Garou into a new era of peace. Only then, as one tribe with one goal, can the Garou hope to destroy the Wyrm and its minions.

Quote: *"You cannot teach a fish to fly, yet some fish do fly. You cannot make cities go away, yet cities do go away. You cannot take a person's love, but they can give it away. You cannot know the truth, but truth knows you. No, I am not deliberately being confusing."*

Uktena

The Uktena are one of the three tribes of Garou that came to America across the Bering land bridge. They believe that open Rage and narrow vision will be the downfall of the Garou. They also believe that, by coming to understand the spirit world, they will be able to spread wisdom and allow the Garou to purify the world of the Wyrm's influence.

The "real" world is not important to the Uktena. They would rather be in the Umbra than on Earth. Since the destruction of the Croatan tribe, the Uktena's maxim is "Know thine enemy." They put their spirits on the line in order to venture into the heart of the Wyrm and discover its foul plans.

The Uktena were once purely Native American, but have since begun accepting those who are alienated from other tribes. They have incorporated many magical beliefs and cultures into their tribal rites and moots.

They are also concerned with fetishes, because they see them as spiritual tools to strengthen themselves as spirit-warriors and protectors. They feel it is their duty to watch over Wyrm-ridden areas and protect other Garou from the Wyrm's influence. They often raid the holdings of mages, Tremere vampires and even Black Spiral Dancers to recover fetishes they believe should be used in service to Gaia.

The Uktena are secretive, and are often accused of allying with the Wyrm because of their close study of it. This is not the case, however; the Uktena are probably among the few tribes that know enough about the Wyrm to have a chance of harming it seriously.

Still, taint by the Wyrm is an ever-present danger, and all Uktena are aware of this fact. It is common practice for all Uktena to undergo the *Rite of Cleansing* regularly in order to purify themselves.

Totem: Uktena

Initial Willpower: Two

Tribe Advantage: Umbral Sight

Uktena can peek into the Umbra from the real world using the same rules as peeking out of the Umbra. This power allows them to see others moving within the Umbra.

Tribe Drawback: Mystic Curiosity

Uktena desire to learn ancient lore and rituals drives them ever deeper into uncharted waters. If an Uktena is not in the process of learning something related to the occult — Lore, Gifts, rites, empowering a Fetish, — she becomes fidgety and short-tempered. Uktena are down three Traits in all Challenges faced under these conditions.

Backgrounds: No restrictions.

Beginning Gifts: *Blur of the Milky Eye, Sense Magic, Spirit of the Fish*

Wolf Form: These wolves have wiry forms in reddish-black hues, with large brown-black eyes that seem to look right through any object of their gaze. Uktena exude an air of mystery and menace.

Organization: Uktena maintain very tightly organized septs, and rely heavily on their own messengers, spirit messengers and the Silent Striders. They also perform regular rituals to renew their connections with the land. It is rumored the Uktena have secret septs in carefully hidden places that are still as pure and as untamed as the land was during prehistoric times. This tribe is ruled by a central lodge that is a collection of elders from all the Uktena-dominated septs, although other Uktena are often invited to attend.

Habitat: The Uktena live as near to their caerns as possible, often building natural-material structures within their bawns. This means they usually live in the wilderness, but many Uktena caerns are located on the repossessed lands of their ancestors.

Protectorate: These Garou consider themselves the guardians of the dispossessed, of people who have lost their lands and spirits to foreign conquest. The tribe also claims rightful ownership of powerful fetishes and talismans. No one else, the Uktena say, could care for them properly.

The Uktena protect a version of the Silver Record that has existed since the early days of the Garou, and they refuse to let it fall into anyone else's hands.

Outlook: The Uktena are constant seekers after mystery and magic. Less implacable in their anger than the Wendigo, Uktena can work with any Garou — not to mention just about anyone else. While outsiders see the Uktena as hamstrung by outmoded traditions, they are actually endlessly innovative, especially when it comes to new ways to combat the Wyrm.

Quote: *"You know your way, I know what the Wyrm is thinking. I will be ready for it and its minions. I will defeat them with powers protected and secret for millennia. While you rely on the tactics that brought us here, each day I learn new ways to combat the Wyrm."*

Wendigo

The Wendigo perceive themselves to be the last of the pure Native American tribes. Once part of the three tribes that called the Americas their home, they are all that remain of the Pure Ones. Because of this, they still harbor resentment toward everyone of European descent, even their Garou cousins, for destroying the land that they love so dearly. Wendigo will, however, reluctantly aid the so-called "Wyrmcomers" in times of need and wage war against the Wyrm.

The Wendigo stay as far away from those of European descent as possible, preferring to live in the wilds or, at the very least, on reservations away from cities. Their pride in their Native American heritage is strong.

The Wendigo are masters of woodland survival, becoming one with the land and letting the spirits guide them through the wilderness. Such prowess has earned them great Renown among other Garou, and they are sought out for their expertise. They are also experts at hit-and-run tactics, and are known as some of the fiercest warriors among the Garou.

Some of the young among the Wendigo believe that the world is not as bad as their elders say and that the differences between the Native Americans and the others can be overcome. They ignore the teachings of their elders and the bloody lessons that history has taught, preferring to go out into the world and learn for themselves. This has caused great unrest among members of the tribe.

Totem: Wendigo

Initial Willpower: Two

Tribe Advantage and Drawback: The Wheel of Seasons

The Wendigo gain one or two positive Traits with each season, but also take one Negative Trait. This change of Traits occurs the moment a season changes and is in effect until the next arrives.

- **Winter** — Physical Traits: *Tenacious* and *Rugged*

Negative Trait: *Callous, Dull* or *Witless*

- **Spring** — Physical Trait: *Energetic*

Negative Trait: *Predictable, Tactless* or *Impatient*

- **Summer** — Social Trait: *Charismatic*

Negative Trait: *Lethargic, Violent* or *Shortsighted*

- **Fall** — Mental Trait: *Reflective*

Negative Trait: *Lethargic, Dull* or *Impatient*

Backgrounds: Wendigo may not buy Influences.

Beginning Gifts: *Call the Breeze, Camouflage, Cutting Wind, Speak with the Wind Spirits*

Wolf Form: Wendigo resemble giant Northern timber wolves. Their fur varies from gray to brown to a mixture of both. Wendigo have strong, short jaws.

Organization: The elders of the tribe are given the utmost respect. They hold ceremonies on sacred ground, much like their Kinfolk have for centuries. Wendigo moots are usually held during the crescent moon.

Habitat: Wendigo tend to live in the northern woods, despite the fact that it is shrinking due to the white man's continuing expansion. They make their homes wherever they roam, just as their ancestors did for centuries. Many of the Wendigo live on reservations, since these provide havens from the Wyrmcomers. One of the reasons the Wendigo are not as powerful as they could be is that one of their most powerful caerns, located in the Black Hills, has been denied them by the United States government. If it were ever to become open to the Lakota people who originally dwelled on the land and worshipped there, the Wendigo would be able to reclaim the powerful caern and potentially cleanse the land all around it. Many Wendigo seek to free the Black Hills for this very reason.

Protectorate: The Wendigo protect Native Americans of all tribes and the lands on which they live. This tribe is famous for organizing war parties with its Native American Kinfolk to drive whites away from their lands. They still believe that the Wyrm is using the white man to manifest itself and eat away the world. Perhaps, some Wendigo say, the best way to destroy the Wyrm would be to destroy its tool as well.

Outlook: The Wendigo see the other tribes as part of the problem, not the solution. Had the others not emigrated and brought the Wyrm with them, the world would be in much better shape.

Quote: *"I am not here to talk. I am here to kill Wyrm-things. Do you intend to help, or are you still undecided as to which side of this fight you're on?"*

Gifts

Gifts are normally taught by spirits. A Garou must either petition a particular spirit to teach him its power or ask an elder to summon that spirit and petition for him. (Further ideas on this process can be found in **Werewolf: The Apocalypse**.) Only spirits allied with the Garou will teach Gifts, and they will not teach them to Garou who have not attained the proper Rank.

Sometimes a Garou may teach another Garou a Gift he knows. Unlike spirit teaching, which takes only a short time, this method can take quite a while. In addition, Gifts learned this way cost an additional Experience Trait. Bonuses received through the use of Gifts, talens, fetishes, rites and Merits, can push characters over their present Trait maximums. The total number of Trait bonuses can never equal more than double the Garou's current Trait maximums.

Additional note: Although many Garou can affect spirits, there is a distinction between spirits and wraiths. A Gift that can affect a spirit will not necessarily have any effect on a wraith.

A Garou must learn all of the Basic Gifts for his breed, tribe or auspice before moving on to the Intermediate ones of that Gift type, and so on.

Breed Gifts

Homid
Basic Gifts
• **Persuasion** — This Gift enhances the Garou's charisma and ability to deal with others in a social situation. The character gains one free retest in a Social Challenge. This Gift may be used once at the beginning of or during a Social Challenge.

• **Smell of Man** — The Garou exudes the well-known scent of danger from her body; sniffing it, animals act accordingly. This Gift can be used only once on the same animal per story line. When the Gift is first activated, the character may make a Simple Test (no Traits are risked) versus all nearby animals (20-foot radius), including ghouled animals. If the Garou wins or ties, the animals flee immediately and will not approach her again that day. Even if she loses, the animal is one Trait down in any challenge it makes against the character.

• **Jam Technology** — The Garou can temporarily disrupt the orderly logic of the Weaver on which technological items depend. It costs at least one Gnosis Trait to activate this Gift. The Garou may choose to affect a single visible item within 50 feet. The exact number of Traits she must expend depends on the complexity of the item she wishes to affect.

One Gnosis Trait	Lever, wrench, knife
Two Gnosis Traits	Automobile, firearm
Three Gnosis Traits	Lock, phone, radio
Four Gnosis Traits	Computer, television

• **Paralyzing Stare** — The Garou may freeze an opponent in place with a piercing gaze. The Garou must make eye contact with the subject and win a Mental Challenge. If the attempt succeeds, the victim is stunned for five turns. A stunned person may not move, speak or initiate a challenge. If the subject is assaulted, he may only defend himself.

Intermediate Gifts

• **Disquiet** — The Garou can cause a deep and profound depression to overcome her target. By expending a Gnosis Trait and winning a Social Challenge, the Garou prevents her victim from recovering any Rage for the session or day. Additionally, this Gift triggers the following Derangements (if already present) in a target: *Manic Depression* and *Regression*.

• **Reshape Object** — This Gift, taught only by Weaver-spirits, allows a Garou to change one cubic foot of once-living material, per Rank level, into a common object instantly. The Garou states the name of what she wants, and performs a Mental Challenge against a number of Traits set by the Storyteller. The more radical the change, the higher the target number. The base material does not change chemical composition or mass, only form. An elk antler can become a spear, a hollow tree might become a small shelter, or flowers may become perfume. Technological items cannot be made, and while plucked vines may be shaped to look like wires, they will not carry electricity. The item lasts in its new form for one scene unless the Garou spends a permanent Gnosis Trait to stabilize the new form. This Gift does not reshape undead creatures. Weapons made through the use of this Gift do aggravated damage only if the Garou expends a Gnosis Trait.

• **Tongues** — By drawing upon the shared knowledge of all intelligent beings, a Garou can attempt to understand languages previously unknown to her. This requires a Mental Challenge against the difficulty of the language. The effects of the Gift last one scene.

Four Traits	Common or modern language
Seven Traits	Obscure or heavy dialect
10 Traits	Unknown or forgotten language

Advanced Gifts

• **Spirit Ward** — By expending a Gnosis Trait and drawing a pictogram in the air, the Garou sets up a guard against spirit attacks. Any spirit within 100 feet must win a Mental Challenge with the Garou in order to attack her. Even if it is successful, the spirit must still risk three Traits each time it initiates an attack. This Gift lasts for one scene.

• **Reduce Delirium**— The Garou can ease the minds of humans, sparing them from the danger of Delirium. The Garou spends a Gnosis and enters a normal Social Challenge with the target, except that the target may not relent; she *must* bid a Social Trait. If the attempt succeeds, the effects of Delirium are ignored for a single scene.

Metis

Basic Gifts

• **Sense Wyrm** — Manifestations of the Wyrm, those who are of the Wyrm and items or places used by these creatures have a trace residue on them which a Garou can sense by using this Gift. The Garou concentrates, wins or ties a Static Mental challenge and then detects Wyrm-taint in the area. This Gift reveals not only Banes and the like, but also vampires who have more than two Beast Traits (see **Laws of the Night**). At Storyteller's discretion, this Gift may also sense mass murderers, psychopaths, socio-paths, vampires of an earlier generation than ninth or recent diabolists as Wyrm-tainted or Wyrm-minions.

• **Create Element** — By expending a Gnosis Trait and succeeding in a Gnosis Challenge (against 7 Traits) the Garou may create one cubic foot (per Rank) of one of the four basic elements: fire, air, water or earth. The element appears either at the Garou's feet or in her hands. The material thus created cannot be poisonous, acidic or even semi-precious — you cannot create earth and then claim that you've got a cubic foot of diamond in your hands.

Fire — This use summons flame, which ignites flammables and causes aggravated wounds. A Mental Challenge is required to attack someone with the summoned fire; if the attack is unsuccessful, the fire ends up on nearby objects, with predictable results.

Air — Summoning air causes a short, slight breeze or refreshes the air for an entombed creature.

Water — The Gift produces enough water to extinguish a small fire or provide a day's worth of drinking water for a single man, wolf or Garou.

Earth — The Gift produces a rock weighing up to about 100 pounds, although objects small enough to be thrown are generally more useful. The rock created tends to be of the same sort as is common in the area.

• **Curse of Hatred**— By focusing the anger and hatred within herself and directing it verbally at her opponent, a Garou may demoralize her foe. This power costs a Gnosis Trait to use. Furthermore, the Garou must defeat her opponent in a Social Challenge. If the Garou wins, her foe loses a Willpower Trait and a Rage Trait for the remainder of the session or day.

- **Shed** — The Garou may suddenly release a layer of fur, making her difficult to restrain. The Garou gains the Physical Traits: *Wiry*, *Lithe* and *Nimble* for use in avoiding being grappled. These Traits last for the remainder of the scene. While the Garou doesn't become completely hairless after repeated uses of this Gift, the amount of hair that she sheds may not endear her to those with allergies.

Intermediate Gifts

- **Gift of the Porcupine** — This Gift (usable in Crinos, Hispo and Lupus forms) makes the Garou's fur sharp and bristly, like a porcupine's quills. If the Garou wins a Physical Challenge in unarmed combat against a foe, she can try to win a follow-up Simple Test (no Traits are risked) to inflict an additional wound. The Garou may make this follow-up challenge even if her foe won the initial combat challenge, but only if the foe attacked without a handheld or distance weapon (claws don't count). This Gift requires the expenditure of a Gnosis Trait and lasts for one scene.

- **Grovel** — When suffering at the hands of another Garou, the possessor of this Gift may draw upon the instinctive surrender reflex of wolves to force the attacking Garou to stop. If the Garou spends a Gnosis Trait and wins a Social Challenge, the attacking Garou must back off and end her attacks. This effect lasts for one hour or until the user makes a move against the Garou who spared her (whichever comes first). The use of this Gift is not particularly glorious, and could result in the loss of an Honor Trait at the next moot.

- **Mental Speech** — The Garou can talk with another character by telepathy (although she cannot read minds). The Garou must win a Mental Challenge against the target to initiate contact (no relent, unless the receiver knows the message is coming). After that the conversation may continue until either party breaks it off. This Gift might work on a stranger (at Narrator discretion) if the Garou has sufficient information about her target or something that belongs to him. The range of this Gift is citywide or about 10 miles. Note that passing notes and employing the aid of a Narrator are acceptable ways to represent the use of this Gift.

Advanced Gifts

- **Wither Limb** — By spending a Gnosis Trait and winning a Mental Challenge against her foe's Physical Traits, the Garou may reduce one of the foe's arms or legs to a useless parody of its former self. The victim suffers an aggravated wound and gains the Negative Physical Trait: *Lame*. Garou, vampires or other regenerative creatures injured in this manner may heal this damage as per aggravated wounds. A normal human affected by this Gift may very well be crippled for life.

- **Madness** — The Garou can cause extreme, but thankfully temporary, insanity in a victim. She must expend a Gnosis Trait and then defeat the target in a Social Challenge. If this is successful, the victim gains a random active Derangement that she does not already possess; the duration is one day or the rest of the session.

• **Totem Gift** — In an act of desperation, the Garou can plead to her totem for aid. With this Gift, a Garou can spend a Gnosis Trait and then petition her tribal totem to intercede on her behalf. Calling upon one's totem always requires a Storyteller/Spirit Keeper. The exact nature of the aid that the totem is willing to give is up to the Storyteller, but should be in keeping with the nature of the totem.

Totem	Type of Assistance
Bear	Peacekeeping, healing, strength in war
Coyote	Trickery, cunning, stealth
Dana	Faerie or Umbral matters
Pegasus	Defense of sacred places
Rat	Stealth, strength in numbers
Unicorn	Health, healing, peacekeeping
Stag	Help during hard times, sensing danger
Fenris	Help with bloodthirsty combat
Cockroach	Adaptability and survival
Griffin	Swiftness, alertness during battle
Thunder	Subtlety, falsehoods, strategy and power
Owl	Stealth, silence, darkness and quiet
Falcon	Honor, leadership and nobility
Chimera	Riddles, enigmas, solving problems
Uktena	Defense, secret lore or knowledge
Wendigo	Help with missions of vengeance

Lupus

Basic Gifts

• **Heightened Senses** — This Gift allows the Garou to try to overhear distant conversations, recognize subtle scents and detect moving targets cloaked by Gifts or vampiric Disciplines by winning a Mental Challenge. Very intense stimuli (sudden blasts of loud music, strobe lights, walking into a warehouse full of Limburger cheese) may result in the particular sense "going numb" for five minutes.

• **Scent of Sight** — If the Garou succeeds in a Mental Challenge (against 6 Traits, though the Storyteller may adjust for distracting scents), he can utilize his sense of smell to compensate for losing his sight, thereby allowing him to attack invisible foes without penalties or roughly navigate in total darkness.

• **Scent of the True Form** — By inhaling the scent of a nearby subject (someone within a few feet), the Garou may attempt to ascertain its true being. Vampires, faeries, mummies, wraiths (who have physically manifested via certain Arcanoi), fomori and other Garou may be detected this way if the Gifted Garou defeats them in a Mental Challenge. If this Gift is used on a mage, ghoul or Kinfolk, the subject wins all ties, regardless of who has the most Traits.

• **Catfeet** — The Garou gains the preternatural agility of this Gift's namesake. She avoids damage from falls of 100 feet or less, and gains the Physical Traits: *Athletic*, *Graceful* and *Nimble*. These Traits can be used only in challenges that deal with balance, agility, dodging and grappling.

Intermediate Gifts

• **Name the Spirit** — The Garou gains the ability to sense the presence and nature of unseen spirits (and to reveal disguised ones). The Garou must first think to activate the Gift, however, and must defeat her target in a Mental Challenge. This Gift allows the Garou to know the type and approximate Trait levels of a spirit.

• **Beast Life** — With the expenditure of a Gnosis Trait and a successful Static Social Challenge, the Garou may call forth a group of a single sort of animal (subject to the availability of the animal). The animals must be given a specific and short-term mission or they will disperse. Missions could include attacking an enemy, guarding a place for a session or destroying an object. The group acts as one creature.

Common animals like rats, insects, snakes, wolves, dogs or cats can be summoned in this way.

• **Gnaw** — The Garou's jaws and teeth take on supernatural strength and resilience. She may chew through and destroy objects that would not normally be affected by bites, simply by chewing on them (remember that objects have Traits and Health Levels just like people). If a Garou with this Gift declares that she is biting an opponent and succeeds, she may try to win a Simple Test (no Traits are risked) to inflict a second wound.

Advanced Gifts

• **Venom** — The Garou can cause her teeth to become coated in a deadly poison. If the Garou successfully bites her foe, the victim must win a Static Physical Challenge each hour or lose a further Health Level. This continues until the target wins or dies.

• **Elemental Gift** — A Garou with this Gift may call upon one of the four primal elemental forces. To do so, the character must expend a Gnosis Trait and win a Static Mental Challenge (against 7 Traits). Use the following profiles for elemental forces:

Fire Elemental: *Brutal* x 2, *Energetic*, *Ferocious*, *Quick*

A fire attack requires a Physical Challenge and inflicts aggravated wounds. If fire and water elementals touch, both are destroyed.

Burn Charm: If the elemental wins a Physical Challenge, it may choose to inflict a second aggravated wound on its target.

Water Elemental: *Enduring*, *Lithe*, *Resilient*, *Tenacious*, *Vigorous*

Engulf Charm: If the elemental wins a Physical Challenge, a breathing opponent suffers a wound from suffocation.

Earth Elemental: *Brawny*, *Enduring*, *Tough*, *Rugged*, *Stalwart*

Entomb Charm: Once the elemental wins a Physical Challenge against a foe, that foe is trapped inside the elemental. The victim may not flee or engage others, and can only fight the elemental from within. If an earth and air elemental touch, they are both destroyed.

Air Elemental: *Energetic, Graceful, Lithe, Quick, Vigorous*

Windstorm Charm: A swirling vortex of air surrounds the summoner, deflecting arrows and thrown objects. The summoner's foes must win a Physical Challenge with the elemental even to close with the Garou.

Note: Elementals are mindless. They do not engage in Social or Mental Challenges. Furthermore, elementals can suffer only three wounds before being disrupted. They do not suffer from wound penalties. The effect of an elemental's Charm lasts for one scene. An entombed character is freed if the elemental imprisoning it vanishes. However, if the earth elemental vanishes after coming in contact with an air elemental, the victim takes an aggravated wound from the explosion.

Auspice Gifts

Ragabash

Basic Gifts

• **Scent of Running Water** — The Garou may completely mask her scent. A foe attempting to use an olfactory sensing power, such as *Heightened Senses*, must first win a Mental Challenge in order to attempt to track the user of this Gift.

• **Blur of the Milky Eye** — The Garou can obscure her presence from others. To activate this Gift, the player must succeed in a Static Mental Challenge and cross her arms in front of herself. At this point, other characters must ignore the hidden Garou and act normally. However, as soon as the Garou speaks or interacts with her environment (she can still move around), the glamour is shattered and she is visible to all. Otherwise, the power lasts for one scene. This Gift affects only other beings, not machines. The Gift may not be activated if the Garou is being watched by others.

• **Open Seal** — By winning or tying a Static Mental Challenge, the Garou may open a single mundane lock or closure. The affected item shows no sign of tampering or the like (except for the fact that it is now is open). Magical or more complex locks (such as computer locks) require a win on the Mental Challenge.

• **Alter Scent** — The Garou may replace her scent with any scent she has experienced before by expending a Gnosis and succeeding in a Mental Challenge. When tracking a Garou thus Gifted, a foe with *Heightened Senses* is allowed a single Simple Test (no Traits are expended). If the foe wins the test, she uncovers her prey's true scent and cannot be fooled again for the rest of the session. Otherwise, the foe falls for the deception.

Intermediate Gifts

• **Blissful Ignorance** — The Garou's powers of invisibility have been developed so well that she can even fool electronic devices and spirits. Otherwise, the Gift works just like *Blur of the Milky Eye* and can still be uncovered by *Heightened Senses*. This Gift costs one Gnosis to activate.

• **Fool's Luck** — The Garou with this Gift has luck on her side. When a Gnosis is spent, she may retest (at no cost) any test she loses as long as it involves trickery, coercion or stealth. A challenge may be retested only once in this fashion. If the Garou loses in this second test, the challenge may not be retested in any other manner. This Gift lasts for one scene.

• **Open the Moon Bridge** — The Garou has the power to open a Moon Bridge without the aid of the caern's totem spirit. A Pathstone fetish is still required, and the Gnosis required to open the bridge must be supplied by the Garou. In all other ways, this Gift functions as the *Rite of the Opened Bridge*.

• **Taking the Forgotten** — This Gift makes the Garou a most daunting thief. If she can steal an item from an opponent (with a Mental Challenge, or through roleplaying), the user and the victim then enter a second Mental Challenge. If the Garou wins, the victim forgets he ever had the item, and forgets that the Ragabash stole from him. If violence is part of the theft, this Gift may not be used. The victim does not realize the item is gone until he next needs it. ("Now where did I put that key to the shed?")

Advanced Gifts

• **Luna's Blessing** — On nights when the moon shines bright in the sky, a Garou with this Gift may petition Luna to spare him the agony of silver. With *Luna's Blessing*, the Garou no longer takes aggravated damage from silver. The effect lasts until morning. In addition, if an attacker loses a combat challenge against the Garou while wielding a silver weapon, the Gifted Garou may call for a second Physical Challenge. If the Garou wins, his opponent takes a normal wound, unless the opponent is also a Garou, in which case the damage is aggravated.

• **Whelp Body** — The Garou may use this Gift to drive strength and vitality from her opponent's body. Using *Whelp Body* is a sure way to initiate a battle to the death; no Garou who suffers this Gift's touch will let her attacker live. The Garou spends two Gnosis and performs a Mental Challenge with the target. If successful, her foe loses a Physical Trait for a month. The victim chooses the Trait lost. This Gift can be used once against an opponent per session. This Gift does not give the user any knowledge of which Trait has been removed.

• **Violation** — A Garou with this Gift can reach deep into the mind of an opponent and shatter his confidence. The Garou must first win a Physical Challenge (in which no damage is inflicted) to touch her foe emphatically. At this point, she must win a Mental Challenge with the target. If she wins this test, she may make another and continue to do so until she loses or ties a test. The victim may not spend Willpower or Rage for a length of time dependent on the number of tests the attacking Garou wins.

Number of tests won	Effect
No tests	No effect, Gnosis wasted.
One test	This scene.
Two tests	This scene and the next.
Three tests	This session.
Four tests	This session and the next (or one week, whichever is shorter).

Theurge

Basic Gifts

• **Sense Wyrm** — As per the Metis Gift.

• **Spirit Speech** — The Garou with this Gift has learned the spirit tongue and may converse with any spirits near enough to hear her. This, of course, is no guarantee that the spirits will be cooperative or will even listen to the character. Some spirits, such as Banes, may be difficult to understand (Storyteller's discretion).

• **Mother's Touch** — The Garou's touch can heal the injuries of other living creatures. The Garou need only touch the subject, concentrate for one minute and expend a Gnosis Trait. A single wound, whether aggravated or not, is healed by this process. The Garou may not use his healing power on himself. This Gift can negate the effects of a battle scar if performed within one scene of the battle in which the scar was received.

• **Sight from Beyond** — The Garou with this Gift is subject to unexpected and uncontrolled visions of the future. Sometimes these visions and dreams warn her of imminent danger or herald great events. More often than not, however, these visions are cryptic and unclear. The Garou must make of them what she will. Once per session, the Storyteller may opt to give the Garou a strange, enigmatic preview of a threat, which is a possible outcome of the evening's play.

• **Name the Spirit** — Same as the Lupus Gift.

Intermediate Gifts

• **Command Spirit** — The Garou can issue a simple, yet compelling command to a spirit. The subject must be able to hear and understand the Garou. The command itself cannot be blatantly suicidal, and must be within the subject's ability to perform. A unwilling spirit must first be defeated in a Social Challenge. This Gift costs one Willpower Trait to use.

• **Exorcism** — The Garou can drive spirits from an area, even persistent spirits or ones bound to items or locations. A Willpower Trait must be expended to make an *Exorcism* attempt. If the spirit has not been bound, driving it off is merely a matter of defeating it in a Social Challenge. If it is bound, however, it must be defeated in a Mental Challenge, but it also receives a number of free Traits to bid equal to the number of Traits assigned to the fetish that houses it. The Garou may not attempt to use this Gift on the same spirit more than once per session.

• **Pulse of the Invisible** — The Garou gains a dramatic insight into the spirit world and its inhabitants. Any time a drastic change takes place, she automatically knows it, but does not necessarily know the nature of the disruption. Storytellers should make characters with this Gift aware of any drastic increases, decreases or changes in the behavior or activity of nearby spirits. For example, with a Simple Test, the Garou could detect if a spirit was just summoned or if someone just stepped sideways. Gaining this information generally requires a Simple Test (no Traits are risked).

• **Grasp the Beyond** — The Garou can reach through the Gauntlet to place objects in the Umbra. This includes humans and animals, both willing and unwilling. The larger the object, the greater the exertion on the Garou's part.

One Gnosis	Small (handheld object)
Two Gnosis	Medium-sized (rifle)
Three Gnosis	Large (man-sized)

The Garou must succeed in a Physical Challenge to touch unwilling individuals. Those unable to sidestep are trapped in the Umbra until they find a place with a Gauntlet of 3 or less. Unless it is moved in the Umbra, an object's position relative to the real world does not change (i.e., this Gift does not provide the Garou with an extra-dimensional duffel bag.)

Advanced Gifts

• **Spirit Drain** — The Garou can tap into the personal energy reserves of a spirit. The Garou must expend a Gnosis Trait to activate this Gift. If she can defeat a spirit in a Mental Challenge, she may continue to attempt to win further Simple Tests (no Traits are risked) until she ties or loses. For every two tests won (rounding down), including the initial Mental Challenge, the spirit loses a point of power and the Garou regains a Willpower Trait. Any Willpower gained over the Garou's original level must be spent immediately, or is lost at the end of the scene.

• **Feral Lobotomy** — The Garou may use this Gift to drive intelligence from her opponent's mind. Garou react to being targeted with this Gift the same way they react to *Whelp Body* — the Garou using *Feral Lobotomy* had better kill his opponent, or he will have made a mortal enemy. The Garou spends two Gnosis and performs a Mental Challenge against the target. If successful, her foe loses a Mental or Social Trait for a month. The attacking Garou chooses which category is affected, but the victim's player chooses the exact Trait. This Gift can be used only once against an opponent per session. This Gift does not give the victimized *character* any knowledge of which Trait has been removed.

• **Malleable Spirit** — Many spirits are fickle and mercurial by nature. A Garou with this Gift can capitalize on that flaw and attempt to warp the spirit completely to suit her needs. The Garou must expend a Gnosis and overcome the spirit in a Mental Challenge. If the Garou wins, she may attempt to win further Simple Tests until she loses or ties. The total number of tests won determines the degree to which the spirit can be altered.

One success	Disposition	(benevolent, hostile, uncooperative)
Two successes	Characteristics	(Traits, Abilities)
Three successes	Role	(type of elemental or spirit)

• **Spirit Vessel** — The Garou can draw upon the powers of the spirits of the Umbra to use as her own. The Garou must expend a Gnosis Trait and win a Static Mental Challenge (number of Traits equals the area's Gauntlet). If the Garou wins, she gains the desired Basic spirit Charm for one scene. A second Gnosis spent and a second test won gains her an

Intermediate Charm, and a third Gnosis allows a third test to attempt to gain an Advanced Charm. If she ties, she gains only the Charms she had won prior to this test, and may not attempt to use the Gift again this session. If she loses the first test, she becomes possessed by a Bane. A Storyteller will then instruct the Garou on appropriate actions and behavior.

Philodox

Basic Gifts

• **Resist Pain** — The Garou may ignore wound penalties for the duration of one scene by expending a Gnosis Trait.

• **King of the Beasts** — The Garou is able to call upon the aid of a single animal type (dogs, big cats, rodents) with which he has a relationship. Specifically, the Garou can control a single animal within sight range. The animal follows the Garou's commands willingly and unconditionally. The Garou must first expend a Gnosis Trait and win or tie a Social Challenge with the animal before giving a command. This Gift affects only normal animals, not Garou in Lupus form or Kindred in animal forms. The effects of this Gift last for one scene.

Actively hostile or ghouled animals win all ties unless an overbid can be called.

• **Truth of Gaia** — The Garou may enter a Mental Challenge against an opponent to determine if the last statement the opponent made was true. This Gift works against pathological liars, but if the person believes something to be true, it will read as a true statement.

• **Scent of the True Form** — As per the Lupus Gift.

• **Strength of Purpose** — Whenever the Garou deals with a challenge that affects or involves the very core of her auspice, pack/sept position or tribe, she may expend Gnosis Traits to regain spent Willpower Traits, at a one-for-one ratio, up to her total. This Gift may be used only once per session.

Intermediate Gifts

• **Call to Duty** — By spending a Gnosis Trait and winning a Simple Test (no Traits are risked), the Garou can call for any spirits within one mile to protect and assist her. The Spirit Keeper (see p. 187.) determines the time the spirit(s) takes to arrive, its type and ability to serve, but in general, only minor spirits answer this call and serve the Garou. This Gift may not be used more than once per session, and lasts for only one scene. If the Garou knows a specific spirit's name, she can call it directly.

• **Weak Arm** — A perceptive Philodox with this Gift can gain valuable insights into a foe's martial prowess by merely observing his style. By witnessing a single combat challenge in which the subject is engaged, the Garou may attempt to ascertain the style's inherent strengths and weaknesses. If the Garou wins a Mental Challenge against the subject, she gains three free Physical retests to use against the subject during that scene. The Garou may not use this Gift on the same individual more than once per scene.

• **Roll Over** — The Garou can exude an aura of power and command. If the Garou calls for a Social Challenge and wins, he dominates his target into submissive behavior. If anyone should attempt an offensive action against the

Gifted Garou, he may opt to demand a Social Challenge before the attack can proceed (regardless of *Celerity* or surprise). If the attacker succeeds, he is not hampered in attacking for the rest of the scene. If the attacker fails, he may not attack the Gifted Garou for an hour.

Furthermore, a defeated foe who returns in the same session must still win a Social Challenge to attack the Garou. Any offensive action taken by the defending Garou negates this Gift's effects. The Gift's range extends about four paces from the Gifted Garou's body.

• **Scent of Beyond** — The Garou can bring all her senses to bear on one spot (even in the Umbra) with which she is familiar. The Garou must succeed in a Mental Challenge against 9 Traits (and win a second challenge against the Gauntlet, if it must be passed through to witness the intended site), and then senses the area as if he were standing in the middle of it. This Gift lasts until the Garou's concentration is broken.

Advanced Gifts

• **Take the True Form** — This Gift allows the Garou to command a shapechanger to assume her breed form instantly. The Gift functions only if the Gifted Garou wins a Social Challenge against his opponent. This Gift also forces a vampire using *Beast Form* to revert instantly to human form. In no case may the shapechanger assume a different form until the next scene.

• **Wall of Granite** — The Garou may instantly erect a stony barrier by expending a Gnosis Trait. This barrier is three feet thick, up to nine feet tall and up to nine feet wide. The wall moves with the Garou and protects him from all sides. It has the Traits: *Stalwart* x 10, and can suffer 10 wounds before being destroyed. It may not be summoned anywhere but in direct contact with the earth. The wall returns to the ground at the end of the scene.

• **Geas** — The Garou can cause others to do her bidding, although she cannot make the targets act contrary to their basic instincts. Thus, she could send a group on a quest, but could not make its members attack each other without provocation. The Garou must first expend a Gnosis Trait and defeat the leader of the group to be affected in a Social Challenge. These commands may not be suicidal and cannot directly endanger the subject. Go *find the Black Spiral Dancers' hive and report back to me*, is an acceptable Geas. Go *subdue Malfeas single-handedly* is not.

Galliard

Basic Gifts

• **Beast Speech** — With a successful Social Challenge, the Gifted Garou can speak with and understand all normal animals (from mice to lions to fish). This Gift does not change the animals' reaction to the Garou, nor does it grant the animals more intelligence than they possess already.

• **Call of the Wyld** — The Garou can issue forth a great howl that is audible to those nearby, but the effects travel beyond that, in some cases reaching Garou miles away. Most often, it is used to summon others to a moot or to herald other important events, but it can serve as a general distress call. A Garou wishing to use this Gift should contact a Storyteller and perform a

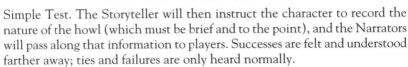

Simple Test. The Storyteller will then instruct the character to record the nature of the howl (which must be brief and to the point), and the Narrators will pass along that information to players. Successes are felt and understood farther away; ties and failures are only heard normally.

• **Mindspeak** — The Garou can forge a telepathic communications link between herself and other willing participants within visual range by expending a Gnosis Trait for each subject to be included. Other creatures, such as a vampire using *Telepathy*, may listen in if they can defeat the Gifted Garou in a Mental Challenge. This Gift lasts for one scene. This Gift cannot be used to forge a link with an unwilling mind.

• **Distractions** — The Garou can harry and annoy his opponent to such a degree that her concentration in other matters suffers for it. If the Garou can defeat the subject in a Mental Challenge, the subject must spend an extra Trait in any challenges, and is down two Traits when comparing on ties. The Distractions must be made at the same time as the tests that are to be affected. The effects of this Gift are not cumulative.

Intermediate Gifts

• **Call of the Wyrm** — The Garou can issue forth a howl that beckons to the minions of the Wyrm. Any minions of the Wyrm that do not win a Social Challenge (the Gifted Garou risks no Traits) must go quickly (but not mindlessly) to the calling Garou. If they win, they may still come, but under their own terms and at their leisure. This Gift is usually used to flush Wyrm-creatures out of their hiding places. The Gift affects only those within hearing range, and the Spirit Keeper must be contacted to use this Gift.

• **Dreamspeak** — If the Garou is successful in a Mental Challenge against a sleeping target, she may enter that person's dreams and affect the course of the dream. If the sleeper wakes up before the Garou leaves a dream, the interloper is unceremoniously thrown back into the real world and loses one Gnosis.

• **Song of Rage** — This power unleashes a fearsome, bestial nature in the target. The Garou must defeat the subject in a Social Challenge in order to use this Gift. If the challenge is successful, the subject flies into an uncontrollable rage for the next turn. A Garou subject immediately regains one Rage Trait. This Gift sends Kindred into frenzy and turns humans into berserkers. If the Garou fails, she may not attempt to use this Gift on the same subject again for the remainder of the session.

• **Eyes of the Cobra** — The Garou can lure the subject to his side and into a docile and amiable state. Eye contact is required to use this Gift. The Garou attempts to win a Mental Challenge against the target, and if he is successful, the target must remain civil and nonconfrontational for the remainder of the scene. If the victim is attacked by any source (including verbal assault), the Gift's power is immediately broken.

Advanced Gifts

• **Bridge Walker** — The Galliard can open a minor Moon Bridge. By spending a Gnosis Trait, the Garou (and only the Gifted Garou) disappears, only to reappear a split-second later a short distance away (only foes with powers that increase speed can attempt to prevent the use of this Gift by catching up to the Garou's new location quickly enough to attack her). Once the Gnosis is spent, the player may take 15 paces in any horizontal direction that she wishes. The character is not hampered by physical barriers, but magical ones cause her to reappear immediately if she attempts to cross them. At the end of her journey, the player must make a Simple Test (no Traits are risked); if she loses, she has caught the attention of a spirit, which appears with her. If it is hostile, the spirit attacks the character immediately.

• **Head Games** — The Garou can drastically alter the subject's emotions. By defeating the subject in a Social Challenge, the Garou can set the character on a new emotional keel. The effects of this Gift last for the remainder of the session. Use of this Gift to make someone fall in love or undergo other such major adjustments usually backfires when the Gift's effects wear off. The victim always remembers his behavior while under the influence, and may well resent it.

• **Song of the Siren** — The Garou can sing an entrancing melody that lulls the unwary into a passive stupor. If the Garou spends a Gnosis and defeats the subject in a Social Challenge, the victim may do nothing else but peacefully listen to the Galliard's singing. The player must actually sing clearly and relatively continually or the Gift's effects end. The effects of this Gift are broken if the subject is assaulted in any way or if the Garou's singing can no longer be heard clearly.

Ahroun
Basic Gifts

• **Razor Claws** — The Garou's claws can be honed to razor sharpness by scratching them across a hard surface, such as a stone floor or metal dumpster. The Garou can retest after successfully striking an opponent to deliver a second level of damage on a win with a Simple Test. This Gift is usable only in Crinos, Hispo and Glabro forms. The benefits are lost if the character assumes another form.

• **Spirit of the Fray** — This Gift allows a Garou to preempt any attack with an attack of her own. This will not work if the Garou is surprised, but can be activated in any normal combat turn. If attacked by a foe who has more than one attack per turn, the Garou may still preempt each attack with one of her own by spending a Gnosis for each. This gift normally costs a Gnosis to activate.

• **Inspiration** — The powerful figure of an Ahroun serves to urge other Garou on to acts of greatness, especially if the Ahroun has this Gift. By spending a Gnosis Trait, the Garou may allow any of his fellow Garou nearby one free retest during the scene. The Garou may not benefit from his own Gift.

• **The Falling Touch** — The Garou can send his foe sprawling to the ground with but a touch. The Garou must spend a Gnosis Trait and defeat the subject in a Physical Challenge in order for this Gift to work. If the attempt is successful, the victim must sit down on the ground for the next four actions or a full 15 seconds (count them out loud, please) if not involved in combat.

The victim may not initiate any Physical Challenges during that time. He may defend himself normally, however. Opponents with *Celerity* or *Speed of Thought* can cut this time to two actions or eight seconds. *Rapidity* or *Speed Beyond Thought* reduces this penalty to one round or four seconds. A vampire with *Fleetness* has no downtime.

Intermediate Gifts

• **Sense Silver** — With a disdainful snort and a Static Mental Challenge (against 3 Traits for a weapon, 7 for a coin, 10 for a bullet) the Garou can uncover the foul scent of the hated metal in the immediate area (up to a 20-foot radius). Tying on the Static Mental Challenge reveals the metal's general presence. Winning reveals exactly where the silver is located. Any nearby characters must then reveal to the Garou the presence of any silver items they possess.

• **Stoking Fury's Furnace** — The Garou may gain Rage as usual when wounded, but does not test to see if she frenzies from injuries. Also, if the Garou spends only one Rage in a turn, her total available Rage does not drop.

• **True Fear** — This Gift allows a Garou to scare a foe into quiescence. The Garou must win a Physical Challenge against the subject. If the Garou is successful, the victim may not initiate any challenges against the user of the Gift for the next hour. If the subject wins, she has faced her fears and may not be the target of the Garou's Gift of *True Fear* for the remainder of the session.

• **Silver Claws** — By spending a Gnosis Trait, the Garou ensorcells his claws so that they inflict the searing agony of pure silver. This Gift can be activated only during a challenge, but can be used before the actual test takes place. If successful, the Garou's victim suffers (if susceptible to silver) an additional aggravated wound. This Gift lasts for one strike only.

Advanced Gifts

• **Strength of Will** — The Ahroun's powers of inspiring confidence in her packmates during battle can reach epic proportions. By expending one of her own Willpower Traits and making a Static Social Challenge (against the number of people she wishes to inspire), the Gifted Garou grants a temporary Willpower Trait to all allies within 100 feet. This Trait may be used only during that scene and only in combat. Any Traits remaining after that scene are lost. This Gift may be used only once per session.

• **Kiss of Helios** — The blessings of the daystar are on the Garou with this Gift, making her totally immune to mundane flame. It costs a Gnosis Trait to activate this Gift, which lasts for one scene, but during that time the Garou cannot be damaged by ordinary flame and ignores half the damage (round down) inflicted by magical flame, napalm or similar attacks. Furthermore, if the Garou wishes, she may immolate herself without suffering harm. However, she does cause aggravated damage to others with blows inflicted by her hands.

Tribe Gifts

Black Furies

Basic Gifts

- **Sense Wyrm** — As per the Metis Gift.
- **Heightened Senses** — As per the Lupus Gift.
- **Sense of the Prey** — The Garou may track down a known quarry while traveling at full speed. A Mental Challenge is required only if the prey is actively attempting to hide. This Gift is often used to track spirits' passage in the Umbra.

Intermediate Gifts

- **Song of the Siren** — As per the Galliard Gift.
- **Coup de Grace** — The Garou with this Gift has the ability to land telling blows regardless of her foe's power. This Gift can be activated by spending a Gnosis Trait in the midst of a challenge *before* the actual test is performed. If the Garou wins the test, she then performs a Mental Challenge against her foe. If she wins or ties (regardless of total Mental Traits), the foe suffers a additional wound (though no additional damage may be added to this wound).
- **Wasp Talons** — The Garou's claws become a lethal ranged attack. The Garou can propel her claws at terrifying speeds, as if they were fired from a ranged weapon. Treat the barrage of claws as a shotgun blast with the Negative Trait: *Painful*. This power can be used only in Crinos, Hispo and Glabro forms. While the Garou waits for her claws to regenerate (in other words, for the duration of the combat), she may not use claws or claw-based powers.

Advanced Gifts

- **Body Wrack** — The Garou can create crippling pain throughout her opponent's body, greatly disabling him. To use this Gift, the Garou must spend a Gnosis Trait and defeat the subject in a Mental Challenge. If successful, the victim is down four Traits for the rest of the scene. (That is, he will be four Traits down if the players have to compare Traits.) In no case will this Gift lower the victim to less than one Trait.
- **Bacchantes' Rage** — This maiming Gift can be used only in the deep wilderness, for it often ensures that the Furies will have the ability to defend those secluded spots. While this Gift is in effect, the Garou wins all ties in any tests involving melee combat without resorting to comparing Traits, and may spend a Rage Trait after successfully hitting an opponent to do an additional level of damage. This Gift can also be linked with *Razor Claws* (but not with any other Gift) for additional damage. It costs two Gnosis to use this Gift, and its effects last for the duration of the scene.
- **The Thousand Forms of Gaia** — The Garou may take the form of any normal animal between the sizes of a sparrow and a bison, gaining all special abilities and weaknesses thereof (flight, gills, speed of movement, etc.). No monsters or extinct animals may be mimicked.

Bone Gnawer

Basic Gifts

• **Blissful Ignorance** — As per the Ragabash Gift.

• **Cooking** — Any Garou with this Gift and a small pot (with ladle) can, with a successful Mental Challenge, make a foul-tasting but edible stew from anything in the area. The difficulty of the transformation to edible food is determined by a Narrator. Common stuff (like bark, grass, tin, glass) is a 6-Trait challenge, while poisons and asphalt would be 10.

• **Scent of Sweet Honey** — The Garou can lay down a scent upon an object or creature that insects and all manner of vermin find irresistible. This Gift costs one Gnosis to use. An object affected by this is swarmed during the scene (within about five game minutes). If the target is a creature, he suffers a 1-Trait penalty on any further challenges for the rest of the session, and temporarily picks up the Negative Traits: *Clumsy*, *Repugnant* and *Witless* as the swarming insects bite, crawl on and generally distract him.

• **Odious Aroma** — By expending a Gnosis Trait, a Garou can put his natural defensive pheromone glands into a sort of overdrive. Anyone who gets within 10 feet of the Garou (and can smell) becomes so overpowered by his stench that she must spend a second Trait in any challenge with the Garou. Those using *Heightened Senses* at the time suffer an additional 1-Trait penalty. The Garou using this power immediately gains the Negative Social Traits: *Repugnant* x 3. The effects of this Gift last for two scenes.

Intermediate Gifts

• **Gift of the Skunk** — The Garou develops a set of musk glands similar to those of a skunk. She can use this musk to spray a subject. The Garou must win a Physical Challenge to hit with the jet of foul-smelling liquid (field of fire like submachine gun — what a revolting image that is). If successful, the target suffers from the Negative Social Traits: *Repugnant* x 2 for the rest of the session, and these Traits can be called by any individual who can smell the victim. Furthermore, if the subject's sense of smell is enhanced (as is the case with a vampire with *Heightened Senses*), he may not initiate a challenge for 10 minutes, being otherwise occupied with retching. A Willpower Trait may be spent to perform one action while incapacitated by this Gift.

• **Gift of the Termite** — The Garou may use this Gift to destroy objects made of wood. The objects rot and weaken until, in seconds, nothing remains except a pile of moist sawdust and splinters. This power costs a Gnosis Trait to use. The Garou must win or tie a Mental Challenge, the difficulty of which depends on the size of the object she wishes to affect.

3 Traits	Stake, bat, cane
7 Traits	Door
10 Traits	Small dead tree
12 Traits	10' x 10' wooden floor

• **Attunement** — While in an urban setting, the Garou can commune with the local spirits for information on the area. To use this Gift requires that the Garou expend a Gnosis Trait and win a Simple Test (no Traits are risked). If she succeeds, she may ask one of the following questions and can expect an honest answer (unless the only spirits nearby are Wyrm-spirits, who will always mislead the Garou). The Garou may continue to make tests and ask questions until she loses. Each test equals one question. The Spirit Keeper must be contacted to use this Gift.

Typical questions include:

— What is the general population of (type of supernatural creature) in this area? (Note, however, that some very powerful creatures cannot be uncovered by these means.)

— Is (a person of a certain description) nearby?

— Are there any (objects of a general type) nearby?

— Roughly how many people have passed by (or have been in) this area in the last day?

The key is to ask general questions about general subjects.

Advanced Gifts

• **Infest** — The Garou may call together a large number of a specific type of vermin in a certain nearby area. The creatures merely arrive and then behave naturally; the Garou cannot create, for example, an army of cockroaches in lockstep. Possible vermin include roaches, ants, rats, flies and so on. The size of the area to be infested determines the Gnosis cost. Normal humans and animals must make a Mental Challenge at a difficulty of 5 Traits to bring themselves to remain in an infested area.

One Gnosis Trait	Small room or car interior
Two Gnosis Traits	Average home
Three Gnosis Traits	Department store

• **Survivor** — The Garou can stand up to some of the most destructive forces known and walk away from them intact. Whenever she suffers damage that would normally have resulted in her death, she may permanently expend three Physical Traits or a Willpower Trait to avoid the killing damage altogether (although this will not mitigate the effects of any nonlethal attacks previously suffered). By spending a Gnosis, the Garou no longer needs to eat, drink or rest, and gains the Traits: *Resilient* x 3. She also becomes almost immune to disease, poisons, normal pressure and temperature variations, radiation and corruption effects from Wyrm-creatures. If affected by any of these things, the Garou gains a free Static Physical Challenge to negate the harm to herself. Use of this Gift lasts for one session.

Children of Gaia

Basic Gifts

• **Resist Pain** — As per the Philodox Gift

• **Mother's Touch** — As per the Theurge Gift.

• **Calm** — By expending two Social Traits and winning a Social Challenge, the Garou may take away one of a target's Rage Traits. (The Trait is gone, but it can be regained as normal. The frustration of losing a Rage Trait will not cause it to be regained.)

• **Luna's Armor** — The Garou can channel the fortifying energies of Luna into her body for a short time. For every Gnosis Trait expended, the Garou gains an extra Health Level. The effects of this Gift last until wounds are suffered (damage is applied to the Gift's wound levels first) or the end of the session. The maximum number of armor Traits that can be added to a Garou is equal to half of her Gnosis total, rounded down.

Intermediate Gifts

• **Eyes of the Cobra** — As per the Galliard Gift.

• **Spirit Friend** — A Garou interacts with spirits more easily than normal when using this Gift. With *Spirit Friend*, a Garou can enter a Mental Challenge with a spirit, and with each victory can call for a retest. Each success reduces, by one step, the spirit's resistance to the Gifted Garou's will; the spirit loses a Willpower Trait each time it loses a challenge. The fewer Willpower Traits the spirit has, the more open it is to the Garou's suggestions and commands. The Gift lasts for one scene, and is not cumulative with other similar Gifts.

• **The Guilty Mind** — The Garou can draw forth a state of guilt or remorse in her target. The Gift requires the Garou to defeat the target in a Social Challenge. If the Garou is successful, the target will do the ethical thing, because of the guilt he feels trying to do anything else. For example, a Get of Fenris might apologize to someone he wronged, or a Shadow Lord could admit to an underhanded plot that she was involved in.

Note: "Ethical" in this case is defined as "Whatever a stereotypical Child of Gaia would think was appropriate."

• **Serenity** — The Garou can inspire a soothing calm in her target. To use this Gift, the Garou expends a Gnosis Trait and then must win a Mental Challenge against the subject. If the user of the Gift wins, the target may not spend any Rage for the rest of the scene.

Advanced Gifts

• **Beast Life** — As per the Lupus Gift.

• **Unicorn's Grace** — The Garou can attain a state of balance and calm not usually found in Garou. By expending a Gnosis Trait, the Gifted Garou can no longer frenzy (voluntarily or otherwise) for the remainder of the session, and may not spend more than one Rage Trait in a single turn.

• **Halo of the Sun** — The Garou projects a glowing nimbus of blinding sunlight from her body. This Gift costs one Gnosis to use and lasts for one scene. The Garou causes aggravated damage with her bare hands, even in Homid or Glabro forms. She may also make a Simple Test to inflict an additional level of damage after a successful strike. Anyone combating her must bid an extra two Traits in any challenges. Vampires within 10 feet of the Garou suffer two aggravated wounds per turn of exposure.

Fianna

Basic Gifts

• **Resist Toxin** — The Garou may call upon incredible recuperative powers to stop diseases and poisons (even Wyrm-toxins) that enter her body. When affected (or infected) by a toxin or disease, the Garou may make a Static Physical Challenge to cancel the effects of the invading substance. In the case of extremely potent or magical diseases or toxins, the Storyteller may call for the expenditure of a Gnosis Trait.

• **Howl of the Banshee** — The Garou issues a terrifying howl that evokes a primal fear in everyone nearby. This power costs one Gnosis Trait to use. When the *Howl* is made, all characters within 20 steps must win (not tie) a Simple Test or flee in terror (the character flees, the player walks away). Victims may stop their flight once they are out of sight of the Garou, but they may not approach her for the rest of the scene. Any assault on the victim cancels this effect. If a victim expends a Willpower Trait, she does not need to flee and is not affected by this Gift for the rest of the session.

• **Persuasion** — As per the Homid Gift.

Intermediate Gifts

• **Faerie Kin** — By expending a Gnosis Trait, the Garou may issue a call to any faeries or changelings within 10 miles. The Spirit Keeper must be contacted for a Garou to use this Gift. The subjects of this call are under no obligation to come unless the Garou also risks Social Traits; in that case, a faerie or changeling must win a Social Challenge to resist the Gift. What any faeries or changelings do if they respond is up to the Storyteller, but they are favorably disposed toward the Gifted Garou, unless he intentionally insults them. (**Note**: If you do not want to have changelings in your game, use spirits with faerielike attitudes).

• **Woadling** — The Garou is knowledgeable the art of the ancient Celtic war-spirit symbols. By painting them on his body and spending a Gnosis Trait, the Garou may release one of these symbols as a spirit to bewilder and confuse his foes when fighting in close quarters. The spirit exists for five turns, unless another Gnosis is spent to revitalize it. While the spirit is active, it harasses and harries a foe, causing him to be four Traits down (when comparing for ties). The effects of this Gift are not cumulative (only one sigil can harry a foe at a time), and it can be used only in Homid or Glabro forms — the effects are immediately canceled if the Garou assumes any other form. The player must mark her face or exposed parts of her body (within reason!) with obviously visible markings in order to use this Gift.

• **Faerie Blood** — The Garou can mystically alter her blood to that of a fae. While this negates the normal Garou penalties from silver, the character now suffers the same penalties from cold iron instead. In addition, any Gifts performed while under the effects of this Gift have their total Gnosis cost increased by one (minimum of one; even if the Gift cost no Gnosis before). The Gift costs two Gnosis Traits to use and lasts for one scene.

Advanced Gifts

• **Troll's Bridge** — This Gift costs a Gnosis Trait to use. With it, a Garou can set up a small, enclosed area as a last line of defense. Examples include the end of a hall, a small room or closet or a ditch or gully. To enter the area, attackers must first beat down the invisible mystical barrier (*Stalwart* x 10) that the Gift creates. Each attacker must defeat the barrier separately, but each one that gets through reduces the barrier's rating by one Trait for all the others. The effects of this Gift last for one scene, and the effects of repeated invocations are not cumulative.

• **Balor's Gaze** — The Garou can evoke mind-numbing pain in a target merely by glancing at him. The Garou must spend one Gnosis Trait and one Rage Trait and defeat the target in a Mental Challenge to use this Gift. If successful, she may try to win a Simple Test (no Traits are risked), and if she does she may try to win more until she loses or ties. For each test won (including the initial test), the target takes the appropriate damage penalty to challenges (this Gift bypasses all Health Levels beyond the first).

The subject does not suffer any actual wounds from the use of this Gift, just the associated penalties. Powers that negate wound penalties are equally effective against this Gift. Furthermore, if in danger of attack, the victim may spend a Willpower Trait to shake off the effects of this Gift for a single conflict. The effects of this Gift last for the rest of the scene, and are not in any way cumulative. If the victim loses tests to the point where he can no longer bid, he is considered to be incapacitated. This state lasts for the remainder of the scene.

• **Gift of the Spriggan** — The Garou can grow or shrink with the use of this Gift. The Garou must spend a Gnosis Trait to grow up to two times normal height or shrink to the size of a puppy. At his largest size, the Garou gains three Physical Traits, an additional Health Level, and causes an additional level of damage in melee. While he is at his smallest, these modifiers are reversed, with one being the minimum. The Garou may use this power only on himself and only once per session. The effects of this Gift last for one scene.

Get of Fenris

Basic Gifts

• **Razor Claws** — As per the Ahroun Gift.

• **Resist Pain** — As per the Philodox Gift.

• **Snarl of the Predator** — The Garou's intimidating growl weakens his foe's resolve and determination. If the Gifted Garou is successful in a Social Challenge, the target must bid an extra Trait against him for the rest of the scene. The effects of this Gift are not cumulative.

Intermediate Gifts

• **Halt of the Coward's Flight** — The Garou can use this on a foe she is already fighting to prevent him from fleeing the fray. If a foe who engages the Garou decides to break combat by any physical means (even with *Celerity* or the like), the Garou may demand a Mental Challenge. If the victim wins, he may flee as normal, and is not subject to this Gift until the next time the two characters cross swords. If the Garou wins, the victim may not flee and must engage in at least one more combat challenge.

Note: The victim can try to flee again next turn, and may be affected by this Gift during that flight as well.

• **Venom Blood** — The Garou can cause her blood to take on toxic properties. Anyone biting the Garou, touched by her blood or partaking of her blood instantly suffers an aggravated wound. If the victim is drinking the Garou's blood, he must make one Simple Test per Blood Trait consumed or suffer damage. This Gift costs a Rage Trait to use, and lasts for one scene.

• **Might of Thor** — The Garou can draw upon deep stores of physical energy, at a price. It costs a Gnosis and a Rage Trait to use this Gift, which lasts for one scene. While the Gift is in effect, a Garou can double her Physical Traits. Furthermore, she does not suffer the effects of wound penalties. However, for the rest of the session after using the Gift, the Garou has only three Physical Traits (regardless of any other powers), and may not initiate any Physical Challenges.

Advanced Gifts

• **Berserker's Song** — The Garou can sing himself into a controlled frenzy. While in this state, the character gains all the benefits of frenzy, but does not attack allies. He may also end his frenzy at any time he chooses. This Gift costs two Rage to use, and the player must sing appropriately (in other words, no Neil Sedaka) while it is being used. The Gift lasts for the duration of one combat.

• **Fenris' Bite** — The Garou can deliver a devastating bite that severely cripples her foe. Once the character successfully bites her opponent, she can choose to spend a Rage Trait immediately to activate the Gift. Once she has done so, she may initiate a Physical Challenge (no Traits are risked). If she wins, she inflicts an additional wound upon her target, making that limb useless (arms and legs only, determined randomly), and may initiate another Physical Challenge. If she wins this second test, the victim loses the limb. A vampire can grow back the limb by resting an hour and spending three Blood Traits and a Willpower Trait. Garou can heal this by retrieving the severed limb and resting for the remainder of the session. In the meantime, the victim should roleplay the loss and has the temporary Negative Physical Trait: *Lame*.

• **Hero's Stand** — The Garou picks a spot, and, while standing on it, declares it to be his stand. He must then succeed in a Willpower test against 10 Traits. If successful, the Garou becomes directly connected to the earth and may not move or be moved from that spot until all foes in the present battle are defeated or retreat. A Garou using this Gift is immune to ranged attacks (he must be fought to be defeated), may not be surprised, and all attacks against him are considered frontal for purposes of determining reach.

Glass Walkers

Basic Gifts

• **Control Simple Machine** — The Garou can control very simple technological items. By spending a Gnosis Trait, she can cause nearby nonelectronic machinery to turn on and off and/or perform its normal range of functions. This Gift affects only one item per Gnosis Trait spent. Each order requires the Garou to win or tie a Simple Test (no Traits are risked). The Gift ends when the Garou loses one of the Simple Tests or the present scene ends. To represent this, the player may actually physically control the item in question (if this is possible and safe).

Items include: locks, doorknobs, pistols, small levers, rifles, safe doors, hydraulic jacks, simple cranes or watermills.

• **Persuasion** — As per the Homid Gift.

• **Cybersenses** — The Garou may use his knowledge of technology and his own senses to alter, to a degree, his access to a range of sensory information that he might not normally comprehend. This Gift costs a Gnosis to use and lasts for one scene.

Some suggested Cybersenses include:

Sight

• Infrared — See heat sources, ignore most darkness penalties, or detect a vampire (unless she's fed in the last hour or has been in a very warm area).

• High band transmissions — Watch television programs as transmissions pass through the air; the Garou must win a Simple Test (no Traits are risked) to find a specific station.

Hearing

• Radio Band — Listen to random radio transmissions; the Garou must win a Simple Test to find a specific bandwidth.

• Radar — See immediate surroundings, ignore darkness penalties.

• Supersonic/Subsonic — See motion sensor beams.

Touch

• Electric (Stream) — Feel the transmission of electricity, find live wires, or tap a phone line or intercom by touching the wiring.

• **Power Surge** — The character can produce a surge of uncontrolled electricity that overloads existing lines, causing a blackout. The Garou must spend a Gnosis Trait and win a Mental Challenge. The target number of Traits depends on the area to be affected.

Three Traits	Medium-sized room
Seven Traits	Small house or single story of a large building
10 Traits	Large building
14 Traits	City block
17 Traits	Neighborhood

Intermediate Gifts

• **Heat Metal** — The Garou can quickly heat a metal object to the point of damaging anyone who touches it. By spending a Gnosis Trait, she may drastically raise the temperature of a small object that she can easily see, such as a knife, pistol, doorknob or wristwatch. The victim must make a Simple Test (no Traits are risked). Winning means the object and anyone touching it avoid damage. A tie means the object heats up, but anyone holding or touching it may release or drop the object to escape harm if they wish. Losing the challenge means the object heats up, and there is no chance to let go before being burned. Each level of *Celerity* (*Alacrity*, *Rapidity* or *Fleetness*) possessed or Rage Trait spent by the victim allows the character to retest a loss, but not a tie. Damage suffered (Narrator discretion as to how much) is aggravated. The object returns to normal temperature in one minute, but if the number of times the object is exposed to this Gift exceeds the number of Traits it possesses, it is ruined.

• **Control Complex Machine** — This functions like *Control Simple Machine*, except electronic devices can be controlled as well. Examples include: phones, calculators, watches, light fixtures, computers, arcade games, TVs, VCRs, cars and industrial machinery.

• **Attunement** — As per the Bone Gnawer Gift.

• **Doppelganger** — The Garou may take on the likeness of an individual she has had the chance to study closely or examine. By spending a Gnosis Trait and performing a Static Social Challenge (against 10), she may assume the subject's exact likeness, including clothes or other belongings (which, if magical or technological, will not function). Someone familiar with the original person senses something is amiss only if he wins a Simple Test (no Traits are risked). Individuals with powers that reveal the hidden Garou may uncover the truth if the individual thinks to use her power on the disguised Garou. The Gift lasts for the rest of the session. This Gift does not grant the Garou any Abilities, languages, armor or powers above and beyond those she already possesses.

Players using this Gift should wear cards or name tags that describe what they are supposed to look like in their new forms.

Advanced Gifts

• **Long Running** — The Garou can take advantage of the time slippage associated with the Umbra to drastically reduce travel time between two points in the physical world. Spending more Gnosis can make the journey quicker. However, once the trip begins, it may not be interrupted or any bonuses for travel are lost. You must utilize a vehicle for this Gift to function.

One Gnosis	Travel time reduced by 25 percent
Two Gnosis	Travel time reduced by 50 percent
Three Gnosis	Travel time reduced by 75 percent

It costs Glass Walkers (who tend to call this Gift *Quick Drive*) one less Gnosis to use this Gift inside a city (traveling on an interstate counts as Weaver, so the discount applies there, too).

• **Phone Travel** — Spending one Gnosis while dialing a phone number allows a Garou to sidestep into the phone net and step out again on the other end almost instantly. Someone must physically pick up the receiver (modems, answering machines and call forwarding do not count) for this Gift to work. If the receiver is on a cordless, the traveler arrives at the base unit. If it is on a cellular phone, the Garou ends up at the switching station where the call is sent to the first tower. This Gift sends a Garou only as far as there are physical phone lines.

• **Calm the Flock** — As per the Homid Gift *Reduce Delirium*.

Red Talons

Basic Gifts

- **Beast Life** — As per the Lupus Gift.
- **Scent of Running Water** — As per the Ragabash Gift.
- **Sense of the Prey** — As per the Ragabash Gift.

Intermediate Gifts

- **Babble** — A Garou can temporarily steal the gift of language from a person. To use this Gift, the Garou must spend a Gnosis Trait and win a Mental Challenge against the target. If the attempt is successful, the victim cannot read, write, speak intelligibly or understand the speech of others. Not even hand gestures are possible — only animalistic grunts are permitted. The effects of *Babble* last for one scene.

- **Beastmind** — The Garou can implant a powerful, animalistic nature in her victim. By defeating the target in a Mental Challenge, the Garou can force the victim to adopt the following temporary Negative Traits: *Bestial* x 2 and *Shortsighted*. The effects of this Gift last for the rest of the scene.

- **Rot Weavertech** — With *Rot Weavertech*, a Garou can ruin the trappings of human science and technology, but not relatively primitive items. Anything developed after the Renaissance is fair game for this Gift. *Rot Weavertech* costs Rage Traits (the more Traits invested, the larger the item that can be affected) and a Mental Challenge to use. Success indicates the destruction of the item. A tie means the item is aged, but still works. A loss means that the device is unaffected and cannot be affected by this Gift for the rest of the story line.

3 Traits	Flashlight, pistol, minor appliance, lock
7 Traits	Rifle, video equipment, stereo, wiring in a single room
10 Traits	Computer, wiring in a small house or car

Advanced Gifts

- **Curse of Dionysus** — The Garou can evoke a powerful transformation, changing her target into a wolf. The Garou must spend a Gnosis Trait and defeat her target in a Mental Challenge. A Garou who is affected can revert to his preferred form after one scene. For normal humans, the effect is permanent. A vampire using *Beast Form* may resume his normal shape after one scene. Vampires without this Discipline must engage the Garou who attacked them in an Extended Challenge. The number of successes the Garou obtains dictates how long the vampire stays in wolf form.

Successes	Duration
1	Until the end of the scene
2	One hour
3	The remainder of the evening's play
4	Until the end of the next session
5	Until the end of the session following the next one

- **Quicksand** — The Garou can transform a patch of ground temporarily into a treacherous quagmire. The Garou must spend a Gnosis Trait and win a Simple Test (no Traits are risked). If successful, she can alter a square of earth or natural stone (not wood, concrete or processed materials) that is ten feet on a side into a sticky trap. Anyone entering or already in the area runs the risk of becoming trapped. These individuals must each make a Simple Test. If they win, they are free from the danger or somehow avoid it. If they tie, they are stuck and may try to test again next turn (or two minutes later, if no combat is occurring). If they lose, they are sucked deeper into the trap and must win an additional test to free themselves. A Physical Challenge risking five Traits allows a person to leap completely over the area (space permitting). The Gift lasts for one scene.

Shadow Lords

Basic Gifts

• **Fatal Flaw** — On a Static Mental Challenge, with the difficulty being the target's total Mental Traits, the Garou learns one of his target's Negative Traits, Flaws or a Derangement (the target chooses which). This Gift may not be used on an individual more than once per session.

• **Aura of Confidence** — On a successful Static Social Challenge (against 7 Traits), the Garou bolsters his natural aura so that *Fatal Flaw* and similar powers do not reveal his weaknesses. Furthermore, those who can see auras find the Garou's emotional state to be solidly confident while the Gift is in effect, unless they win two successive Social Challenges against the Gifted Garou. This Gift does not hamper other powers of *Aura Perception* whatsoever, and its effects last for one scene.

• **Clap of Thunder** — By clapping his hands together forcefully, the Garou can produce a stunning shock wave. Everyone within five steps of the Garou must make a Simple Test (no Traits are risked). If the defender wins, he is unaffected. If the defender ties, he is stunned and may not initiate a Physical Challenge for one turn. If the defender loses, he cannot initiate any sort of challenge for the rest of the scene. This Gift costs one Gnosis to use, and the Garou must be in Homid, Glabro or Crinos form (i.e., must have hands instead of paws) for it to work.

• **Disfigurement** — With a whisper, the Garou can create an unsightly blemish or mark upon her target. By spending a Gnosis Trait and defeating her opponent in a Social Challenge, the Garou can bestow upon the target the Negative Social Trait: *Repugnant*. The effects of this Gift last for one scene and are not cumulative. Repeated successes with this Gift can extend the effect's duration, however.

Intermediate Gifts

• **Luna's Armor** — As per the Children of Gaia Gift.

• **Icy Chill of Despair** — As per the Philodox Gift: *Roll Over*.

• **Paralyzing Stare** — As per the Homid Gift.

• **Open Wounds** — The Garou can cause the victim to bleed profusely from the next wound she inflicts upon him. Immediately after wounding a target, the Garou may spend a Gnosis Trait and make a Simple Test (no Traits are risked). If the Garou wins, the target suffers another normal wound. A vampire affected by this Gift does not suffer another wound, but does lose a Blood Trait.

Advanced Gifts

• **Strength of the Dominator** — The Garou may steal Rage from another Garou. If the Gifted Garou defeats her opponent in a Mental Challenge, the target loses a Rage Trait to the Garou. If the defender wins, the Gifted Garou may not try to steal her Rage again that session. Stolen Rage, if it is not spent, returns to its user at the end of the session. This Gift may be used on the same target only once per session.

• **Obedience** — The Garou can spend a Gnosis Trait and issue powerful mental commands to an individual. The Garou must defeat her target in a Mental Challenge. If she does so, she may attempt to win Simple Tests until she loses. The number of successes indicates the degree to which the victim obeys.

One Success	Perform a preferred act or one directly in line with the target's Nature
Two Successes	Perform unlikely actions or ones that do not oppose the target's Nature
Three Successes	Perform disliked actions or ones completely against the target's Nature
Five Successes	Perform dangerous actions but not suicidal or possibly fatal ones
Seven Successes	Perform dangerous, potentially fatal actions

Silent Striders

Basic Gifts

• **Blissful Ignorance** — As per the Ragabash Gift.

• **Sense Wyrm** — As per the Metis Gift.

• **Speed of Thought** — The Garou may spend a Gnosis Trait to double his land speed, and gains the following Traits, which can only be used in reference to land movement: *Quick* x 2 and *Tireless*. If these Traits are not used within one scene, they are lost.

• **Messenger's Fortitude** — The Garou may travel great distances without experiencing hunger or fatigue. The essential matter is that the Strider must continue to run. The Garou can run for up to three days nonstop, but must sleep for one full week afterward. The power costs one Gnosis to use and, for another Gnosis, another being may benefit from this Gift as well. In-game, this means that Garou using this Gift can cover long distances in a third of the normal time required.

Intermediate Gifts

• **Summon Talisman** — The Garou may summon forth an item that has been dedicated to her by the Rite of Talisman Dedication. This power costs a Gnosis Trait to use, and cannot access items currently in the Umbra, unless the Gift: *Grasp the Beyond* is also known and used by the Garou (or unless he is in the Umbra).

• **Adaptation** — The Garou can overcome the harshest of conditions and survive in environments that would kill lesser beings. He can resist the effects of high and low pressure, poisonous atmospheres, vacuum, diseases, toxins and extremes of temperature. The Gift costs one Gnosis to use and lasts for one session. For an additional Gnosis Trait, the Gifted Garou may extend the benefits of this Gift to another.

• **Tongues** — As per the Homid Gift.

• **Speed Beyond Thought** — The character possesses a supernatural degree of speed and coordination, one that outstrips humans and even her fellow Garou. If the character is aware of an upcoming physical threat, she may spend a Gnosis Trait to preempt the actions with an action of her own. Some examples of such threats include: melee attacks, falling objects, gunfire, oncoming cars and thrown objects.

A character may spend a Gnosis Trait to activate this Gift during combat, which gives her an additional chance of harming her opponent (i.e., an extra attack). After the first test is resolved, the character with *Speed Beyond Thought* may perform an additional test to attempt to damage her opponent. This is a Simple Test (no additional Traits are risked) — the Garou is successful on either a win or a tie. Note that the use of *Speed Beyond Thought* must be declared at the beginning of a challenge.

This Gift allows the Garou to travel at 10 times normal running speed for up to eight hours. At the end of this time the Garou must eat (immediately!) and rest for eight hours.

Advanced Gifts

• **Attunement** — As per the Bone Gnawer Gift, except it works only in the wilderness.

• **Open Moon Gate** — As per the Ragabash Gift.

• **Reach the Umbra** — By using this Gift, the Garou may simply and easily move from this world to the Umbra. The Gauntlet does not matter, and a reflective surface isn't necessary to facilitate travel.

Silver Fangs

Basic Gifts

• **Sense Wyrm** — As per the Metis Gift.

• **Lambent Flame** — The Garou emanates a silvery shower of light from her body, illuminating an area up to a hundred-foot radius. The light itself is harmless, but those engaged in melee in the illuminated area must bid three Traits to attack. Anyone making a ranged attack into the lit area from more than 20 steps beyond it, on the other hand, functions as if she had two additional Traits. The Gift costs one Gnosis Trait to use and lasts for the rest of the scene.

• **Luna's Armor** — As per the Children of Gaia Gift.

• **Paralyzing Stare** — As per the Homid Gift.

Intermediate Gifts

- **Roll Over** — As per the Philodox Gift, but it costs no Gnosis Traits to use.
- **Silver Claws** — As per the Ahroun Gift.
- **Wrath of Gaia** — The Garou can evoke terror and panic in minions of the Wyrm. He must spend a Gnosis Trait and defeat the target in a Social Challenge to use this Gift. If successful, any creature of the Wyrm must flee in terror (some vampires are affected by this) from the Garou for the duration of the scene.

    Note: If the Garou is facing multiple Wyrm-creatures, Mob Scene rules apply to the challenge.
- **Mastery** — A Garou can call upon the ancient rites of leadership and demand that another Garou obey her. She must defeat her opponent in a Social Challenge, but if she is successful, the subject must obey the command, as long as it is not suicidal, is straightforward and can be executed without breaking the Litany or Traditions of the Garou Nation. The effects of this Gift last for the rest of the session, but the victim may make a Static Mental Challenge versus the Social Traits of the Gifted Garou every full hour, in order to disobey.

Advanced Gifts

- **Ignore Wound** — After suffering a grievous wound, the Garou can choose to ignore it and thus dispel its effects entirely. Immediately after suffering the effects of a single combat challenge, the Garou may spend a Gnosis Trait to totally disregard those effects. No other aspect of the challenge is altered. This Gift may be used only once per scene.
- **Mindblock** — The Garou can fortify her mind against the manipulations of others. Anyone who attempts to affect or harm the Garou mentally must defeat her in a challenge twice instead of once. This Gift protects against any form of supernatural control derived through Mental or Social Challenges. Furthermore, the Garou wins any ties in challenges to resist control.
- **Paws of the Newborn Cub** — The Garou can temporarily cancel out any special or supernatural powers of a foe. The Gift costs a Gnosis Trait to use, and the Garou must defeat the victim in a Mental Challenge. Once the Garou has done so, the target is as helpless as a newborn cub, and has only mundane powers at his disposal. (The powers that can be stripped include: aggravated damage, claws, Gifts, vampiric Blood Pool, ghostly Arcanoi, regenerative powers, special attacks — all selected at Narrator discretion.) The vanished power returns after one scene.
- **Luna's Avenger** — The Garou can transform into a fierce engine of destruction in times of great need. By spending a Gnosis Trait, the Garou transforms her body into purest silver. In this form, the Garou doesn't suffer the ill effects of silver, gains an extra Health Level and augments her in hand-to-hand combat so that she inflicts damage in the same manner as the Gift: *Silver Claws*. The Gift lasts for one scene.

Stargazers

Basic Gifts

- **Sense Wyrm** — As per the Metis Gift.
- **Catfeet** — As per the Lupus Gift.
- **Inner Strength** — The Garou can meditate for 15 minutes. If he then succeeds in a Mental Challenge against 8 Traits, he can transform one Rage Trait into a Willpower Trait to replace one he has spent.
- **Surface Attunement** — If the Garou succeeds in a Static Physical Challenge (against 7 Traits), he may pass effortlessly over mud, water, grease, oil, snow, ice, quicksand or similar substances without leaving a trace. This Gift also allows the Garou to resist Gifts that mimic the effects of these surfaces. This Gift lasts for one scene.

Intermediate Gifts

- **Merciful Blow** — If the Garou wins a normal *Brawl* challenge to strike a foe, she may choose to stun her opponent instead of inflicting damage. If so, she must expend a Gnosis Trait. The foe is stunned for the rest of the scene and cannot initiate any actions, unless snapped out of it by a touch from someone else.
- **Clarity** — With a successful Mental Challenge (difficulty is Narrator discretion), the Garou can see through obscurement, such as fog, smoke, complete darkness or even magical obscurement or illusions (*Chimerstry*). The Gift lasts for the rest of the scene. This Gift can be used to see through someone else's personal disguise (*Obfuscate*), but the Garou must defeat the individual in a separate Mental Challenge first.
- **Preternatural Awareness** — The Garou gains uncanny insight into danger directed at her person. When an attack is initiated against the Garou, she may spend a Gnosis (even if she does not know the attack is coming) to force anyone wishing to attack her to make a Simple Test first (no Traits are risked). If the attacker wins, he is unhindered in his assault and challenges as normal. If he ties, he loses any ties when attacking the Garou during that combat. If he loses, his first attack misses completely (neither party suffers a wound or loses Traits), and he still loses all ties for the rest of the combat when attacking. This Gift lasts for one scene.

Advanced Gifts

- **Wisdom of the Seer** — The Garou can contemplate the night sky for the answer to a single, direct question. The cost is one Gnosis Trait, and answers are often cryptic or unclear. The Storyteller must answer the question correctly, but not necessarily or totally clearly. For example:

Q: "Where are the Bane spirits hiding in that factory?"

A: "They like the cold wind," meaning that they are hiding in the kitchen, where the massive freezer doors are open.

- **Circular Attack** — The Garou can turn the supposed advantage of numbers against his attackers. This Gift works only if the Garou himself is attacked by two or more assailants. For every attacker beyond the first, the Garou makes a Simple Test to avoid and redirect each of the supporting attackers. If he wins, that assailant must test against one of the other assailants. Mob Scene rules apply only if more than one assailant is coordinating an attack on the Gifted Garou. This Gift costs one Gnosis Trait to use.

• **Spirit Drain** — As per the Theurge Gift.

Uktena

Basic Gifts

• **Sense Magic** — If the Garou succeeds in a Mental Challenge (difficulty is Narrator discretion), he can tell whether or not an item, person or a particular area is magical or enchanted. The Garou can sense the use of Garou rites or Gifts, vampire Thaumaturgy, mage Spheres, Numina, fetishes and other magical items or phenomena. This Gift reveals the type of supernatural powers present, but nothing specific beyond that.

• **Spirit of the Bird** — The Garou may hover and float in the air. The Gift costs one Gnosis to use each hour, and allows the Garou to travel 20 miles. Maneuvering requires a Physical Challenge against 7 (*Occult* allows a retest).

• **Spirit of the Fish** — The Garou may breathe water and travel unhindered underwater as quickly as he can run in Hispo form. The Gift costs one Gnosis Trait to use, and lasts until the end of the scene.

• **Blur of the Milky Eye** — As per the Ragabash Gift.

Intermediate Gifts

• **Call Flame Spirit** — The Garou can summon forth a flame spirit from an existing fire source to attack a foe of the Garou's choosing. The Garou must spend a Gnosis Trait and perform a Simple Test (no Traits are risked) to use this Gift. If she loses the test, the spirit doubles in size and attacks her instead. Use the statistics for fire from the lupus Gift: *Elemental Gift*.

• **Secrets** — The Garou may unearth one of a subject's secrets, ranging from relatively mundane knowledge to deep dark secrets. The Garou must spend a Gnosis and win or tie in a Static Mental Challenge against 9 Traits. He may continue to make tests until he loses. The more successes he obtains, the deeper the secret revealed. If the target knows the Garou is going to use this Gift, a Mental Challenge must also be won before the inquisitor learns anything.

Degree of Success	Type of Secret Learned
One Success	Creature type, minor treachery or wrongdoing
Two Successes	Real name, embarrassing fact, sire, parents
Three Successes	Alliances, affair with another Garou
Four Successes	Earth-shattering revelations

• **Call Elemental** — As per the lupus Gift: *Elemental Gift*.

Advanced Gifts

• **Hand of the Earth Lords** — With the expenditure of one Gnosis, the Garou can move objects weighing up to 500 pounds. A successful Mental Challenge (against 6 Traits, +1 per 100 pounds) is required to redirect the object successfully.

- **Pointing the Bone** — The Garou can channel energy into an old bone to cause her foes damage at a distance (within sight). The Garou must spend a Gnosis Trait and defeat her foe in a Mental (versus target's Physical) Challenge. If the Garou wins, the victim suffers an aggravated wound and the Gifted Garou may make a second challenge (without either party risking Traits) to cause a second aggravated wound. If the Garou fails in the first test the victim is unharmed and may not be affected by this Gift for the remainder of the session.

- **Fetish Doll** — The Garou can create a small doll with which she may damage a foe over great distances and with little risk to herself. The doll requires part of the victim (or a close personal effect), one week of work to construct and a Gnosis Trait to create. The Garou then makes five Mental Challenges (against 15 Traits) to inflict damage upon the target. Each win inflicts an aggravated wound, while a tie or loss inflicts no damage. The doll is destroyed at the end of this effect.

Wendigo

Basic Gifts

- **Call the Breeze** — The Garou may call up a strong, cold breeze (20 mph) at will. This breeze lasts only for a moment, but it blows away insects or loose paper, disperses gases and extinguishes candles, torches and oil lamps.

- **Camouflage** — As per the Ragabash Gift: *Blur of the Milky Eye*, but only usable in wilderness settings.

- **Cutting Wind** — A painfully frigid wind blasts forth from the Garou, chilling opponents to the bone. The area of effect is 10 steps around the Gifted Garou. Individuals within this area must make a Physical Challenge against the Gifted Garou's Mental Traits (his own Mental Traits are not risked). If a defender wins, he suffers a 1-Trait penalty on any Physical Challenges for as long as the Gift's effects last. If he loses, he suffers a 2-Trait penalty on any Physical Challenges for as long as the Gift's effects last. The Gift costs a Gnosis to use and lasts for the rest of the scene.

- **Speak with the Wind Spirits** — The Garou may beckon nearby air spirits to bring him information about a nearby area. He may also use this Gift to listen in on the conversations of others nearby (50 feet or so), as long as they are not obstructed from his view. This Gift costs a Gnosis Trait to use and lasts for the rest of the scene. The Garou may also send the air spirits to look at a place and come back. If he succeeds in a Simple Test, the air spirits will be able to answer a single question about the area they have just scouted (their attention span is too short for anything more).

Intermediate Gifts

- **Chill of Early Frost** — The Garou calls forth wind spirits of biting cold from the domain of the Wendigo itself. This mystical chill covers a five-mile radius around the Garou, and causes all creatures not adapted to cold (unlike Crinos and Lupus Garou) to suffer while exposed. Those braving the hostile weather must make a Simple Test (no Traits are risked) for every scene they remain outside. If they succeed, they are two Traits down on all challenges. If they tie, they are four Traits down (minimum of one) on all challenges. If they lose, they are four Traits down and also suffer a wound. Characters must spend half an hour warming up indoors to cancel the penalties inflicted by the bitter cold. This Gift takes an hour to evoke and costs one Gnosis. It can be used to full effect only in winter, early spring or late fall if the location is anywhere other than the Arctic or Antarctic regions. If this Gift is activated any other time, the temperature drops to below freezing and everyone is simply cold. In that case, no penalties are incurred, but crops and plants may be damaged. This effects of this Gift last for the rest of the session.

• **Counting Coup** — The Garou can perform great feats of bravery when faced with a superior foe. She attacks as normal but instead of inflicting damage she makes a Simple Test (no Traits are risked). If she wins, the victim loses a Glory Trait (if he has any) until the next full moon, or until he bests the Gifted Garou in some challenge (whichever comes first). Furthermore, if the Gifted Garou goes on to overcome her opponent, she may petition for a Glory Trait at the next moot. This Gift may be used only in real life-or-death combat, not in brawls or mock fights. No foe can be the subject of this Gift more than once per session.

• **Sky Running** — By concentrating for one turn and spending a Willpower Trait, the Garou can literally run across the sky at 50 miles per hour. He must move continuously, however, or he will fall. The Garou leaves a trail of fire in the sky behind him. This Gift lasts for four hours.

Advanced Gifts

•**Attunement** — As per the Bone Gnawer Gift, but it works only in wilderness.

• **Invoke the Spirits of the Storm** — The Garou may call up any type of weather possible in the area at that time of the year. The Gift costs one Gnosis to use and takes one to three hours to activate, depending upon the severity of the weather change. For each extra Gnosis spent, the Garou may call a damaging weather effect (e.g., lightning) down on a foe, after making a Mental versus Physical Challenge to hit. This effect causes two levels of aggravated damage. The weather change lasts for one full day or for the rest of the session (whichever is shorter).

• **Heart of Ice** — The Garou can direct the icy vengeance of Wendigo himself into the heart of his foe. To use this power, the Garou must first know the victim's full, real name. She must then spend one Gnosis Trait and defeat the foe in a Mental Challenge (or a Narrator serving as proxy; there is no range limit on this Gift). If successful, she may then try to tie or win a Simple Test (no Traits are risked) to inflict an aggravated wound upon the victim. The Garou may continue to do this each turn until she loses a challenge or the victim dies. Instead of suffering wounds, a vampire loses five Blood Traits each time he is successfully attacked with this Gift. This Gift may not be used more than once on the same individual in the same session.

Rites

Rites are the formal yet highly individualized mystic ceremonies of the Garou race. They are like recipes, utilizing the bounty of Gaia to create a spiritual repast for Her most beloved children. The rites bear the flavor of the auspices and tribes that perform them. No one would mistake the reflective meditations of the Stargazers for the savage pageantry beloved by the Get of Fenris.

Regardless of the trappings of a set of rites, they share a common direction and bent, and are often recognizable by other Garou in even the most unfamiliar forms.

Rites can be broken down into several categories according to their nature. The categories are assigned as Accord, Caern, Death, Mystical, Punishment, Renown, Seasonal and Minor, although Garou are hardly limited to one particular type of rite. As one might expect, different auspices show affinities for particular categories. Most noteworthy among these are Theurges (Mystical, Seasonal and Caern Rites) and Philodox (Accord and Punishment Rites). Other auspices often learn assorted rites befitting their natures, but not nearly as often as do Philodox and Theurges, who are expected to learn this ancient lore from spirits or their elders.

How to Throw a Rite

Most of the rite descriptions below are deliberately devoid of step-by-step instructions ("First you howl at the moon, then you scratch behind your left ear..."). Such rote roleplaying isn't fun for anyone, and can turn a game of **Apocalypse** into nothing more than a glorified game of Simon Says.

Instead, Storytellers and Ritemasters are encouraged to improvise or pre-script their rites, taking into account their settings, characters and cohorts. A personalized rite is always more appropriate than a generic one.

Enacting a Rite

All but the simplest of rites are performed by a group of three or more Garou, one of whom coordinates the effort and is designated the Ritemaster. The Ritemaster is the only member of the group who must know the rite. As a result, she directs the actions and channels the energies of the others.

Performing a rite takes about 20 minutes for each level of the rite. Minor Rites take 15 minutes. An untested or inexperienced Garou can take twice as long to perform a rite that is unfamiliar to him.

Each rite requires a minimum number of Traits, which can be determined by cross-referencing the rite type and level on the chart on page 126. The Garou who attempts to lead the rite must meet or exceed this minimum Trait requirement to perform it. These Traits are not spent in the process of the rite. Rather, they are merely the minimum which the Ritemaster must have to perform the ceremony. If the Ritemaster does not have enough Traits, but is within three Traits of the total needed, he can still attempt the rite. However, it will take him twice the usual amount of time to do so.

Additionally, a rite can take less time to perform if the Ritemaster has more Traits than needed. For every two Traits over the minimum number required, the Ritemaster can subtract 10 percent from the time it should take to perform the rite. No more than half the time needed for a rite can be shaved off in this manner.

The more Garou there are involved in a rite, the easier the rite is to perform. For every two Garou beyond the minimum number required to perform the rite, the Ritemaster gains a free additional Trait to use in the ceremony.

The following table shows the types of Traits that are used in different types of rites.

Minimum Number of Traits

If a ceremony requires a minimum number of Traits of the Garou present, this pool of Traits is separate from the Traits that are actually risked. This pool is not part of the actual test, and the Traits of attending Garou are not actually part of the bid. The Traits risked in a rite are those of the Ritemaster only.

Minimum Number of Participants

Some confident or desperate Garou attempt rites even when they do not have the necessary resources to perform the rite properly. If a group attempting a rite does not have the minimum number of Garou necessary to do it properly, the Ritemaster must spend a number of Mental Traits equal to the number of participants he is lacking in order to perform the rite successfully.

Rite	Trait and Challenge Type
Accord	Social
Caern	Varies
Death	Social
Mystical	Mental
Punishment	Social
Renown	Social
Seasonal	Physical
Minor	None

Rite Level	Minimum Number of Traits	Minimum Number of Participants
Basic	Five	One
Intermediate	Eight	Three
Advanced	Eleven	Five

Rites of Accord

These rites draw their power from connecting to the primal state of Gaia. That cycle is characterized by harmonious coexistence and rejuvenation. To channel this power, the Garou must utilize a talen, fetish or an object that is unspoiled by the ravages of man or the Wyrm. Rites of Accord are based on the Ritemaster's Social Traits for making Challenges.

Basic Rites

Rite of Cleansing: The Wyrm and its minions leave their indelible taint on everything they touch. While this rite cannot affect the Wyrm or its minions directly, it can remove the taint of their presence. Once the taint is removed, the area, person or object once tainted may not be further infected for the rest of the session. The Gnosis cost of this rite varies with the size of the target the Garou wishes to affect. The challenge is made against the Power Traits of the contaminator-spirit.

No Gnosis   One person or one man-sized object

One Gnosis   A small room or two people

Two Gnosis   A large building or three people

If a minion of the Wyrm is present in the contaminated object or area, it must first be defeated in order for the rite to work. Also, if the minion is not banished in time, it can re-infect the target.

Rite of Contrition: This rite is a form of apology for an affront (whether real or imagined); it is often used to soothe the enmity of spirits or Garou whom an individual has annoyed, or to prevent war between septs or tribes. It eases anger, and attacking the Ritemaster becomes difficult. The Garou performing this rite must have a present for the subject (or piece of the material aspect of a spirit). The Ritemaster then performs a challenge against the subject. Success on the part of the Ritemaster dictates a 3-Trait penalty is levied against any challenge the rite's subject engages in, if they choose to ignore the rite. The effects of the rite end when the performing Garou initiate any sort of attack against the subject or insult the subject, or when the story ends.

Rite of Renunciation: This rite allows a Garou to take on a new auspice while leaving her old auspice (and any previous Rank) behind. It is also used by those wishing to move beyond some great shame and experience a rebirth of sorts. Those partaking of this rite are often frowned upon by the more conservative factions of Garou society, and may (as a so-called Shifting Moon) even experience open hostility as one who would not bear the weight of his burdens assigned by Luna. This rite requires no challenge or Gnosis, but it must be entered into freely.

Once the rite is complete, the subject is a fostern of her new auspice, with the minimum number of Renown Traits. A Shifting Moon can no longer learn Gifts of her previous auspice, but does retain any old ones, and may now learn Gifts of her new auspice.

Intermediate

Rite of the Opened Sky: When this rite is performed, a cool, cleansing rain showers down on the caern. The cost and effect of this rite are the same as those of the *Rite of Contrition*. However, for every additional Gnosis Trait spent by the Ritemaster, all Garou present are healed of a single wound, aggravated or normal. The casting Garou must sacrifice something of personal value in order to enact this rite.

Caern Rites

These rites are aligned with the most sacred sites of the Garou and Gaia. Caerns are the bosom from which all Garou are nourished. If the caerns were left to ebb and die out, the Garou race would not be long in joining them.

Caern Rites may be performed only within the bounds of a caern. This condition implies that those performing a rite have the permission of the presiding Garou, as caern piracy is one of the foulest breeches of Garou etiquette. Furthermore, for every level of the caern, the Ritemaster receives a free Trait to use in the rite's contest, in addition to any other bonus Traits she might have.

Basic Rites

Moot Rite: This rite is required to open a moot. It must be performed at a caern at least once per month, or the caern will wane. During the course of the rite, two Gnosis Traits must be sacrificed for each level of the caern. For every month this rite is ignored, the caern drops one power level until it is dormant. The Gnosis Traits sacrificed may come from any Garou present for the moot.

Rite of the Opened Caern: Caerns are fonts of enormous mystical energy. Each caern has its own power; Knowledge, Strength, Healing, Gnosis, Rage and Defense are some examples. A brave Garou can attempt to harness those energies with this rite. In order to do so, a Garou must enter a Social Challenge against the caern's rating (one to five in Traits), with the benefit of the caern's bonus Traits as well. If she wins, the Garou can utilize one level of the caern's power in future challenges appropriate to the caern's special purpose. This bonus lasts until the Garou travels more than 100 miles away from the caern. If the Garou fails, she suffers a number of aggravated wounds equal to the caern's rating divided by two (round up).

See "Caerns", pp. 208-209.

Intermediate Rites

Rite of the Badger's Burrow: The Garou can use this rite to forge a mystic sensory link between herself and the area around the caern. No challenge is necessary to enact this rite, but interpreting its results can be difficult. For every Mental Challenge (against 14 Traits) the Garou wins or ties after enacting the rite, she can ask a short yes/no question of a Narrator. Questions can concern only the caern, the bawn and their surroundings, contents, current state and history.

Rite of the Opened Bridge: This well-protected rite has served the Garou since ancient times, helping distant septs keep in touch with each other and providing a means of quick travel (1/1000th normal time) in times of need. The rite, which must be performed at two caerns simultaneously, works through a Lune-spirit to establish a bond between the two locales.

In order to perform this rite, a Pathstone (also called a Moongem) is needed at both caerns. The two performing Garou must win or tie the challenge to open the bridge. If successful, either the *Rite of the Opened Caern* or the Gift: *Open Moon Bridge* will be able to activate the bridge throughout the next twelve months. If either Garou loses, the two caerns may not be linked for a full year, and the Ritemasters may be subjected to the *Rite of Ostracism*. The maximum range of the bridge is 1000 miles.

See "Caerns" for Moon Bridge distances, p. 209.

Rite of the Shrouded Glen: The Garou (five minimum for this rite) can create an effect within the Umbra that conceals the caern, so that observers outside of the field see the area as empty and unremarkable. Ten Gnosis Traits must be spent to make the effect last as long as the caern remains active. The cost increases two Traits per square mile to be protected. In other words, to make a caern and an average-sized bawn appear normal to all observers, in or out of the Umbra, the cost is 20 Gnosis (total accumulated Gnosis spent by all involved).

Creatures with exceptional powers of perception can try to penetrate the shrouded area by picking the right place to look and winning a Mental Challenge (against the Gnosis spent in the veil's creation).

Advanced Rites

Rite of Caern Building: This rite creates a caern, a power base for Gaia. It can be performed only at locations that have inherent potential to become caerns; stretches of tarmac and high-school soccer fields generally don't fit the bill. The initial setup for this rite tells the Garou about the area's potential. Once the intent to perform this rite has been announced and a site has been selected, the Storyteller must decide if a caern can be made in the area, and if so, how powerful it could be (Rank 1 to 5). The Garou can then decide if they wish to attempt to build the caern at that spot or look elsewhere.

Once engaged in the rite, which must be performed after nightfall, the Ritemaster is helpless and must be defended from any minions of the Wyrm, which almost invariably arrive to disrupt the rite. If any Banes, fomori or Black Spiral Dancers are within 20 miles of the event, they home in on it and attack the Garou mindlessly, fighting to the death to prevent the caern's creation. This includes vampires "of the Wyrm," but not those who are merely "Wyrm-tainted." For every hour of the rite, the Ritemaster may make up to five Simple Tests (a maximum of 40 tries). At dawn, the number of successes is tallied, and if the total is 20 or more, all is well. See below for the newborn caern's rating. Excess successes are discarded; a caern's rating can't be raised above its maximum potential. In other words, even if the Ritemaster scored 40 successes on a site with potential to be only a Level One caern, it would still be only a Level One caern.

20+ Successes — Level One
24+ Successes — Level Two
28+ Successes — Level Three
32+ Successes — Level Four
36+ Successes — Level Five

When the 20th success is made, a total of 50 Gnosis Traits must be spent by the Garou present (minimum of 13 Garou). If less than 50 Gnosis Traits are available from *within* the Garou participating (stored Gnosis doesn't count), each suffers an aggravated wound. Each wound thus taken provides three more Gnosis points, and the process continues until the requisite 50 is reached. Once the caern's level is established, the Ritemaster must also spend a permanent Gnosis point for each level of the caern.

If fewer than 20 successes were made to create the Caern, divide the number of successes that were achieved by the number still needed; these get divvied up evenly among the participating Garou as aggravated wound levels. The rite has failed, the Gnosis has been wasted, and those who failed must pay the price. Wounds received this way inevitably leave a single tear-shaped scar. A "Tear of Gaia" makes one worthy of one Glory Renown Trait.

To have participated in a successful *Rite of Caern Building* is a legendary feat deserving of three Glory and two Honor Renown. The Ritemaster also deserves four Wisdom Renown, even though these might be posthumous rewards. The Ritemaster for a *Rite of Caern Building* cannot initiate challenges, defend, flee, use Gifts or fetishes or otherwise act while the rite is in progress. If he does so, the rite ends instantly, with results as described above.

Rites of Death

Having spent their lives so close to the spirit world, Garou understand death as an essential part of Gaia's cycle, and show appropriate homage to it.

Basic Rites

Gathering for the Departed: The rite eases the passage of a fallen Garou to the Umbra and his totem. It consists of reciting the tales of the departed's life, remembering his good qualities and allowing all present to make their farewells without undue sorrow. If this rite is neglected, the spirit may become lost and haunt his old companions until they give him this honor. Treat such Garou as wraiths.

Intermediate Rites

Rite of the Winter Wolf: This rite is performed by a Garou who is too wounded or aged to serve the tribe. In a solemn and serious ceremony, the tales of his life are sung by his fellow Garou. The ceremony ends as the Garou retires to a secluded place where he takes his own life with a silver klaive (or knife). This rite is immediately followed by the *Gathering for the Departed*.

Mystical Rites

These rites call spirits and Umbral entities to the Garou who performs them. These are considered solitary affairs, performed by a lone Ritemaster (a ceremony can be performed elsewhere). The results often manifest only in complete privacy.

Basic Rites

Baptism of Fire: This rite is used to help Garou keep track of their young, who will one day share in the task of defending Gaia. It leaves a spiritual mark on a child and is only lifted upon the completion of the *Rite of Passage*. Until that time, a marked cub who is lost or absent may be found as if the performer were using the *Ritual of the Questing Stone*. Rumor has it that Black Spiral Dancers (and worse) may take advantage of this rite to track down Garou young for their own purposes.

Rite of Spirit Awakening: This rite awakens the spirit in an object or place. If the rite is performed on an object, the sleeping spirit "wakes up" and is now visible in the Umbra. The object's spirit is now available to be communicated with, commanded or bound. An object's spirit is usually a Gaffling or Jaggling. If this rite is performed on a fetish or Talen that has been discovered, it allows the Ritemaster to speak briefly with the inhabiting spirit and perhaps learn some of the item's secrets. Glass Walkers are particularly adept at speaking to technology spirits, and often awaken even the floppy disks they use.

In addition, natural herbs that have been specially dried and treated with this rite gain special powers of various kinds. These herbs are assigned a Gnosis Trait rating depending on the quantity of the herbs gathered. For example, plantain can heal a number of Health Levels equal to its Gnosis Pool; a single leaf might contain only one Gnosis, while a five-pound bundle could hold five Gnosis. The Storyteller will have to decide what sacred foods and herbs do in the context of her story, and must list what is available in a given area.

Rite of the Cup: This rite allows two or more entities to exchange or otherwise transfer Gnosis, either receiving or giving it. The rite requires at least one Garou. Other participants can be Garou or spirits.

The *Rite of the Cup* requires that each Garou participant spends one of the following Mental Traits: *Calm*, *Disciplined*, *Insightful*, *Intuitive*, *Patient*, *Reflective* or *Wise*. If the Garou in question does not possess one of these Mental Traits, he may not take part in the rite.

The actual order of the rite is as follows: A ritual cup is prepared, which can be any kind of container, from a styrofoam coffee cup to a crystal goblet to a beer stein. The container is filled with water. At this point, everyone involved in the rite decides to whom his Gnosis goes. If there is a dispute, the person who is performing the rite decides how the Gnosis is shared. Once the rite begins, the Gnosis cannot be removed or redirected. The Gnosis "travels" through the water into the appropriate individual and the rite ends. The passage of the Gnosis into the water is purely symbolic; no one needs to take an actual drink to get his Gnosis.

Gnosis may be stored by performing this rite with the assistance of an invested, bound spirit who agrees to hold the Gnosis, which is accessed again by another use of the rite (investiture is discussed under *Rite of Binding*). There is no effective limit to the amount of Gnosis that can be transferred, but a Garou or an invested, bound spirit cannot hold more Gnosis than his Gnosis Pool allows.

Ritual of the Questing Stone: By enacting this rite, the Garou forms a sympathetic magical link between the subject item or person and himself. The Garou must know the name by which the item or person is called. He then holds out a small stone tied to a string. If he succeeds in a Simple Test, he feels a slight tug on the stone from the direction of the subject. After the rite has been performed, the player of the Garou may ask any other player or Storyteller (out of play, of course) where the subject was last seen. The person who answers must answer honestly. The rite's effect lasts for the duration of the session if the Garou has either a piece of the subject or one of his treasured possessions. Otherwise it only lasts for one out-of-game hour.

It is recommended that those who perform this rite carry some sort of Narrator-approved identification, such as a card or a prop, to indicate that the rite has been cast and that pertinent questions should be answered truthfully.

Rite of Talisman Dedication: When a Garou changes forms, her possessions are normally left behind or destroyed. This rite binds items to the Garou so that they will change with her and go with her into the Umbra. The cost of the rite is one Gnosis per five pounds or cubic foot of material. Items such as a set of clothes, a handgun, a knife, a small electronic device or jewelry cost one Gnosis. Something the size of a rifle, body armor, a laptop computer or a backpack costs two Gnosis. Rocket launchers, full backpacks or anything up to man-size costs three. The final determination of cost is up to the Storyteller.

The rite is permanent, unless the Garou ends the effect. In no case may a Garou have more Gnosis Traits' worth of items bound to her than her total Gnosis score. (Note that if an "inappropriate" technological item, such as a Nintendo Game Boy or a power drill, is bound by a Garou who isn't a Bone Gnawer or Glass Walker, that individual may lose Renown.)

Rite of Becoming: This powerful rite can be performed only at an Anchorhead domain. It allows the Garou to travel into the Deep Umbra. The Umbra is a potentially dangerous place; the Deep Umbra is worse. Garou hurling themselves into this realm better be well-prepared and capable of dealing with malefic entities. In addition to the normal challenge, this rite costs three Gnosis to use.

Rite of Binding: This rite binds a spirit to a specific real-world object or a specific place in the Umbra. The object must be brought into the Umbra after being dedicated by the *Rite of Talisman Dedication*.

There are three kinds of binding:

Anchoring: This prevents a spirit from leaving and gives the Ritemaster the power to communicate with the bound spirit at will. Thus, the spirit can use its senses to report to the Ritemaster. This binding, which allows the spirit to use its Charms, Abilities and Traits, is temporary, although it can be made permanent later (see "Imprisonment," below). Septs often bind spirits in this manner to have them watch over their bawns.

This kind of binding costs one Gnosis Trait, plus one extra Gnosis Trait if the bound spirit is a totem or Incarna avatar. The Ritemaster must ask and receive permission to bind the spirit in such a fashion. This can either be a result of roleplaying or of several successful Mental and Social Challenges. This version of the *Rite of Binding* gains the Ritemaster no Notoriety. This is the equivalent of "working a part-time job" to a spirit.

Investiture: A spirit is bound into an item, which then becomes a specific talen. The enchanting Garou spends a Gnosis Trait and one other appropriate Trait in the investiture, and must get permission from the spirit so invested (see "Anchoring," above). The result is a talen. A talen must have a spirit of an appropriate affinity (Bane Arrows must have spirits of War in them, etc.). The spirit stays bound until the talen is used.

Imprisonment: A spirit is bound into an item, which subsequently imprisons that spirit. The spirit cannot break free unless someone breaks the object or the binding. A Garou wishing to imprison a spirit usually beats the spirit into submission and then, when the spirit has only a little Power remaining, enacts the *Rite of Binding* and imprisons it. The Garou can communicate with a spirit bound in this manner, although the prisoner cannot use its Charms. It can, however, use its Gnosis in Social and Mental Challenges, particularly with unsuspecting Garou who might be persuaded to break its prison and set the spirit free. By the time a spirit is freed after many years of imprisonment, it is usually restored to full health and Power, and is quite angry at the person who originally bound it.

Regardless of whether a spirit is evil when it is bound, a Ritemaster gains an automatic Notoriety Trait just by performing this version of the *Rite of Binding*.

The *Rite of Binding* requires 10 minutes of game time and the attention of the Spirit Keeper.

Rite of Summoning: One of the most potentially powerful of rites, the *Rite of Summoning* enables a Garou to call up a spirit from the Umbra. The *Rite of Summoning* is possible only because of the respect that most spirits have for the Garou; they are, after all, the Defenders of Gaia. It is only when this respect is abused or when Garou do not return the spirits' respect that problems develop.

The *Rite of Summoning* takes 30 minutes of game time. It is not something that is done in the middle of combat, nor can it be done off the cuff. Summonings should only be thoroughly thought out, prepared and re-searched. Casual or frivolous summonings can be considered disrespectful by spirits, and will have far-reaching repercussions.

The *Rite of Summoning* begins with the would-be Ritemaster informing the Spirit Keeper that he is preparing for a *Rite of Summoning*.

The Spirit Keeper then asks the Ritemaster the following questions:

What type of spirit are you trying to summon?

What is the affinity of the spirit you are trying to summon?

Have you summoned this spirit before? If so, do you know its name?

Are you searching for a spirit that meets this particular description, or are you willing to accept any spirit that comes?

The answers to these questions determine how successful the ritualist's summoning is likely to be. The Keeper then performs a Static Gnosis Challenge against the performer. The type and affinity of the spirit being called determines the difficulty. Here are some guidelines:

Note: The Spirit Keeper needs to tailor the difficulty to fit the situation. Certainly, a Ritemaster should not be able to prepare *too* much for this sort of thing.

Spirit Type	Basic Difficulty
Jaggling	4
Gaffling	5
Totem avatar	6
Incarna avatar	7

Affinity	Difficulty Modifier
Healing	+1
War	+2
Enigmas	0
Tribal totem	-3
Pack totem	2
Wyrm	+3
Weaver	+2
Wyld	+3

Miscellaneous Factors	Modifier
Summoned the spirit before	-1
Knows spirit's name	-3
Lupus breed	-1
Theurge auspice	-1
On a mission for Gaia	-2
To fight the Wyrm	+2
To fight another Garou	+3
Will take any spirit	-4
Per extra Gnosis Trait spent	-2
Each Notoriety Trait of the summoner	+3

A Garou can choose to spend Gnosis Traits before the challenge to reduce the difficulty. Each Gnosis spent reduces the difficulty of the challenge by two.

Unless the Garou is in the Umbra, she must first defeat the Gauntlet in order to summon a spirit. This is done by succeeding in a Mental Challenge or by spending a Gnosis Trait. Summoning while in the Umbra is therefore much easier, but has more limited application.

After approximately 30 minutes has passed from the time the Ritemaster first contacted the Spirit Keeper, she will approach the ritualist with a "spirit sheet" for this rite. She may wish to roleplay initial contact with the spirit.

A Garou usually chooses one of six basic tactics to get a spirit to serve him:

He may politely request that a spirit do something. This is usually followed up by an offer of reward (bargaining requires a Social Challenge). Chiminage (in the form of a Ban) may be thrown into the pot as an initial bid or added later to an offer or counter-offer. This is the preferred method for both spirits and Garou, and actually sets up a potential future relationship between them.

The Ritemaster may command a spirit to do something, appealing to its sense of duty. This is usually followed up by a threat of some kind. (*Leadership*, Social Challenge)

The summoner may challenge the spirit to a riddle game or some other contest to vie for control, usually with some offer of a Ban burden made by the summoner to balance out the service of the spirit. (*Enigmas*, Mental Challenge)

He may use a Gift to command the spirit. Of course, this has its own potential problems.

He may use his prowess and strength to intimidate the spirit (*Intimidation*, Social Challenge). *

He may attack the spirit and force it to agree to serve him. ("Bullying" requires a Physical Challenge).

* Indicates that Notoriety may be gained by using these methods.

If the spirit wins the initial challenge, it may depart immediately. If the spirit loses, it will usually serve the summoner to the best of its ability and then depart. A Ritemaster may continue to use commanding tactics to get the spirit to continue to serve him.

The amount of knowledge that the Spirit Keeper passes on to the summoner concerning the spirit he's attracted is determined by the relationship between the Garou and the spirit. If it's a good one, and the spirit is likely to do anything that the summoner asks, the Spirit Keeper can simply give a "spirit sheet" to the summoner. Otherwise, she has to arrange with the summoner exactly what he wants from the spirit and decide what happens as a result of the spirit's decision to obey or disobey.

Intermediate Rites

Rite of the Totem: This rite binds a totem to a group of Garou (henceforth called a pack). The group begins the *Rite of the Totem* and steps into the Umbra, where it finds some trail of the spirit animal it has chosen as its pack totem. The Garou must then track the spirit animal; this is usually just a formality.

When the spirit is found, it can either agree to take the pack as its fosterlings or ask for the Garou to prove themselves worthy of recognition as a pack by performing a quest. The latter option is rare, but can make for some excellent roleplaying opportunities.

The new pack howls as one at the end of this rite, and goes immediately to the nearest tribe or sept elder to announce its new pack name and members. A feast or hunt is often planned for this occasion. If a pack of Garou want to add a member at a later time, members must agree to the addition. No challenge is needed to perform this rite, but the subject Garou must collectively purchase at least one point in the Totem Background in order to benefit from this rite.

Rite of the Fetish: The *Rite of the Fetish* takes a spirit and binds it permanently into a prepared object. The object then becomes a magical thing, a fetish with specific powers. The object must be appropriate to the fetish being created. Furthermore, the item must be "purified" for three consecutive nights before it is ready to become a fetish. Fetish creation is not to be undertaken lightly; an impure object offered to house a spirit can have unpredictable and unfortunate effects.

During the actual *Rite of the Fetish*, a spirit is either summoned or released near the Ritemaster in the Umbra. The spirit must be of a type and affinity appropriate to the fetish being created. The Ritemaster formally asks the spirit to enter the fetish, and sacrifices an appropriate Trait (Physical for a war fetish, Mental for a mind fetish, etc.). If the spirit complies of its own accord, the fetish behaves normally.

If the spirit is compelled in any way, however, there is a chance that the fetish will become cursed or possessed. A cursed fetish is unpleasant to use, and can lead to Wyrm-taint in anyone who wields it. On the other hand, a cursed fetish can be cleansed through repeated *Rites of Cleansing* and Gnosis sacrifices.

A possessed fetish, on the other hand, uses its powers only when it deems them to be necessary. Garou cannot argue their fetishes into performing; only a Narrator or Storyteller can decide when the fetish feels like working.

The Spirit Keeper decides whether a fetish is cursed or possessed.

Casting this rite requires an hour of ritual and the sacrifice of one permanent Gnosis Trait per "level" of spirit required. See the guidelines below for required spirit types.

Gnosis Cost	Type
1	Gaffling, Jaggling
2	Totem avatar
3 to 5	Incarna avatar

Once the rite is finished, the fetish must be wrapped in red cloth (preferably silk) and must sit for an entire month. This gives the Spirit Keeper time to devise rules and game elements for the fetish, but also helps players come to grips with the level of sacrifice necessary to wield a fetish.

Punishment Rites

In a race as proud and honorable as the Garou, the regard and fellowship of one's peers is of paramount importance. It is no surprise, then, that Garou punishments for transgressions rely heavily on the pack, tribe and sept. Most of the time, offenders are simply punished physically or socially, but not supernaturally. The guilty party takes his lumps, accepts his punishment, and gets on with his life. This is usually enough, but for truly heinous or repeated offenses, certain rites may be brought to bear. These rites are never used lightly.

Note: If a Ritemaster performs a Punishment Rite on a Garou he *knows* to be innocent of her supposed crime, the rite affects the Ritemaster and any cohorts he has instead, but the rite's effects last twice as long as normal. Those who punish the innocent accidentally do not suffer this penalty.

Basic Rites

Rite of Ostracism: This rite serves as a punishment by peers for those Garou who commit lesser crimes. The duration of the rite's effects varies with the severity of the crime. It can be permanent, if necessary. The Garou is ignored by other Garou, not allowed to participate in any functions, and may not use her Renown Traits while under the sentence of Ostracism. For all practical purposes, the guilty party ceases to exist.

Players whose characters are subjected to this rite find themselves left out of plots and unable to participate in Garou sections of a session. Conversely, the ostracized Garou may wish to put his solo time to good use.

Stone of Scorn: This rite is one of the more creative forms of punishment among the Garou and is reserved for crimes against honor. The rite binds minor spirits of suffering and shame to a large rock, to which the offender is bound. Any member of the tribe may hurl Physical attacks as well as verbal insults at the guilty Garou. The punishment lasts one night, during which the subject loses a Renown Trait. This Trait is not regained until the end of the next session. No challenge is necessary for this rite.

Voice of the Jackal: A Garou can be subjected to this rite if found guilty of an act of cowardice, or of one shameful not just to herself, but also to her sept or tribe. When the rite is performed, the Garou is cursed with a shrill, high-pitched voice (which she must roleplay), and is two Traits down on any Social Challenges involving speech. The effects of this rite last for two lunar cycles.

Intermediate Rites

The Hunt: This rite is commonly used on a Garou who is guilty of a terrible crime against his people, and when amends can be made only through his death. Victims of this rite are denied shelter or aid by any other Garou. Furthermore, it is the duty of all Garou taking part in the rite to hunt down and execute the Hunt's target. After the object of the Hunt is caught and killed, his Honor is restored to him. Those few who escape the Hunt are never welcomed back, and will be killed on sight.

Satire Rite: A favorite rite of the Half Moons and Moon Dancers, this ritual heaps ridicule and shame upon the Garou subject. These poignant insults and ribald tales become part of the permanent oral history of the Garou. No challenge is necessary, and the Garou who is subjected to this rite loses a Glory or Honor Trait permanently.

This rite, obviously, must be roleplayed. It is important to remember that japes and insults are directed at a character, not at a player. If it looks like the *Satire Rite* is causing tempers to flare, a Social Challenge can be substituted instead.

Advanced Rites

The Rending of the Veil: When used on a human, this rite dispels the protection of the Veil so that she can see the Garou in all their glory. The effects of the rite last for an entire night, but few spectators survive the fury of the Garou for that long. Remember, only Crinos form causes a Delirium reaction.

Gaia's Vengeful Teeth: This rite is reserved for those Garou guilty of the foulest and most horrible crimes, such as consorting with the Wyrm, or killing or causing the death of Garou. The rite has a permanent effect, and causes any natural surface the victim comes in contact with to be transmuted momentarily into razor-sharp slivers of silver. Furthermore, the effects of the rite prevent the Garou from stepping sideways. Garou thus cursed are typically chased into the ground — literally. Every turn requires a Static Physical Test against 10 Traits, or the victim takes an aggravated wound. Victims of the rite who stand still suffer injuries at a rate of one aggravated wound level every three rounds.

Rites of Renown

These rites serve to reward those Garou who distinguish themselves in any of the Garou virtues. Many Garou dream of receiving the accolades of these rites. If a Garou is so honored for an action he did not perform, these rites fail and remove Renown in equal measure to what they might have bestowed.

There is no rules mechanic for the performance of any of these rites. Instead, they are a vital part of the experience of roleplaying Garou. The details and forms of these rites are left to individual Storytellers; what is important is what the rites stand for.

Basic Rites

Rite of Accomplishment: When a Garou performs a great deed against the Wyrm or shows uncommon valor, her peers may choose to perform this rite in her honor. The *Rite of Accomplishment* is generally enacted in the stories and songs portion of a moot, and is almost invariably presided over by Galliards. Its purpose is to award a Garou Renown for a recent deed. The Ritemaster extols the virtues of the supplicant, and while no challenge is made, any Garou who dispute the claim to Renown can do so. If the majority of Garou present agree, the subject receives the Renown Trait.

Rite of Passage: This rite serves as the "coming of age" ceremony for Garou. It is the time when a Garou's true nature is awakened, and she is introduced to her fellows as well as her heritage. Usually, some quest or trial must also be performed instead of a challenge, though the details of this trial can vary greatly. Before she passes through this rite, a young Garou may not question or challenge her elders, and she has no voice within Garou society.

Rite of Wounding: This rite is held in high regard by the more martial tribes and auspices. It celebrates the first wound a Garou receives in true battle. The rite is generally presided over by Ahroun, regardless of the subject's auspice. The performance of this rite is important; if it is neglected, other Garou will seriously doubt the new warrior's competence and prowess. This is particularly true of Ahroun, who will challenge any *Rite of Accomplishment* until the *Rite of Wounding* is performed.

Seasonal Rites

In ancient times, the Garou — men, women and wolves — had to stay keenly aware of the seasons. Failing to do so meant starving in the bitter winter cold, broiling in the summer heat or not being prepared to take advantage of the fertile spring or abundant autumn. On a grander scale, the seasons reflect Gaia's own eternal cycle of yearly renewal.

Basic Rites

Rite of the Hunting Grounds: The Garou using this rite may choose to mark an area as her own, her pack's, her sept's or her tribe's. After the rite is finished, Garou and natural wolves instantly recognize the ritualist's mark for what it is. Others with enhanced sensory powers realize something is strange, but do not recognize its importance without winning an *Occult* Mental Challenge (against 8 Traits and risking 2).

Rite of the Winter Winds: This rite, performed on the night of the winter solstice, ensures that the minions of the Wyrm do not harm Gaia during the long nights and short days. Other than the initial challenge, there are no game mechanics associated with this rite.

Rite of Reawakening: This rite takes place during the vernal equinox. The Ritemaster leads the assembled Garou into the Umbra where they search out seven tests to represent the seven gates to the underworld. Their hunt lasts until dawn, when they return and seek out their Kinfolk to "reacquaint themselves." It is a rite celebrating the return of spring, and life, to the Earth.

There are no game mechanics for this rite beyond the initial challenge, but the performance of the ritual certainly can provide a creative Storyteller with some good story ideas. There are no hard and fast definitions of what the seven tests might be; they vary for each group of Garou performing the rite.

In Garou legend, it is stated that if seven tests are found and passed by a pack of Garou, and if a single Garou of the pack manages to pass every one while relinquishing something of himself at each, he can then renew the Earth. To date, no Garou has ever succeeded at passing seven tests, or has even come close.

The Great Hunt: Garou perform this rite on Midsummer's Eve. At exactly midnight, the Ritemaster calls upon Gaia to bring creatures worthy of the *Great Hunt* to the attention of the sept. At dawn, the sept is shown a clear sign of the target of the *Great Hunt*, which can be anything: an animal, a vampire, a Wyrm-creature — anything. The sept has until the following midnight to complete the hunt and slay the target. If the hunt is successful, all who participate gain two Glory Traits. Those involved in a failed *Great Hunt* lose one Glory Trait.

Rite of Keres: This rite takes place during the night of the autumnal equinox. It honors Garou who have fallen to the minions of the Wyrm. In particular, it honors the legendary Garou Keres and her packmates, who died killing a great horde of Wyrm-creatures. (Keres herself, the last standing, consumed her fallen packmates to prevent them from being tainted, and then slew nine times nine great Wyrm-beasts before being killed.) If a Garou participating in this rite releases her own fear and grief over a personal situation and throws a representative figurine into the fire (and wins a Simple Test), she may receive a Willpower Trait (at the Storyteller's discretion). If the Storyteller decides that the character (or player) was just after the Willpower and not roleplaying, he may take away an Honor Renown instead.

Minor Rites

These rites each take about 15 minutes to perform, during which time the Garou character must be out of play. The modifiers these rites grant are not cumulative, but an individual Garou can receive the modifiers from a number of different Minor Rites equal to her Rank.

Bone Rhythms: If a Garou taps out this mystic rhythm to her personal totem spirit for 15 minutes over three consecutive sessions, she gains one free retest that can be spent on any challenge in the spirit realms.

Breath of Gaia: If a Garou performs this rite (which involves taking 15 deep breaths without interruption) once each session over four consecutive sessions, he gains two free retests that can be spent on any healing or detection-related tests.

Greet the Moon: If a Garou performs this rite, which consists of howling an elaborate greeting to the moon, over three consecutive sessions, she gains a free retest that can be spent on any Social Challenge.

Greet the Sun: This rite is identical to *Greet the Moon*, but is done at sunrise. This gives the Garou one free retest when sensing for Wyrm-taint or Wyrm-creatures. This free retest returns each session so long as the Garou does not miss performing the greeting each session.

Hunting Prayer: The Garou chooses a common item (a bowl, knife or candle will do) and prays in praise to Gaia over the item for three consecutive sessions. The Garou thereafter receives one free retest per session when hunting. If the item is lost or is not taken hunting with the Garou, he must start the process over with a different item.

Prayer for the Prey: The Garou steps into the Umbra just after making a kill and thanks the spirit of her prey for giving its life for the Garou. This is considered a sign of respect to Gaia, Her children and to life itself. If a Garou does this for four consecutive sessions, the Garou gains one free retest whenever dealing with nature-related spirits. To keep this advantage, the Garou must perform this rite over every beast of Gaia (not including Wyrm-spawn) that she slays.

Merits and Flaws

Merits and Flaws are optional defining Traits that give you a way to make your character unique. A Merit is a descriptive Trait that applies to your character and gives him a slight advantage in some area, while a Flaw gives your Garou a slight disadvantage. You may buy Merits only during character creation, unless you earn them during a story (and with Storyteller approval). To buy Merits during character creation, you may spend only Traits from Flaws (maximum of seven), Backgrounds (maximum of five), Abilities (maximum of five) or Traits earned by taking Negative Traits (maximum of five); the maximum number of Merit Traits allowed is 22. Your character will not suffer if you do not have any Merits or Flaws, but putting all your points into Merits and Flaws will assuredly handicap you in other areas.

You can also take Flaw Traits and use them to buy other Traits — Abilities and Backgrounds — at a one-for-one ratio.

Merits and Flaws might be restricted in some stories, or not purchasable at all. Make certain that you talk with your Storyteller before buying any Merits or Flaws, as some of the ones listed below may be disallowed. Merits and Flaws are optional parts of a character, and **Apocalypse** can be played quite well without a single Merit or Flaw.

Remember that you must have Storyteller approval on all Merits and Flaws you want for your character. Once gameplay starts, Merits and Flaws may be purchased or bought off only with Storyteller approval, and at double the Trait cost listed in Experience.

You may never purchase a Flaw that duplicates a Flaw already inherent in your character because of breed, tribe, etc. You are also not allowed to double up an already existing advantage with a Merit.

Aptitudes

Ability Aptitude (1 Trait Merit): You have a natural affinity for a particular (but not combat-related) Ability. You are two Traits up on all tests directly related to that Ability.

Ambidextrous (1 Trait Merit): You take no penalty for doing things with your off hand. If fighting with two weapons, you must bid one Trait for your good hand and two for your off hand. **Note:** Individuals without this Merit must bid two Traits for their good hand and three for their off hand when using multiple weapons.

Pitiable (1 Trait Merit): There is something about you that others pity. It may cause them to care for you as if you were a cub (see "Natures and Demeanors," pp 29-31). Some Natures are totally unaffected by this Merit (i.e., Deviant and Fanatic), and some Demeanors may pretend they are not. You must decide what it is about you that attracts such pity, and how much (or little) you like it. You may use this Merit as a bid in any challenge to defend yourself from those intent on doing you harm — and nothing more. This Trait cannot be lost as a result of a test, and you cannot use it more than once per situation.

Daredevil (3 Trait Merit): You are good at taking risks, and aren't too bad at surviving them, either. You are one Trait up on any challenge in which you try something particularly dangerous.

Note: This Merit does not always apply to combat, only to fights in which you are obviously outmatched and wade in anyway.

Jack of All Trades (5 Trait Merit): You have a large pool of miscellaneous skills and knowledges obtained through your extensive travels, the jobs you have held or too much time spent watching public television. You may automatically attempt any action, even if you do not have the appropriate Ability. You need to spend an extra Trait to do so, however. If you lose this challenge, the Traits you bid are also gone unless you spend a Willpower Trait to avoid the loss.

Natural Peacemaker (5 Trait Merit): As per the Children of Gaia Tribal Advantage.

Outmaneuver (5 Trait Merit): As per the Shadow Lord Tribal Advantage, but you may chose Social, Mental or Physical.

Illiterate (1 Trait Flaw): You are unable to read or write. Storytellers should increase the Trait rating of this Flaw for homid characters

Inept (5 Trait Flaw): You are not attuned to your natural aptitudes. You start the game with no Abilities, and cannot buy any Trait of Ability or Influence above one until this Flaw has been bought off.

Awareness

Acute Sense (1 Trait Merit): You have an exceptionally sharp sense (choose one: hearing, smell, taste or vision), even for a wolf. You automatically have two free Traits on all perception challenges related to that one sense.

Pulse of the City (5 Trait Merit): As per the Bone Gnawer Tribal Advantage *Rumors*.

Umbral Sight (5 Trait Merit): As per the Uktena Tribal Advantage.

Weak Sense (1 Trait Flaw): You have a defective sense (choose one: hearing or vision). You are automatically down two Traits on perception tests related to that one sense. You may not have the Merit *Acute Sense* and Flaw *Weak Sense* on the same sense.

One Eye (2 Trait Flaw): You have one working eye (you can choose which one). You have no peripheral vision on your blind side, and are two Traits down on any test requiring depth perception. This includes all forms of ranged combat.

Deaf (4 Trait Flaw): You cannot hear sound. This Flaw is exceedingly difficult to roleplay properly.

Blind (6 Trait Flaw): You have no sense of vision, and automatically lose all challenges related to sight. This Flaw should be roleplayed to the best of your ability, but not to a point where it endangers anyone's safety.

Garou Ties

Favor (1 - 7 Trait Merit): An elder owes you a favor because of something either you or your pack once did for him. The extent of the favor depends on how many points you spend: One Trait indicates a relatively minor favor, while seven Traits indicates that the elder owes you his life.

Twisted Upbringing (1 Trait Flaw): A major part of what you think you know about the Garou is wrong. Perhaps you were taught this way out of malevolence, or you came to your conclusions through erroneous information. It will take repeated efforts on the part of a very patient teacher to correct what you think, and even then you may think that she is trying to trick you.

Enemy (1 - 5 Trait Flaw): You have an enemy, or perhaps a group of enemies, who seek to do you harm. The value of the Flaw determines how powerful these enemies are. The most powerful enemies (Methuselah vampires or potent mages) are worth five Traits, while someone near your own power would be worth only one Trait. You must decide who your enemy is and how you became enemies in the first place. All enemies are subject to Storyteller approval.

Social Outcast (3 Trait Flaw): As per the Bone Gnawer Tribal Drawback.

Unworthy (3 Trait Flaw): As per the Shadow Lord Tribal Drawback.

Human Society

Weaver's Children (5 Trait Merit): As per the Glass Walker Tribal Advantage.

Persistent Parents (2 Trait Flaw): Your parents refuse to let mystery of your disappearance lie, and actively use missing children programs to search for you. They also use hired detectives to hunt for you. The Storyteller determines how close they are on your trail, but the chase is hot enough to cause you some discomfort. Implicit to this Flaw is the fact that you cannot simply tell them what has become of you for some reason: Maybe your father is a loyal Pentex Employee, or your parents are so mundane they'd have you taken away for persisting in your "delusions."

Ward (3 Trait Flaw): You are devoted to the protection of a human. You may describe your Ward, though the Storyteller will create her and assign her Traits. This character may be a friend or relative from your pre-Change days, or simply a human you admire and consider important. Wards have a way of getting caught up in the action of stories, and are frequently irresistible targets for a character's enemies. If the Ward is Kinfolk, then she must be one with whom your character has a special relationship (lover, childhood friend, etc.).

Hunted (3 Trait Flaw): You are pursued by a fanatical werewolf-hunter who believes you are a dangerous slavering beast inimical to humanity (not that he's necessarily wrong). Everyone you associate with may be hunted by the same individual as well. Though this hunter seeks the destruction of all Garou, there is something about you that drives him. In addition, the hunter is, for some reason, immune to the Delirium.

Mental

Time Sense (1 Trait Merit): You have an innate sense of time and its passage. You can estimate the time of day and the passage of time with 99-percent accuracy. You are off about two minutes in every 24 hours.

Light Sleeper (2 Trait Merit): You awaken instantly at any sign of trouble or danger, and do so without any sleepiness or hesitation.

Calm Heart (3 Trait Merit): You are naturally calm and well-composed, and never fly off the handle. You are always one Trait up on all tests to resist frenzy, no matter how you are provoked.

Iron Will (3 Trait Merit): Once your mind is made up, nothing can thwart you from achieving your goals. You are extremely resistant to powers that affect your mind or emotions, and gain one free retest in such challenges.

Untamable (5 Trait Merit): You are a wild wolf who has never bowed his head to the leash. You are six Traits up on any challenges versus Mental or Social control. Attempts to control you emotionally, however, are an entirely different matter.

Warrior's Heart (5 Trait Merit): As per the Get of Fenris Tribal Advantage.

Deep Sleeper (1 Trait Flaw): It is very difficult to waken you from a sound sleep. If awakened unexpectedly, you are one Trait down for all challenges during the rest of the scene.

Amnesia (2 Trait Flaw): You are unable to remember anything about your past. However, that doesn't mean your past won't come back to haunt you. You may buy up to five more unidentified Flaws and leave it to the Storyteller to spring them on you at dramatically suitable moments.

Confused (2 Trait Flaw): You are often confused, and the world seems to be a very distorted, twisted place. Sometimes, you are simply unable to make sense of things. You need to roleplay this behavior to some extent all the time, but your confusion becomes especially strong whenever you're in the presence of intense stimuli (such as when a number of different people talk all at once, or you enter a nightclub with loud, pounding music). In such situations you are two Traits down on all challenges. You may spend a Willpower Trait to override the effects of your confusion, but only for the rest of the scene.

Absent-Minded (3 Trait Flaw): Though you do not forget such things as Knowledges and Skills, you do forget names, addresses and where you were two hours ago. In order to remember anything more than your own name, address and phone number during stressful situations, you must win a Static Mental Challenge (against a number of Traits set by the Storyteller) or spend a Willpower Trait.

Blind Commitment (3 Trait Flaw): As per the Get of Fenris Tribal Drawback.

Low Self-Control (3 Trait Flaw): As per the Fianna Tribal Drawback.

Weak-Willed (3 Trait Flaw): You are highly susceptible to Dominate and other forms of intimidation by others; you are three Traits down on all related challenges. Furthermore, you can employ your Willpower only when survival is at stake or when it is appropriate to your Nature.

Physical

Double-Jointed (1 Trait Merit): You are unusually supple. You gain one free retest per session on a challenge related to body flexibility. This includes slipping loose from bonds, squeezing through narrow windows and so on. The Storyteller is the final arbiter on what sorts of tests are applicable.

Bad Taste (2 Trait Merit): Your flesh exudes oils which taste so bad that anyone (Garou, fomori, vampire, Wyrm-creature, over-affectionate significant other) who tries to bite you is instantly nauseated. The biter must spend Willpower every turn, or retch. Lupus and wolves will not lick your hands or face.

Fair Glabro (2 Trait Merit): Your Glabro form can pass for Homid. You do not acquire the normal Negative Social Traits when in Glabro.

Lack of Scent (2 Trait Merit): You produce no scent, or your scent is extremely faint. Those attempting to track you are automatically down two Traits.

Longevity (2 Trait Merit): You are extremely long-lived. You can expect to live to be 120 or even 130 years old, barring death in combat.

Huge Size (4 Trait Merit): You are abnormally large in size, possibly over seven feet tall in Homid form, or extremely heavyset. You therefore have one additional Health Trait before becoming *Bruised*.

Metamorph (6 Trait Merit): You find it extremely easy to change forms, and can do it in your sleep. You do not need to test to shift forms, nor do you need to spend a Rage point in order to assume a desired form instantly. In addition, if you are ever knocked unconscious (due to wounds, etc.), you can make a Mental Challenge (against eight Traits) to assume whatever form you wish instead of reverting to your breed form automatically.

Animal Musk (1 Trait Flaw): You smell like an animal, even in Homid form. You must bid two Traits in Social Challenges (those not related to *Intimidation*) in which your smell is obvious (indoors or at a cocktail party, for example, but not while rooting around in a junkyard). This scent does not bother wolves, only humans.

Strict Carnivore (1 Trait Flaw): You derive no nourishment from vegetables, and must rely solely on meat — preferably the raw variety. Subsistence in areas where game is scarce or at salad bars is difficult for you.

Disfigured (2 Trait Flaw): A hideous disfigurement makes you ugly and easy to notice, as well as remember. You may never have Social Traits related to beauty.

Monstrous (2 Trait Flaw): There is something wholly monstrous about you, something that makes you hideous in the eyes of fellow Garou. Your Homid form scarcely looks human, and your Crinos and Lupus forms look horrendous; in what manner you differ from the norm is up to you. Perhaps you have taken on reptile features and appear as a creature of the Wyrm to certain literal-minded Garou. You may never have Social Traits related to beauty, or Gifts related to positive social interaction.

Short (2 Trait Flaw): You are noticeably below average height, and have trouble seeing over high objects. Your Crinos form does not gain as much mass and size as normal; you are just under average human height when in this form. You and your Storyteller should make sure your height is taken into account in all situations. In some circumstances, it will give you a concealment bonus, in others, a decided disadvantage.

Deformity (3 Trait Flaw): As per the Metis Breed disadvantage.

Partially Crippled (3 Trait Flaw): Your legs are permanently injured or otherwise prevented from working effectively. You lose all ties in challenges involving movement. Your character may also need assistance in walking, such as a pair of crutches or a wheelchair. Movement in Lupus form is no easier, and switching forms does not alleviate the problem.

Wolf Years (3 Trait Flaw): You age in wolf years, not human years like most Garou. In other words, you have 12 to 20 years to live at most. You begin to suffer the effects of aging at eight years if you are lupus, or within five years of the Change if you are a homid character.

One Arm (4 Trait Flaw): You have only one arm. You can choose which one, or determine this randomly at character generation. The Flaw could stem from a birth defect, pre-Change injury or battle scar. It is assumed that you are accustomed to using your remaining hand, so under normal circumstances you have no off-hand penalty. However, you lose all ties in challenges involving tasks that would normally require two hands.

Mute (5 Trait Flaw): Your vocal apparatus does not function, and you cannot speak at all. You can communicate through other means, typically writing or signing.

Psychological

Code of Honor (1 Trait Merit): You have a personal code of ethics to which you adhere strictly. Even when you are frenzying, you gain two Traits on all challenges to resist any temptation or persuasion to break your code. Your personal code must be approved by the Storyteller before gameplay begins.

Higher Purpose (1 Trait Merit): You have a goal that drives you in everything. Although this may cause you to behave contrary to your survival instincts, it also grants you great personal strength. You gain two extra Traits on all challenges dealing with this higher purpose, which must be approved by the Storyteller. (You may not have this Merit and the Flaw *Driving Goal*.)

Berserker (2 Trait Merit): You may enter frenzy at will, during which time you take no penalties from wounds. Unfortunately, you still have the same chance of being thrown into frenzy involuntarily as a normal Garou, and take all the penalties of being in frenzy, no matter how it's inspired.

Inner Peace (5 Trait Merit): As per the Stargazer tribal Advantage.

Compulsion (1 Trait Flaw): You have a psychological compulsion that causes you a number of different problems. Your compulsion may be cleanliness, perfection, bragging, stealing, gaming, exaggeration or just talking too much. You may defeat your compulsion for one scene by spending a Willpower Trait.

Dark Secret (1 Trait Flaw): You have a secret that, if uncovered, would embarrass you immensely and make you a pariah in the Garou Nation. While it weighs on your mind at all times, the secret surfaces only occasionally in stories (otherwise, it will lose its impact). And in case you are wondering, no, your dark secret cannot be that you are metis.

Intolerance (1 Trait Flaw): You have an unreasonable dislike for a certain thing, and are one Trait down in any challenge dealing with the object of your intolerance. It may be an animal, a class of person, a color, a situation or just about anything else you can imagine. Some dislikes may be too trivial to be worth a Trait — a dislike of pomegranates or tissue paper will have little effect on play in most chronicles, and as such should not be permitted. The Storyteller is the final arbiter on what *Intolerances* are permissible.

Nightmares (1 Trait Flaw): You experience horrendous nightmares every time you sleep, and memories of them haunt you during your waking hours. Sometimes the nightmares are so bad that you are one Trait down on all your challenges for the next day or night (Narrator discretion). Some of the nightmares may even become so intense that you mistake them for reality, which certainly won't endear you to the rest of your pack. Storytellers who plan on taking great advantage of this Flaw should adjust its point value accordingly.

Overconfident (1 Trait Flaw): You have an exaggerated and unshakable opinion of your own worth and capabilities. You always trust your own abilities in any matter, even in situations when you risk defeat. Because you may not always be correct in your convictions, such overconfidence can be very dangerous. When you do fail, you quickly find someone or something else to blame — after all, it couldn't *possibly* have been your fault. If you are convincing enough, you can infect others with your overconfidence.

Shy (1 Trait Flaw): You are distinctly ill at ease when dealing with people, and try to avoid social situations whenever possible. You are one Trait down on all challenges concerned with social dealings. You are also one Trait down on any challenges in which you are the center of attention for a large group of people (over 10).

Speech Impediment (1 Trait Flaw): You have a stammer or some other speech impediment that hampers verbal communication. You should roleplay this impediment most of the time, though not to the point of offensiveness or parody.

Pack Mentality (2 Trait Flaw): You pride yourself on being a member of a pack. It is your life. Your identity is tied to that of your pack, so much so that you always think in terms of "us" rather than "me." You are one Trait up in all challenges when working with at least two other members of your pack. The flip side is that you are down one Trait the rest of the time. You are so dependent on your packmates that you sometimes cannot make decisions without them, even if you are the alpha. A Simple Test may be required to make decisions in stressful situations when you're acting without suitable backup.

Soft-Hearted (2 Trait Flaw): You cannot stand to watch others suffer, not necessarily because you care about what happens to them, but simply because you dislike the intensity of emotion. If you are the direct cause of suffering and you witness it, you will experience days of nausea and nights of sleepless grief. You avoid situations in which you might have to witness suffering, and will do anything you can to protect others from it. Whenever you are forced to view others' pain, you are one Trait down on all challenges until the end of the next scene.

Vengeance (2 Trait Flaw): You have a score to settle. You are obsessed with wreaking vengeance on an individual (or perhaps an entire group), and you make revenge your first priority in all situations. This need for revenge can be overcome only by spending a Willpower Trait, and even then it subsides only temporarily.

Driving Goal (3 Trait Flaw): You have a personal obsession that compels and directs you in sometimes startling ways. The goal is always limitless in depth, and you can never truly achieve it. It could be to reform the Black Spiral Dancers or to resurrect the lost Croatan tribe from the spirit world — truly an impossible dream. Because you must work toward your goal throughout the chronicle, your single-minded devotion will get you into trouble and may jeopardize other goals. You may avoid your driving goal for one scene by spending a Mental Trait, and for one session by spending a Willpower Trait.

Hatred (3 Trait Flaw): You have an unreasoning hatred of a certain thing. This hate is total, and largely uncontrollable. You may hate a species of animal, a class of person, a color (*"ARRRGHHH! IT'S IN EARTH TONES! I **HATE** EARTH TONES!"*), a situation — anything. When confronted with the object of your hatred, you must test your current Willpower against your current Rage (no Traits are risked). If you fail this test, you immediately frenzy and attack the hated object. You constantly pursue opportunities to harm the hated object or to gain power over it, so much so that your reasoning is clouded.

Low Self-Image (2 Trait Flaw): You lack confidence in your own abilities. You are two Traits down in situations where you don't expect to succeed (at Narrator discretion, though the penalty might be limited to one Trait if you help the Narrator by pointing out times when this Flaw might affect you). At Narrator option, you may be required to use a Willpower Trait in order even to attempt things that require strong belief in oneself.

Phobia (Mild) (3 Trait Flaw): An overpowering fear of something causes you to avoid it both instinctively and illogically. You must expend a Mental Trait to remain in the vicinity of the object you fear; however, once that Trait is spent, that particular object doesn't bother you for the remainder of the session.

Quirk (3 Trait Flaw): As per the Silver Fang Tribal Drawback. Quirks cannot be bought off.

Short Fuse (3 Trait Flaw): You get angry fast. You are down two Traits when attempting to resist frenzy. Alternately, this can be played as per the Black Furies Tribal Disadvantage, except you and the Storyteller pick the specific object of your ire.

Territorial (3 Trait Flaw): You are extremely territorial. You do not like to leave your territory, nor do you like to have strangers enter it. In fact, you get so nervous and disoriented when outside your own turf that you are down one Trait on all challenges. You must make a frenzy test to avoid automatically attacking intruders who enter your territory, unless they have obtained your permission to do so beforehand.

Phobia (Severe) (5 Trait Flaw): You fear something so much that you must resist frenzy or run (fox frenzy) when faced with it. The Storyteller chooses the object of your phobia — and might not inform you of its identity beforehand.

Supernatural

True Love (1 Trait Merit): You have discovered a true love, a rare thing in a world where such savagery rules. Whenever you are suffering, in danger or dejected, just the thought of this true love is enough to give you the strength to persevere. In game terms, this love allows you two extra Traits in a challenge when you are actively striving to protect your true love. Also, at Storyteller discretion, the power of your love may be powerful enough to protect you from other supernatural forces.

Danger Sense (2 Trait Merit): You have a sixth sense that warns you of danger. When in a perilous situation that would potentially surprise you, you have six seconds to react, instead of the normal three seconds.

Faerie Affinity (2 Trait Merit): Your presence does not frighten changelings; indeed, it attracts them, and you are naturally attuned to their ways.

Magic Resistance (2 Trait Merit): You have an inherent resistance to the spells of mages, Tremere rituals and other forms of magic (or magick). All such spells and rituals cost an extra Trait when directed at you.

Note: This resistance includes spells of a beneficial nature as well; you cannot pick and choose which spells you will allow to affect you.

Medium (2 Trait Merit): You possess the natural affinity to sense and hear wraiths. Though you cannot see them, you feel their presence and are able to speak with them when they are in the vicinity. It is even possible

for you to summon them (through pleading and cajoling) into your presence. Wraiths will not simply aid you or give you advice for free, however; they have their own agendas. In most cases, a wraith will want something in return for her assistance.

Moon Bound (2 Trait Merit): You are especially tied to your auspice, and when your moon is in the waxing phase (in game), you receive a bonus Trait in all ties. However, when your moon is waning, you are down one Trait in all ties.

Luck (3 Trait Merit): You were born lucky. Either you have a guardian angel or the Devil looks after his own. You may call for a retest against any challenge made by anyone in your presence, once per session.

Natural Channel (3 Trait Merit): You find the Gauntlet between worlds thinner than most do. The difficulty for stepping sideways is one less than normal for you, and you gain one free retest per session when dealing with spirits' reactions to you. Even if you are not a Theurge, you will not find it difficult to obtain training from Garou shamans.

Spirit Mentor (3 Trait Merit): You have a wraith as a companion and guide. Otherwise, this Merit is just like the Silent Strider Tribal Drawback, *Haunted*. You cannot leave this wraith behind, and you are one of the wraith's Fetters. For more information on wraiths, see **Oblivion**.

Destiny (4 Trait Merit): You are here for a reason, though you do not know what it is yet. Your birth was attended by many powerful omens, and much is expected of you by your sept. You did not suffer any trauma from the Change, as your parents (Kinfolk) had prepared you for it. When the time came, you were fully ready to take up the mantle of your destiny. You begin the game with two additional Renown Traits.

Your Storyteller should decide your destiny, and make it more apparent to you as the game progresses. Prophecies and dreams may guide your way and grant you clues to your ultimate goal. It is as if you are being directed to fulfill a quest (which you are). This Merit can be taken only with Storyteller approval.

Charmed Existence (5 Trait Merit): As per the Silent Strider Tribal Advantage *The Omen of Doom*.

Gaia's Fury (5 Trait Merit): As per the Red Talon Tribal Advantage.

Totem's Siblings (5 Trait Merit): As per the Black Furies Tribal Advantage *Artemis*, except it relates to your tribal totem.

Resistant to Wyrm Emanations (5 Trait Merit): You get one free retest versus the contaminations and toxins of the Wyrm. This Merit also protects you against radiation, balefire, Wyrm elementals and possession by Banes. Your sept will recognize this and thrust you into many perils, expecting you to use your resistance for the good of others. This retest can be called every time there is a challenge against any of these contaminants.

Silver Tolerance (5/7 Trait Merit): You have partial immunity to the adverse effects of silver. With five Traits in this Merit, only every other Health Level of damage received from silver is aggravated damage. At seven Traits, none of the damage you receive from silver is aggravated.

Mysterious Guardian (6 Trait Merit): Someone or something watches over you, protecting you and aiding you on random occasions. The Storyteller decides why you are being watched over, and by what — and what else this entails.

True Faith (7 Trait Merit): You have a deep-seated faith in and love of Gaia, God or whatever name you want to use for the Almighty. You begin the game with one Trait's worth of Faith. Your belief provides you with an inner strength and comfort that continues to support you when all else fails. It can be used just like Willpower Traits. The exact effects of *True Faith*, if any, are completely up to the Storyteller (though it will typically repel Kindred); they vary from person to person, and are never obvious. The nature of any miracles you perform is usually tied to your Nature, and you may never realize that you have been aided by a force beyond yourself.

You must not have any Derangements in order to choose this Merit, and if you ever get a permanent Derangement, you instantly lose all Faith Traits. You may recover them only through extensive penitence and work (and then only after your Derangement has been removed). No one may start the game with more than one Faith Trait. Additional Faith Traits can be purchased only at the Storyteller's discretion.

Slip Sideways (1 Trait Flaw): You cannot always control your passage into the Umbra. If, during any stressful situation, you confront a mirror, you must win a Mental Challenge against the Gauntlet to avoid involuntarily stepping sideways. You must still make all appropriate tests to cross over, but you do get an extra Trait for breaking ties when doing so.

Foe from the Past (1 - 3 Trait Flaw): An enemy from one of your Past Lives (which you must also purchase in order to buy this Flaw) pursues you for revenge. A vampire, wraith or spirit is worth three Traits, otherwise the Flaw is worth only one or two Traits. How powerful the enemy is and how frequently he appears determine the Trait cost.

Forced Transformation (1 - 4 Trait Flaw): Some event forces you to shapeshift. You must spend a Willpower Trait in order to prevent the change or to change back, so long as the triggering event is in effect. Some examples include:

- Every full moon you must assume Crinos form (2 Trait Flaw).
- When your auspice waxes, you assume Crinos (2 Trait Flaw).
- When drunk or angry (but not in frenzy): Glabro (1 Trait Flaw), Crinos (2 Trait Flaw).
- When sexually aroused: if you are homid: to Glabro (1 Trait Flaw), to Crinos (2 Trait Flaw); if you are lupus: to Homid (2 Trait Flaw).

- When you frenzy, you take a form other than Crinos: Glabro or Hispo (2 Trait Flaw), Lupus (3 Trait Flaw), Homid (4 Trait Flaw).
- When entering the Umbra: Glabro, Crinos, Hispo (1 Trait Flaw), Homid or Lupus (2 Trait Flaw).
- At the sight of wolfsbane: Homid (3 Trait Flaw).
- At the sign of a vampire: Crinos (1 Trait Flaw), Homid (3 Trait Flaw).
- When you sense Wyrm-taint: Crinos (1 Trait Flaw), Homid (2 Trait Flaw).

Banned Transformation (1 - 6 Trait Flaw): Some event prevents you from changing forms. Some ideas and costs include:

Soothing music (1 Trait Flaw), wolfsbane present (1 Trait Flaw), silver present (3 Trait Flaw), cannot see moon (6 Trait Flaw), during the day (5 Trait Flaw), without spending a Rage Trait (2 Trait Flaw).

Mark of the Predator (2 Trait Flaw): Herbivores fear you, and carnivores consider you a threat. You cannot possess the Ability *Animal Ken*.

Sign of the Wolf (2 Trait Flaw): In Homid form, you have all the signs of being a werewolf according to the old wives' tales. Your eyebrows have grown together, there is hair on your palms, your second and third digits are the same length, and so on. A pentagram may even form on your right palm just before and during your auspice. All this makes it hard to hide from werewolf-hunters.

Haunted (3 Trait Flaw): As per the Silent Strider Tribal Drawback.

Limited Affinity to Gaia (3 Trait Flaw): As per either the Red Talon or Glass Walker Tribal Drawback.

Pierced Veil (3 Trait Flaw): As per the Children of Gaia Tribal Drawback, *Weak Veil*.

Dark Fate (5 Trait Flaw): Within the year you will either experience a most horrible demise or, worse, suffer eternal agony. No matter what you do, you are doomed. All the signs and portents clearly show that your fate is certain. Even more ghastly, you have partial knowledge of this, and occasionally have visions of your fate.

When and how you will indeed meet your destiny face-to-face is completely up to the Storyteller. Though you cannot do anything about your fate (unless you buy the Flaw off beforehand), you can still attempt to reach some goal before it occurs, try to ensure that your packmates are not destroyed as well or turn your doom into a noble sacrifice.

Taint of Corruption (7 Trait Flaw): You are touched by the Wyrm and corrupt in the eyes of your fellow Garou. You are detectable as a Wyrm-creature to anyone using the Gift: *Sense Wyrm*. You suffer nightmares as manifestations of the Wyrm come to you in your sleep and try to lure you to the other side completely. Your pack may be your only hope, if it will stand beside you. Ridding yourself of this corruption should be a major undertaking.

Sample Character

Step One

Lori, who's gotten tired of her Toreador vampire character, decides she wants to try something a bit different, and sits down with **Laws of the Wild** to create a Garou character instead. Pondering her choices, she settles on a female lupus character named Returns-to-Wilderness, who grew up happily in the wild until development and "progress" encroached on her home, and she and her pack were carted off to a zoo. Lori has a few ideas about the character's history, but decides to save them for later, when it's time to flesh out that sort of thing. She does, however, note her character's Rank of Cliath, which is the default for a new character.

The first thing Lori has to do is pick a Nature and a Demeanor. Explorer seems like a natural choice for a wolf who wants to get back to the pure wilderness. Demeanor is a bit harder, but in the end Lori settles on Survivor. After all, she reasons, Returns-to-Wilderness has seen a lot of hard times and has adopted a tough attitude in order to deal with them.

Lori has already chosen lupus as Returns' breed, which means that the character starts off with three initial Gnosis. As for a breed Gift, *Scent of the True Form* seems appropriate for a lupus trying to get out of the city and back to the woods. After all, she wants to know who she's dealing with.

Next comes auspice. Lori reads over the choices and, after some heckling from her Narrator (who's stopped by to watch), settles on Theurge. Returns-to-Wilderness is a child of the wild trying to get back in touch with the spirit of the land. She's not really interested in combat or in socializing much, but the idea of talking to spirits really appeals to Lori, so Theurge it is. This decision sets the character's starting Rage at 1. Then there's the question of an Auspice Gift; because *Name the Spirit* seems to fit well with *Scent of the True Form*, Lori marks that one down and moves on to tribe.

After reading over the various tribe descriptions, Lori ponders for a bit, torn between Red Talons (she's angry over the destruction of her home and the kidnapping of her wolf pack) and Child of Gaia (she wants to show the humans the error of their ways). Child of Gaia wins in the end, primarily because it fits better with Returns' *Explorer* Nature. Thus, the character's starting Willpower is 2. As for a Tribe Gift, Lori decides *Calm* would be best for a Garou in Returns' position. It will keep her out of unnecessary fights and let her talk to people who might otherwise be inclined toward violence.

The basics of the character are set. Now it's time for Traits.

Step Two

Returns-to-Wilderness is a curious character (note her Gifts), so Lori sets up Mental as the Garou's Primary Traits. A wolf accustomed to life in the wilderness would probably have Physical as her Secondary category, Lori reasons, so that leaves Social for last. That's just as well; Returns-to-Wilderness is happy with wolves but doesn't really know how to deal with humans yet.

Starting from the top, Lori selects the following Physical Traits: *Clever, Dedicated, Determined, Insightful, Patient, Rational* and *Reflective*. She briefly considers doubling up *Determined* but ends up giving Returns *Reflective* instead, wanting to explore all facets of the character's personality instead of focusing on just a few at the outset.

Next, it's time for Physical Traits, and Lori goes for *Athletic, Enduring, Energetic, Robust* and *Tough*. All of these reflect a youth spent in the wilderness, and captivity hasn't made Returns soft yet.

Finally, Lori gives her character three Social Traits: *Charismatic, Diplomatic* and *Empathetic*. She ponders taking some Negative Traits as well to reflect Returns' relative ignorance of Garou and human social customs, but decides against it.

Step Three

Next on the agenda are Abilities. *Animal Ken* is a natural choice, as is *Meditation* (for those long nights spent admiring the beauty of the moon). *Survival* seems appropriate, considering the character's history, as does *Primal Urge*. Finally, *Enigmas* seems like a good choice for a Theurge who'll be dealing with the mysteries of the spirits on a regular basis.

Breed, Auspice and Tribe Gifts are already taken care of, so it's time for Backgrounds. A Theurge should know at least one rite, so Lori immediately marks down a Trait in *Rites* (and selects *Ritual of the Questing Stone*, which makes sense for a Garou trying to find her way home). Two more go to *Pure Breed*, which gives the character a sense of connection to her heritage and ancestors. Her other two Background Traits go to *Totem*, a suitably spiritual assignment for a Theurge character.

Returns' Renown depends on her auspice, so Lori checks her options. It turns out that she gets two Wisdom and one of either Glory or Honor. With that in mind, she selects *Inventive, Spiritual* and *Dutiful*. Rage, Gnosis and Willpower have already been taken care of, so it's time to move on to the Final Touches.

Final Touches

Looking over her character, Lori isn't quite satisfied with her Traits. She decides to add a pair of Negative Social Traits—*Naive* x 2 seems to fit—to reflect more accurately the fact that Returns isn't at all comfortable with human society, or even homid Garou. In social situations, Returns-to-Wilderness is likely to be at a severe disadvantage....

On the bright side, however, Lori now has a couple of extra Traits to play with. One of them goes to an additional Physical Trait: *Tenacious*. The other she decides to spend on a Merit: *Higher Purpose*. After all, Returns isn't in this just for herself; she wants to preserve the wilderness for all Garou.

At this point, the stats are all taken care of. Lori now gets to flesh out the character, deciding that Returns escaped from the zoo early on but has been wandering around the city ever since, trying to figure out how exactly to get home. She's spending more and more time in Homid form (under the name "Shanti"—she got it from a billboard) and trying to connect to other Garou. She still has a lot of Garou habits—scratching herself, sitting on the floor and whatnot—which make humans look at her oddly, but she's doing her best in this strange new world.

Satisfied, Lori takes the character off to show her Narrator. He suggests a few basic items that Returns-to-Wilderness might have, but likes the character and clears it for the next session of the game in which he and Lori take part. Now it's time to play.

Mental Traits
Clever, Reflective, Dedicated, Determined, Insightful, Patient, Rational

Social Traits
Charismatic (Naive), Diplomatic (Naive), Empathetic

Physical Traits
Athletic, Enduring, Energetic, Robust, Tough, Tenacious

Fetishes/Talens

Influences

Merits/Flaws
Higher Purpose

Backgrounds
Past Life, Totem
Past Life, Totem
Rites

Abilities
Animal Ken, Primal Urge, Survival
Enigmas, Meditation

Gifts
Scent of The True Form
Name The spiriT
Calm

Gnosis
● ● ● ○ ○ ○ ○ ○ ○ ○
☒ ☒ ☒ □ □ □ □ □ □ □

Willpower
● ● ○ ○ ○ ○ ○ ○ ○ ○
☒ ☒ □ □ □ □ □ □ □ □

Rage
● ○ ○ ○ ○ ○ ○ ○ ○ ○
☒ □ □ □ □ □ □ □ □ □

Rites
RiTual of The QuesTing STone

Laws of the Wild

Player _Lori_

Character _ReTurns-To-wilderness_

Chronicle _The Brass Menagerie_

Nature _Explorer_

Demeanor _Survivor_

Breed _Lupus_

Auspice _Theurge_

Tribe _Children of Gaia_

Rank _Cliath_

Renown

Honor _DuTiful_

Glory _____

Wisdom _InvenTive, SpiriTual_

Chapter Three: Rules

> When I hear any man talk of an unalter-
> able law, the only effect it produces on me is to
> convince me that he is an unalterable fool.
> — Sydney Smith

There are times when a player wants to have her character do something that can't be accomplished through simple roleplaying, such as attacking another person, picking a lock or searching for a file in a computer system. When this happens, you need rules.

Rules are an imperative part of any game; they define what characters can and cannot do. Still, the primary focus of this game is to tell a good story, and it's always best to try to defeat your opponents through roleplaying and manipulation rather than by direct confrontation. Only when confrontation does occur are rules necessary to govern those situations.

Time

Time in **Mind's Eye Theatre** works as it does in real life. It moves forward inexorably, relentlessly. For the most part, everything is played out in real time, and players are expected to stay "in character" unless they have a rules question.

It is assumed that a player is always "in character" during the course of a story. A player should never drop character when interacting with other players. Doing so ruins the atmosphere for everyone involved. Challenges may be talked through, but a player is always considered to be active in the game. If a player needs to take a break, he should inform a Narrator. That player should not interact with any of the other players while out of character.

The only other exception to the "in-character rule" is when a Narrator calls for a "time-out." This may be necessary to resolve a dispute or to change the scene if the story calls for it. When "Time-out!" is called, all players within hearing distance must stop whatever they are doing until the Narrator calls out, "Resume." Time-outs should be kept to a minimum, since they interrupt the flow of the story.

Challenges

He only employs his passion who can make no use of his reason.
— Cicero

During the course of most stories, there comes a time when two or more players come into conflicts that cannot be resolved through roleplaying alone. The system detailed in this chapter allows for the resolution of conflicts simply and quickly, whether they're firefights or tests of will. This sort of face-off is called a challenge, and it makes for a very simple system of conflict resolution. In most cases, a Narrator does not even need to be present when a challenge is played.

Roleplaying does not necessarily have to end when a challenge begins. Experienced players can seamlessly integrate a challenge into their roleplaying so that outsiders don't know that anything unusual is going on. At the players' option, hand signals can be used to indicate when certain Traits and powers are being employed.

In order for this system to work, players need to work together. They have to educate each other on the rules and agree on what Traits can be used in a challenge. Compromise and cooperation are the bywords of the game. Arguments over whether or not a particular Trait bid is appropriate wreck both the momentum and the mood of a game.

The challenge system presented in this chapter is part of the basic rules for the **Mind's Eye Theatre** system. By combining **Laws of the Wild** with other games in the series, players can have werewolves interact with vampires, wraiths, mortals and other types of characters. This system of challenges is also included in **Laws of the Night** and **Oblivion**.

Using Traits

Before you can begin to learn how challenges work, you must first understand what defines a character's capabilities. A character is created by choosing a number of adjectives that describe and define that person as an individual. These adjectives are called Traits, and are fully described in Chapter Two. These Traits are used to declare challenges against other characters or against static forces represented by a Narrator.

Initial Bid

A challenge begins with a player "bidding" one of her Traits against an opponent. At the same time, she must declare what the conditions of the challenge are — firing a gun, attacking with a klaive, etc. The defender must then decide how she will respond. She can either relent immediately or bid one of her own Traits in response.

When players bid Traits against one another, they may use only Traits that could sensibly be used in that situation. Essentially, this means a player can usually use only Traits from the same category as her opponent's Traits. Most challenges are categorized as Physical, Social or Mental, and all Traits used in a challenge must be from the same category. Experienced players may offer each other more creative leeway, but that sort of arrangement works strictly by mutual agreement; don't try it out on an unsuspecting newcomer.

If the defender relents, she automatically loses the challenge. For example, if she were being attacked, she would suffer a wound. If she matches the challenger's bid, the two immediately go to a test (described below). The Traits she has bid are put at risk, as the loser of the test not only loses the challenge, but also the Trait she bid for the rest of the evening.

Testing

Once both parties involved in a challenge have bid a Trait, they immediately go to a test. The test itself is not what you may think — the outcome is random, but no cards or dice are used. The two players face off against one another by playing Rock-Paper-Scissors. It may sound a little silly, but it works.

If you lose the test, you lose the Trait you bid for the duration of the story (usually the rest of the evening). Essentially, you have lost some confidence in your own capabilities and can't call upon them for a while. You can no longer use that Trait effectively, at least until you regain confidence in it.

The test works like the moment in poker when the cards are turned over and the winner is declared. The test produces one of two possible outcomes — either one player is the victor, or the result is a tie.

In the case of a tie, the players must then reveal the number of Traits that they currently have available in the category used (Physical, Social or Mental). The player with the lower number of Traits loses the test and therefore loses the challenge. Note that the number of Traits you've lost in previous challenges, or lost for any other reason, reduces the maximum number of Traits you can bid in ties. The trick to the declaration is that you may lie about the number of Traits you possess, but only by declaring fewer Traits than you actually have — you may never lie and say that you have more Traits than you actually do. This allows you to keep the actual number of Traits you possess a secret, although doing so may be risky. The challenger is always the first to declare his number of Traits. If both players declare the same number of Traits, then the challenge is a draw, and both players lose the Traits they bid.

Example of Play: Helen, a Black Fury, is attacking Grady, a Bone Gnawer. Helen begins by bidding the Physical Trait: *Ferocious* ("I am Ferocious as I sink my teeth into your shoulder."). Grady, who is only interested in surviving her attack and escaping, bids the Trait: *Resilient* ("But even as you bite through my three layers of dirty T-shirts, I know I'm Resilient enough to shrug it off!"). Helen and Grady decide to test. They both play "Rock" — a draw. Helen, who is the attacker, must decide how many of her seven Physical Traits she wishes to declare. She has nothing to hide, so she declares all seven. Grady, who is a

Ragabash, only has five Physical Traits. He loses the test. Grady also loses his Physical Trait of *Resilient* and takes one wound. Furthermore, Grady does not escape, and Helen can attack him again if she chooses to continue.

Incidentally, certain advanced powers allow some characters to use gestures other than Rock, Paper and Scissors. Before players can use the gestures in a test, however, they must explain what they are and how they are used.

Rock-Paper-Scissors

If you do not happen to know (or remember) what we mean by Rock-Paper-Scissors, here's the concept: You and another person face off and, on the count of three, show one of three hand gestures. "Rock" is a basic fist. "Paper" is just a flat hand. "Scissors" is represented by sticking out two fingers. You then compare the two gestures to determine the winner. Rock crushes Scissors. Scissors cuts Paper. Paper covers Rock. Identical signs indicate a tie.

Adjudication

If you have a question or argument about the rules or the conditions of a challenge, you need to find a Narrator to make a judgment. Try to remain in character while you look for a Narrator. Any interruption in the progress of the story should be avoided if at all possible, so work out problems with other players if you can. If you do not know the correct application of a certain rule, it's usually better to wing it rather than interrupt the flow of the game. Cooperation is the key to telling a good story.

Complications

There are many ways in which a challenge can be made more complicated. The basic rules are enough to resolve most disputes, but the following rules add a few bells and whistles.

Negative Traits

Many characters have Negative Traits; these are Traits that can be used against a character by his opponent. During the initial bid of any challenge, after you have each bid one Trait, you can call out a Negative Trait that you believe your opponent possesses. If he does indeed possess the Negative Trait, your opponent is forced to bid an additional Trait, although you only have to risk your one Trait as usual. If he does not possess that Negative Trait, *you* must risk an additional Trait. You may call out as many Negative Traits as you wish during the initial bid phase of a challenge, as long as you can pay the price if you're wrong.

If your opponent does not have additional Traits to bid, then your Trait is not at risk during the challenge. Additionally, if you guess more than one Negative Trait that your opponent cannot match, you gain that many additional Traits in the case of a tie or an overbid (See p. 161). The same works in reverse, favoring your opponent if you do not have additional Traits remaining to match incorrect Negative Trait guesses.

Example of Play: Ray, a Shadow Lord Galliard, is using his *Persuasion* Gift and challenging Camille, a Toreador vampire, in a Social Challenge. He is trying to get her to abandon her position and walk over to where he's standing.

He bids his Trait: *Commanding* ("My Commanding tone of voice overwhelms you and you feel compelled to approach me."), and she responds with *Alluring* ("I stand by the door, aloof and Alluring, forcing you to come to me instead."). Ray then suggests that she is also *Condescending* ("You may be Condescending, but I can tell you're intrigued."). However, Camille does not possess this Negative Trait ("I'm not Condescending, I merely detest your arrogance and I'm going to leave."). Therefore Ray would have to risk an additional Social Trait, such as *Persuasive* ("Perhaps I can be Persuasive enough to convince you to stay and hear me out?"), if he wished to continue the challenge.

It can be risky to bid Negative Traits, but if you're sure about what you're doing, you can raise the stakes for your opponent, possibly even to the point where she relents rather than risking additional Traits. Just make sure your sources of information are dependable.

Overbidding

Overbidding is the system by which elder Garou (who often have considerably more Traits than less-experienced opponents) may prevail in a challenge, even if they lose the initial test. An elder Garou with 18 Social Traits should be able to crush a cub with five. This system is designed to make that possible.

Once a test has been resolved, the loser has the option of calling for an "overbid." In order to call an overbid, you must risk a new Trait; the original one has already been lost. At this point, the two players must reveal the number of applicable Traits they possess in the appropriate category, starting with the player who called for the overbid. If you have double the number of Traits as your opponent in that category, you may attempt another test. As with a tie, you may state a number of Traits less than the actual number you have and keep your true power secret. This can be dangerous though, unless you are completely confident in your estimation of your opponent's abilities.

Example of Play: Sir Godfrey, a Silver Fang Ahroun, has decided to crush a whelp Fianna Ragabash like a bug. A test was called, and Sir Godfrey lost. At this point, Sir Godfrey, confident of his abilities, calls for an overbid. Sir Godfrey is in Crinos form and has 15 Physical Traits, while the poor Fianna, Gerry, is in Homid form and has only five Physical Traits. Sir Godfrey risks an additional Trait: *Relentless* ("As I show my contempt for your insolence, I Relentlessly swing again!"). They do a second test. This time they tie. Sir Godfrey clearly has more Traits, and therefore wins. At the end of this challenge, Sir Godfrey has lost the initial Trait he bid from the first test. However, because he overbid, he has won the challenge and wounded Gerry. Gerry has also lost the initial Trait he bid because Sir Godfrey has won the second test ("Show mercy on a poor Ragabash! I was only joking!").

A challenger who fails on a Social or Mental Challenge must wait five realtime minutes (and not spend them arguing over the results of the previous challenge — you can't protest a ruling with a Narrator for 4:58, then drop your argument and say, "Oh look, time's up,") before repeating the failed challenge. This does not include trials that are failed but then redeemed through overbids.

Static Challenges

Sometimes you may have to undergo a challenge against a Narrator rather than against another player, such as when you are trying to pick a lock or summon a spirit. In such circumstances, you merely bid the Trait that would be appropriate, then immediately perform a test against the Narrator. Before the test is made, the Narrator decides on the difficulty of the task that you are attempting — in other words, the number of Traits you are bidding against (so you can overbid if you fail). The test proceeds exactly as it would if you were testing against another character. Of course, you may overbid in a Static Challenge, but beware, because the Narrator can overbid as well. The number of Traits attached to the challenge should represent the difficulty and danger inherent in the challenge.

Sometimes Narrators may leave notes on objects, such as books, doors or even fetishes. These notes indicate the type of challenges that must be won for something to occur (such as understanding a book, picking a lock or identifying a fetish). With experience, you may learn how difficult it is to open a locked door. However, difficulty ratings can be as different as lock types.

Simple Tests

Simple Tests are used to determine if you can do something successfully when there is no real opposition. Simple Tests are often called for when using Gifts. Most Simple Tests do not require you to risk or bid Traits, although some may.

When a Simple Test is called, a test (Rock-Paper-Scissors) is performed against a Narrator. In most cases, the player succeeds on a win or a tie, although in some cases, it may be necessary for the player to win for him to receive any benefit from the challenge.

Health

A character in **The Apocalypse** has five Health Levels; these represent the amount of injury the character can endure. These levels are: Healthy, Bruised, Wounded, Incapacitated and Mortally Wounded. If a healthy character loses a combat challenge, she becomes Bruised. If she loses two, she becomes Wounded, and so on.

• **Bruised** — When a character is Bruised, she is only slightly injured, having perhaps suffered a few scrapes and bruises, but little more. In order to enter a new challenge, she must risk an additional Trait. Thus, even to have a chance in a challenge, a Bruised character must bid at least two Traits.

Example of Play: Howls-at-Dawn has just been on the losing end of a challenge, and is again assaulted by his foe, Logarann. However, this time, Howls-at-Dawn must now risk two Traits in order to defend himself. Logarann, however, needs to risk only one Trait.

• **Wounded** — When a character is Wounded, she is badly hurt. She might be bleeding freely from open wounds, and may even have broken bones. She must bid two Traits to have a chance in a challenge. In addition, she always loses during a test on a tie, even if she has more Traits than her opponent. If she has fewer Traits, her opponent gets a free extra test. (**Note:** If Traits permit, a character can always attempt to overbid, even in a situation such as this.)

Example of Play: Howls-at-Dawn has now been Wounded by Logarann, who continues to press the attack. Howls-at-Dawn is in pretty bad shape now. He must risk two additional Physical Traits to have a chance in the challenge. However, he has also lost the past two challenges to Logarann. Because of this, Howls-at-Dawn has already lost three Physical Traits. He has considerably fewer Physical Traits than Logarann, so he will not only lose on ties, but Logarann now gets two tests to see if he can Incapacitate Howls-at-Dawn. If Logarann wins or ties either of these two tests, Howls-at-Dawn will be Incapacitated (see below).

• **Incapacitated** — When a character is Incapacitated, she is completely out of play for at least 10 minutes. Once awake, the character is still immobile, and may not enter into challenges until she has healed at least one Health Level. She is at the mercy of other characters. She may not change forms until she is conscious.

• **Mortally Wounded** — When a character is Mortally Wounded, she is near death. She also immediately reverts to her breed form (her "natural form"). One Physical Trait is lost for every 10 minutes that she is without medical assistance. Ten minutes after her last Physical Trait is expended, she dies.

Battle Scars

Every time a character is mortally wounded, she gets a battle scar. These battle scars can add up; each one is nastier than the last. However, battle scars are also worthy of Renown, for they show, indisputably, that the Garou has faced great peril and survived. The first three battle scars are light scars. Light battle scars are rarely bothersome — they occasionally itch during the winter. The next two battle scars are deep scars. Deep scars offer a one-Trait penalty if an opponent specifically targets them. However, if an opponent does that, she will probably lose Honor Renown. Finally, once a character has been Mortally Wounded six times, serious permanent injuries result. The following list includes some possibilities. The players or Narrators can choose one injury that they feel is appropriate for the circumstances, or the effect can be chosen randomly.

• **Improper Bone Setting** — A limb has been set improperly. The character has the added Negative Physical Trait: *Lame*.

• **Skull Head** — At some point, the side of your head was bashed in, and even though the wound has healed, part of your skull can still be seen. The character gains the Negative Social Trait: *Hideous*.

• **Broken Jaw** — Your jaw was broken and did not reset properly. You have trouble speaking and cannot always make yourself understood verbally. This should be roleplayed.

• **Missing Eye** — One of your eyes is gone. You lack depth perception. You must risk twice as many Traits involving any vision-based challenges or range-based challenges, such as noticing something hidden or operating a firearm at anything other than close range.

• **Collapsed Lung** — Your lung was punctured in battle, and you now have trouble breathing. You wheeze a lot, and you also gain a Negative Physical Trait (either *Decrepit* or *Lethargic*).

• **Missing Fingers** — One of your hands has lost several fingers. Your claw attacks will do aggravated damage only if you risk an additional Physical Trait in a challenge. You also gain the Negative Physical Trait: *Clumsy*.

• **Severe Damage** — If a character already has several major battle scars, the Narrator may elect to give her more extreme damage. This could mean completely losing a limb, suffering from spinal cord damage or even sustaining brain damage. The exact nature of the battle scar and its impact on the character are at the discretion of the Narrator.

Healing

Werewolves heal wounds at a very rapid pace, recovering one Health Level every five minutes, unless the damage is aggravated (see below). However, Garou in breed form do **not** heal faster than a normal human or wolf; the lone exception to this rule is metis in Crinos. Additionally, a Garou must remain still while healing. While healing damage, a Garou may not engage in any other actions or participate in any challenges. Should a Garou in the process of healing be challenged, the healing process is considered to be interrupted and no partial benefit accrues from it.

In other words, a Garou who is two Health Levels down and who rests for seven minutes before being discovered and challenged by a roving Black Spiral Dancer receives the benefit of the first five minutes' rest (one Health Level) but that's all. Furthermore, assuming the Garou defeats the Dancer and resumes resting, the two extra minutes from the first period of rest don't carry over to the Garou's second bout of R&R.

Aggravated Wounds

Wounds that cannot be healed by the Garou's natural healing powers are called aggravated wounds. Such wounds are usually caused by injury from fire, silver or the claws or teeth of a supernatural creature, such as another Garou or a vampire. A Storyteller can also deem any injury to be aggravated, depending on the circumstances. A full night of rest is required to heal one level of aggravated damage.

Silver

Silver is the bane of all Garou. All Garou suffer one Health Level of aggravated damage for every 10 seconds they remain in contact with silver. Likewise, any wounds caused by silver weapons result in aggravated damage.

Lupus and homid Garou do not take aggravated damage from silver in Breed Form. Likewise, silver does not do aggravated damage to Garou in Homid.

Carrying a silver object (such as a klaive) reduces a Garou's current Gnosis by one. This effect lasts for 24 hours after the object is discarded.

Mob Scene

During the course of many stories, there will inevitably be situations that involve challenges in which several people want to take part. Multiparty challenges can be confusing, but if you follow these simple guidelines, you shouldn't have much difficulty. These rules are most useful in combat situations, but they can be used with nearly any sort of group challenge.

The first thing you need to do is decide who is challenging whom. This is usually obvious, but when it's not, you need a quick way to work things out. Simply have everyone involved count to three at the same time. On three, each player points at the individual he is challenging.

The first challenge that must be resolved involves the person who has the most people pointing at him. Determine what the appropriate category of Traits would be — Physical, Social or Mental. Each player pointing at the defender must bid one appropriate Trait. The attacking group must also choose a leader. The defender must bid as many Traits as there are people opposing him. If he does not have enough Traits to do so, he automatically loses the challenge. If he does have enough Traits, a test is performed between the defender and the chosen leader of the attackers. The rest of the challenge continues as normal, although any comparison of Traits or overbidding may **only** be done by the group leader. In other words, only the leader's Traits come into play at this point — the rest of the mob doesn't affect the action.

If the defender wins the test, he is unharmed, but he can choose to affect one member of the attacking group. Usually, as in the case of a combat, this would mean inflicting one wound. Additionally, all the Traits bid by the attackers are lost. If the attackers win, they may inflict one wound on the defender, and he loses all the Traits he had risked.

After the first challenge is concluded, go on to the next one. Continue the process until each character who declared an action has been the target of a challenge or has donated Traits.

Even in a mob scene, no more than five people can attack any single individual at once. There's only so much room around a single target, after all. (**Note**: If this number is exceeded during the initial "pointing" stage, the Narrator decides who has to choose a new target or action.)

Order of Challenges

Some people question exactly how a player can respond when challenged. Typically, if someone initiates a Physical Challenge, the defender can only respond with Physical Traits, unless he possesses a Gift or some other Ability that is considered to be always active. He cannot respond with the activation of a Gift or another Ability until after the first challenge has been completed. Social and Mental Challenges work the same way.

Note: Gifts and other powers that allow for a pre-emptive strike (such as *Spirit of the Fray*) give the Gifted character the chance to initiate a challenge that occurs under surpise conditions *before* the stated challenge.

Movement in Combat

Note: These rules can also be added to **Masquerade** or **Oblivion**.

Anyone in or just entering combat is subject to the "three step rule." You may take three steps during any combat action and still attack. Moving one step is considered walking cautiously, two steps is moving directly (down one Trait in Physical Challenges), and three steps is running (also down a Trait in Physical Challenges). Any Gift, fetish, etc., that allows greater movement or multiple actions in combat affects movement accordingly. Two actions equal six steps — a Gift that allows for an additional action would allow you to take three additional steps, and so on.

Chapter Four: Systems

Men, at some time, are masters of their fates. The fault, dear Brutus, lies not in our stars but in ourselves
— William Shakespeare, *Julius Caesar*

This chapter discusses some of the additional rules and complications that sometimes come into play in **Laws of the Wild**. It also describes a multitude of different systems for resolving character interactions. However, this chapter is more a set of permutations than a set of rules. There is nothing contained in the next several pages that you *need* to know, only things that you might *want* to know. These are complications that can add more detail and depth to the game.

Combat

To be prepared for war is one of the most effectual ways of preserving peace.
— George Washington

The basic challenge system used in **Laws of the Wild** has already been presented in Chapter Three. This section contains a few basic modifications to the combat system, as well as some elaboration on it.

Combat is the usual intent behind Physical Challenges. Essentially, combat involves two characters in physical conflict. The players agree what the outcome of the challenge will be, each player bids an appropriate Trait, and a test is performed to determine the victor. The following section allows for variations on those basic rules, such as situations involving surprise or weapons.

The agreed outcome of a Physical Challenge is often the loser being injured. This is not the only possible result, though. For instance, a Garou could say that he wants to wrest a weapon from his opponent's hands or try to trip him. The result can be nearly anything the two parties agree on, whether it's simply raking someone with claws or throwing him through a window. The results of a combat challenge may also be different for both participants. (For example, if a frenzied Get of Fenris elder is trying to rake a Child of Gaia fostern with his claws, the Child of Gaia might try to restrain her opponent instead of hurting him.)

Surprise

If a player does not respond within three seconds of the declaration of a Physical Challenge, the character is considered to have been surprised — he is not fully prepared for what's coming. Sometimes a player is busy with another activity, doesn't hear a challenge or is playing a character who just isn't prepared for the attack (i.e., the character is led into an ambush). It is considered highly improper to sneak around whispering challenges to try to get the element of surprise.

Surprise simply means that the outcome of the first challenge in a fight can only harm the surprised defender, not the challenger. For instance, if a player did not respond in time to an attack, but still won the challenge, the challenger would not be injured. Furthermore, if the challenger loses the test, she may call for a second challenge by risking another Trait, since she was operating from the benefit of surprise. With the second challenge, play continues, and winners and losers of a challenge are determined as normal. Overbidding is permitted for both challenger and challenged in surprise situations.

Surprise is only in effect for the first challenge of a conflict; all further challenges are resolved normally, as explained below.

Weapons

For obvious reasons, no real weapons are ever allowed in **Mind's Eye Theatre** games. Even nonfunctional props are forbidden if they can be mistaken for weapons. This system does not use props of any kind, nor are players required (or allowed) to strike one another. Weapons are purely an abstraction in this game. Instead, characters should use weapon cards, which display the Traits and pertinent details of a particular weapon. The damage a weapon inflicts is limited only by mutual agreement, although it is generally assumed that an injury incurred from a blow reduces the target by a Health Level.

A weapon gives its wielder extra Traits for combat or other appropriate challenges. Sometimes this advantage is offset by a disadvantage in terms of a Negative Trait. Each weapon has one to three extra Traits; these Traits may be used in any challenge in which the weapon is employed. These Traits *cannot* be used in place of Traits when placing an initial bid. Instead, they add to the user's total when she is comparing Traits, such as in the case of a tie during a test or an overbid. In addition, some weapons have special abilities that may be used, such as causing extra levels of damage or affecting more than one target.

Disadvantages are weaknesses inherent to a weapon. These can be used by the wielder's opponent in precisely the same way as Negative Traits. The weapon's Negative Traits can only be used against the wielder of that weapon. Negative Traits for a weapon must be appropriate to the situation. For instance, if you are firing a gun and your opponent wants to use the gun's Negative Trait: *Loud* against you, that Negative Trait could be ignored if you have taken the time to find some means of silencing the weapon.

If a Negative Trait of your weapon is named by your opponent, and that Trait applies to the situation, you suffer a 1-Trait penalty (i.e., you are required to risk an additional Trait). If your opponent calls out a Negative Trait of your weapon that doesn't apply to the situation, your opponent suffers a 1-Trait penalty in the challenge.

Statistics for weapons are written on cards and carried along with your character card. Weapon cards specify the capacities of each weapon. Weapon cards allow other players to see that you actually possess a weapon — when you have a weapon card in your hand, you are considered to be holding the weapon. Each weapon has a concealablity rating. If the weapon is not concealable, you must have that card on display at all times. You cannot, for example, pull a rifle out of your pocket. Instead, you must carry that card in hand at all times or, optionally, you could pin the card to your shirt, indicating that the rifle is slung over your shoulder.

Bidding Weapon Traits

During a normal hand-to-hand fight, characters bid Physical Traits against their opponents' Physical Traits. However, if a character is using firearms, he uses Mental Traits instead. If his opponent is also using a firearm, she bids Mental Traits as well. If the opponent is not using a firearm and is merely trying to dodge, then the attacker uses Mental Traits to attack, while the defender uses her Physical Traits to dodge. This is one of the few instances in which Traits associated with different Attributes may be used against one another.

Weapon Examples

Knife — This easily-concealed weapon is very common.
Bonus Traits: 2
Negative Traits: *Short*
Concealability: Pocket

Club — This can be anything from a chair leg to a tree limb.
Bonus Traits: 2
Negative Traits: Clumsy
Concealability: Jacket

Broken Bottle — A good example of a weapon made from scratch.
Bonus Traits: 1
Negative Traits: *Fragile*
Concealability: Jacket (ouch!)

Sword — This long-edged blade is nearly impossible to conceal, unless you have long years of experience.

Bonus Traits: 3

Negative Traits: *Heavy*

Concealability: Trenchcoat

Klaive — An artistic, powerful weapon favored by the Garou.

Bonus Traits: 3

Negative Traits: *Bulky* (this Trait does not apply when the character is in Crinos form)

Concealability: Jacket

Pistol — This covers nearly any sort of handgun.

Bonus Traits: 2

Negative Traits: *Loud*

Concealability: Pocket

Rifle — Favored by many types of hunters.

Bonus Traits: 3

Negative Traits: *Loud*

Concealability: You've got to be kidding.

Shotgun — This powerful weapon fires a spray of pellets, making targets easy to hit and ballistics checks nearly impossible.

Bonus Traits: 3

Negative Traits: *Loud*

Concealability: Trenchcoat

Special Ability: A shotgun may affect up to three targets if they are standing immediately next to each other and are further than 20 feet from the person firing the shotgun. This is resolved with a single challenge against the group. The Traits are risked against the entire group. Up to three separate tests are performed (one test for each target). In this fashion, it is possible to simultaneously wound up to three opponents in a single challenge. The Trait risked by the attacker is used against all three opponents. If any of the three opponents win, the attacker loses that Trait. However, that Trait still applies to all three tests within that group challenge. Thus, a character can challenge up to three opponents while only risking one Trait with this weapon. Also, a shotgun can cause two levels of damage to a single target standing within five feet.

Submachine Gun — This weapon is very powerful, though difficult to conceal.

Bonus Traits: 3

Negative Traits: *Loud*

Concealability: Jacket

Special Ability: A submachine gun may affect up to five targets if they're standing immediately next to each other and are further than 10 feet from the person firing the gun. This is resolved with a single challenge against a group (as described under the section on shotguns).

Ranged Combat

Many weapons allow a character to stand at a distance from a target and engage him in combat. In such situations, the character must still go over to the target (after shouting "Bang!") and engage in a challenge.

If a character surprises her opponent, even if she loses the first test, she has the option of calling for a second test. Once the second challenge is called, play continues as normal with that new challenge. The target is considered to be surprised for the first attack, and if he has no ranged weapon with which to return fire, he is considered "surprised" for as long as the aggressor can attack him without facing resistance (that is, if she wins on a challenge, she doesn't take damage).

If the target is aware of the attack before it happens and has a ranged weapon of his own, he is not considered to be surprised for the first attack. He may shoot back right away, and challenges are resolved as stated below.

After the first shot is fired (and the first challenge is resolved), the target may attempt to return fire (assuming he is armed). The loser of a firefight challenge loses a Health Level.

If the defender is unarmed, he may declare his victory condition as escape (providing he is not cornered). If the defender wins the challenge, the attacker is still unharmed, but his target, the defender, has escaped from view and must be searched out if the attacker decides to press the attack. In instances such as this one, a new challenge cannot be made for at least five minutes.

Cover

Fighting with hand-to-hand weapons — clubs, knives, klaives, swords and whatnot — requires that combatants be within arm's reach of each other. Fighting with ranged weapons allows combatants to stand some distance apart; therefore, participants can "dive for cover." When resolving each ranged combat challenge, each combatant can present one Trait of cover to add to his total number of Traits. These cover Traits may not be used for bidding, but they do add to a player's total if Traits are compared. This cover can take the form of whatever obstacles are around and within reach (*don't* actually dive for them). A Narrator might be required to describe what cover is around, but if combatants know the area, they can agree upon what cover is available. In some instances, there may be no cover around, leaving a combatant in the open with only his own defensive Traits for protection.

If cover is extensive (a brick wall, perhaps) it may be worth more than one Trait. The number of Traits available for cover is left for challengers to agree upon, or for a Narrator to decree. Hiding behind a car, for example, might be worth two Traits, while hiding behind a piece of sheetrock might count only as one. If one combatant goes completely under cover (he cannot be seen at all and is thoroughly protected), he is considered impossible to hit. The attacker must change his position to get another clear shot.

Specialized Fighting Styles

Buying a specialized fighting style under the Melee Ability allows you to describe how your character moves to allow retests, but does not allow you to do extra damage or specific injuries.

Renown

Renown governs ranking among the Garou. Rank determines what level of Gifts a Garou is able to learn, how powerful she may be and how well she is respected and known throughout Garou society.

There are three kinds of Renown Traits that characters can collect: Honor, Glory and Wisdom. Each auspice has its own requirements for rising in Rank. In general, Garou try to excel in the areas of Renown that are favored by their particular auspices.

Honor is adherence to the Litany and an indication of how well a Garou upholds his own word and code of ethics. It is also traditional "chivalry," as well as the idea of remaining true to yourself and your ideals. The Philodox of a sept are chiefly concerned with matters of Honor, and they are the ones who nominate a Garou to receive Honor Renown.

Glory is willingness to throw yourself headlong into the fight against the Wyrm. It represents bravery, prowess and success in the face of certain doom. A truly glorious Garou has fought well and often, and continues to make a name for himself by defeating the Wyrm in a manner that shows style. The Ahroun of a sept are chiefly concerned with matters of Glory, and they nominate a Garou to receive Glory Renown.

Wisdom is inner strength and knowledge. When disputes are solved without bloodshed, when the Wyrm is defeated by simple means rather than violent ones, when a Garou devotes himself full-time to the service of his totem or to spiritual meditation, the Garou is considered Wise. Since the Theurges of a sept are chiefly concerned with matters of Wisdom, they are the ones who nominate a Garou to receive Wisdom Renown.

Nominations

Nominations of Garou for Renown can be decided on by the auspices responsible for the particular aspects of Renown. This can either be done as a majority-rule vote, or by having one elder of the auspice decide who gets the Renown. It is really up to the characters as to how they do this, but a Storyteller may step in as an angered elder or spirit if Renown is dealt out too easily or is not given when truly deserved.

The general rule about Renown is this: A Storyteller can tell you, as a player, what your character's auspice, tribe or breed would normally do, but she cannot make your character give or refuse to give Renown. Only Narrator characters can interact with your character to attempt to influence such matters — and you can bet they will if you are abusing this system.

For more on awarding Renown in-game, see Moots (p. 210).

Renown Awards

The following list can be used as a guideline for circumstances that could warrant Renown awards. These situations are by no means set in stone, and they are always up to the individual interpretation of the characters involved.

Remember, as a character earns Renown, it becomes more difficult to outdo past actions to gain more Renown (i.e., a character may earn Glory the first time he kills a 13th-generation vampire, but the second time this happens his packmates and the sept will not be so impressed). Such successes will be expected from the character. To translate this into the game, each player should keep a written list of what he did to earn each Renown Trait. In order to earn another point for the same general action, the character must excel or succeed in an extremely diverse way. (i.e., teaching several young Garou of the importance of the basic tenets of the Litany will not be worthy of more than one Wisdom Renown. Mediating a conflict between two Garou fairly, then doing the same later, but for two elder Garou and several vampires instead, would be worthy of a second award of Wisdom Renown for the same general action).

Losing Renown, however, can be a very simple — and speedy — process. Every time a Garou takes an action that is dishonorable, inglorious or unwise, she can lose Renown. An appropriate Renown Trait is removed from her list, and the Garou must successfully once again perform the general action that earned the Renown in the first place in order for her to be eligible for that Renown Trait again.

If Narrators notice that a character is on an endless cycle of gaining and losing Renown over one particular action or set of actions, they may wish to intervene and declare that the character is no longer eligible for Renown from that source. Constant repetition of a pattern of actions indicates that the Garou has not learned from her past mistakes, and as such is not truly worthy of Renown.

Glorious Actions

Surviving an incapacitating wound

Gaining a battle scar

Surviving a toxic waste attack

Attacking a minion of the Wyrm without regard for personal safety

Defeating a minion of the Wyrm (if there was some real personal risk involved)

Traveling beyond the Near Umbra to another Realm and surviving

Performing or participating in a *Rite of Caern Building*

Owning a klaive (this is awarded once, after three moons of use)

Helping to prevent a caern from being overrun by anyone

Dying while defending a caern (posthumous)

Preventing the Wyrm from taking over a caern (a Garou can receive more than one Glory Trait for this action if it is done without any assistance)

Accepting a sept position

Telling a good story at a moot

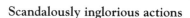

Scandalously inglorious actions

Cowering from a foe

Begging a minion of the Wyrm for your life

Participating in a failed Great Hunt

Suffering the *Rite of Ostracism*

Failing or refusing to prevent a caern from being overrun by the Wyrm

Refusing a sept position

Suffering from a fox frenzy (running in fear)

Honorable Actions

Showing restraint in the face of certain death

Performing a *Moot Rite* (first time only)

Performing a *Rite of Passage* (first time only)

Performing a *Rite of Caern Building* (earned again only if the subsequent caern is of higher Rank than the last)

Performing a Punishment Rite (only one per rite)

Owning a klaive (only once, after three moons of use)

Consistently helping to guard a caern, even when you'd rather be somewhere else

Helping to prevent a threat of the caern being overrun by the Wyrm before things come to blows

Teaching another Garou a valuable lesson

Reciting part of the Silver Record at a moot (once per each evening-long part)

Gaining the position of pack leader (awarded once)

Serving in a sept position faithfully for one year

Upholding the Litany during a controversial issue

Mediating a dispute fairly and impartially

Consistently keeping your promises

Being truthful in the face of adversity

Telling an epic story at a moot

Showing mercy to a wayward Garou

Protecting a helpless human or wolf

Supporting a person who is accused of a crime (who is later proven innocent)

Making sacrifices to protect the Veil

Repairing the Veil

Scandalously dishonorable actions

Falsely accusing anyone of being of the Wyrm

Refusing to perform a *Moot Rite*

Suffering the *Stone of Scorn*

Suffering the *Rite of Ostracism*

Accidentally breaking or losing a klaive

Not staying on watch at a caern when a more tempting activity presents itself

Refusing to help guard a caern

Failing to prevent a caern from being overrun by the Wyrm

Refusing any sept position

Challenging someone too far above or below your own Rank

Mediating a dispute unfairly

Failing to keep your promises

Being deceptive

Speaking poorly of the Garou as a whole

Speaking poorly of one's tribe, auspice or pack

"Crying Wolf" (i.e., summoning the Ahroun of a sept when there is no
   real danger present)

Not protecting a helpless Garou

Not protecting a helpless wolf or human as appropriate

Performing heinous acts while in the thrall of the Wyrm

Abandoning your pack in a time of need

Harming/rending the Veil

Wise Actions

Besting someone (even a spirit) in a riddle contest

Showing restraint in the face of certain death

Ending a threat without serious harm to any Garou

Revealing with certain proof that a Kinfolk or Garou is "of the Wyrm"

Purifying a Wyrm-tainted object, person or place

Successfully completing a spirit quest in the Umbra

Giving a prophetic warning that later comes true

Discovering ancient Garou lore

Performing a *Rite of Caern Building*

Discovering/creating a new rite or ritual

Discovering/creating a new Gift

Creating a fetish

Sacrificing a fetish for the good of the sept or tribe

Keeping a caern safe through trickery or imagination

Teaching another Garou a valuable lesson

Upholding the Litany

Consistently giving good advice

Healing a fellow Garou (not a pack member) selflessly

Scandalously unwise actions

Attacking a much more powerful force without aid

Falsely accusing another of being "of the Wyrm"

Failing to complete a spirit quest in the Umbra

Giving a prophetic warning that does not come true

Giggling, joking or otherwise being disrespectful during a rite (leeway is
   given on this one for a Ragabash)

For a homid, ignoring one's wolf nature for too long

For a metis, attempting to hide one's deformity

Living alone or away from your pack

Breaking the Litany

Consistently giving bad advice

Having trickery backfire

Injuring a fellow Garou during a frenzy

Having poor relations with nearby Kinfolk

Teaching Garou knowledge to one of the Wyrm's minions

Confirmation

When all is said and done, and all Renown nominations have been made at a sept, the elders of each auspice present the Galliards with their nominations. At that point, the Galliards must make a decision. Will they confirm the nominations by singing of the subject's new Renown, or will they negate the nomination by refusing to recognize the story that the Renown Trait represents? Ultimately, the eldest Galliard has veto power, and can cancel a nomination at any time. In games without enough players to fill all these roles, they can either be played by the Storyteller or the Renown must be determined by vote of the characters. Do not punish characters by denying Renown just because the group is missing a key elder from an auspice.

Renown can also be earned at Moots. See pp. 213-214.

Scandal

Finally, even after a Renown Trait has been awarded, a Ragabash can attempt to destroy a character's Renown by speaking scandalously. These scandals must have an element of truth, and must be agreed upon by the Ragabash elder of the sept. So, in a sense, the Ragabash must prove the truth of the scandalous rumors. Still, it is the Galliards who must also confirm the scandal, thus authorizing the loss of Renown. Only one Renown Trait can be affected per scandal.

The Wyrm often finds out when a scandal has occurred among the Garou. A Bane might approach a Garou to "help" him through his crisis by offering him revenge or more power to gain back his lost Renown.

Loss of Rank

It is possible for a Garou to gain Rank and then lose it later through scandal. This is the way of the Garou — a werewolf must purify himself before attempting to rise in Rank.

Benefits of Renown

Aside from the fact that a Garou needs to accumulate Renown Traits in order to be able to challenge for Rank, Renown Traits give a character other benefits.

First of all, an appropriate Renown Trait can be used in place of Social Traits during any Social Challenge. In order to use a Renown Trait, the Garou must somehow work the Trait into the roleplaying appropriately. For example, an Ahroun trying to intimidate someone might say, "You must realize what you are doing. Are you going to deny Alaric the Glorious? I've killed a Nexus Crawler!" Even if a Renown Trait is temporarily lost during a challenge, such a loss is only temporary and does not reduce the character's Rank.

Note: A player attempting to use a Renown Trait instead of a Social one must make it clear exactly what he is doing; otherwise it can be difficult to distinguish a legitimate bid from character braggadocio.

Each Renown Trait that a Garou gains also gives her the opportunity to learn a new Gift, as long as the character has sufficient Experience to do so (for more information on spending Experience on Gifts, see p. 203). A character must also petition the spirits to teach her a Gift. Gifts are taught, not acquired instantaneously. Moreover, a character cannot learn a new Gift unless she has a new Renown Trait to demonstrate her eligibility. If the character wishes to learn a Gift that is outside her tribe, auspice or breed, she must have two Renown Traits to gain permission.

Tokens

A Garou can represent "favor" by creating a token, a small gift of some kind, usually a necklace, bracelet or other piece of jewelry. A token can also be as simple as a keyring, a computer disk, a trading card or a seashell, so long as it is easily identifiable. Each token a Garou makes should look roughly the same so that it can be identified as being the mark of a particular Garou. By creating a token, a werewolf can temporarily loan *one* of his Renown Traits to another Garou, to be used in Social Challenges or to lend the token's creator's "support" to other enterprises. So long as a Garou holds a Token, the creator of the token may not use that Renown Trait in challenges; it's out "on loan" and is inaccessible.

The number of tokens that a character can create is determined by her Rank (see below). A fostern can make only one, an adren can make two, an athro can make three, an elder can make five and a legend can make seven. A token does not permit its recipient to learn a new Gift, and it does not count toward his total Renown Traits; after all, it is just on loan. A token does grant its bearer more authority, however, and many adren who hold sept positions receive tokens from elders.

The Ranks

In general, the Garou method of gaining Rank is based on auspice, but Rank is also a measure of the respect and loyalty that the Garou feel for one of their own. Rank has its privileges, as well as its duties.

Cub - Rank Zero

This is the lowest Rank, and it is not the normal starting-point for an **Apocalypse** character. However, it can be fun to play someone who's just gone through her First Change. You have to roleplay learning all about the Garou, and discover the secret lore of your character's auspice and tribe.

There are benefits to being a cub. First, no one is allowed to challenge a cub, on the grounds that cubs just aren't worth the effort. Second, everyone will likely come to a cub's aid if he gets into danger. However, cubs are only allowed to learn their breed and tribe Gifts; they learn their auspice Gifts after their *Rite of Passage*. Many septs include a Garou with the title Den Mother or Den Father. Such Garou watch over the cubs to make sure that they respect their elders and don't get into *too* much trouble.

Note: Playing a cub is an excellent way to be introduced to the game as a whole. If a local troupe is set up with a Den Mother, a new player can easily join the story and be tutored in the game as a matter of course while still playing. Learning about the Garou this way can be a lot of fun.

Gifts Available: None (at start, but may learn Basic from their breed and tribe)

Maximum Traits per Category: 10

Maximum Willpower, Gnosis and Rage: 3

Renown Requirements: None (must earn Cliath Rank Renown for auspice to be considered ready for *Rite of Passage*)

Duties: Cubs are required to learn as much as they can.

Cliath - Rank One

As soon as a Garou passes her *Rite of Passage* she is considered a "teenager" in the Garou Nation, and must prove herself worthy of promotion to a position of responsibility. A cliath cannot hold a sept office or take command of any group projects. It is the cliath's responsibility to find her place and become proficient enough in her auspice to be considered worthy of authority.

Gifts Available: Basic

Maximum Traits Per Category: 11

Maximum Willpower, Gnosis and Rage: 4

Renown Requirements

• **Ragabash**: Any Three Renown
• **Theurge**: Two Wisdom and One Glory or Honor
• **Philodox**: Two Honor and One Wisdom
• **Galliard**: One Glory, Two Wisdom or Honor
• **Ahroun**: Two Glory, One Honor

Other Requirements: A Cliath must learn three initial Gifts and swear an oath of loyalty to her sept or tribe, usually at a ceremony that takes place after the completion of her *Rite of Passage*.

Duties: Cliath are required to give service to the sept on a regular basis. This service can entail minor jobs, such as aiding the Keeper of the Land with his duties or patrols, accepting guard duty, or helping an adren or elder with an upcoming rite. Essentially, the job description is "other duties as required," and since cliath are lower in Rank than most Garou, a cliath usually has little choice but to obey.

Privileges: A cliath can petition for justice, challenge for higher Rank (when she has enough Renown), and can enter the caern (usually).

Note: This is the starting Rank for a player. Garou expect a cliath to go out and make a name for herself; one who hangs around the caern and doesn't try to find her own way won't be well-liked. Cliath are always getting into trouble, but that's just part of being a cliath. The elders give cliath a fairly long leash, intervening only when it looks like she will screw up so badly as to be denied fostering.

Fostern - Rank Two

This is typically the most common rank at a sept. A fostern has earned some Renown outside of his *Rite of Passage*, and now stands as an adult among the Garou. A fostern is expected to attend moots, fulfill the duties as described by his auspice, and learn the ways of his breed and tribe.

Gifts Available: Basic

Rites Available: Basic

Maximum Traits Per Category: 12

Maximum Willpower, Gnosis and Rage: 5

Renown Requirements:

• **Ragabash**: Any Seven Renown
• **Theurge**: Three Wisdom, One Glory
• **Philodox**: Five Honor, One Wisdom, One Glory
• **Galliard**: Four Glory, Three Wisdom
• **Ahroun**: Five Glory, Three Honor, One Wisdom

Duties: A fostern is required to give service to the sept on a regular basis. This service can entail all the same minor jobs he performed as a cliath, only now he is expected to be competent and responsible.

Privileges: A fostern is allowed to perform Basic Rites, can petition for justice, can challenge for higher Rank (when he has enough Renown), and is usually allowed access to the caern. He can also request that a Moon Bridge be opened to the destination of his choice, but the request will not always be heeded — Moon Bridges are sacred things and are not to be used frivolously.

Note that the word "fostern" is also used to refer to pack brothers and sisters, the Garou family by choice. In the sense that all members of a pack are "family," the members of a Garou's pack can be referred to as his "fostern," regardless of their Rank. Unity is sometimes more important than social standing.

Adren - Rank Three

Adren have gained in prestige and Renown, and now are expected to take a larger part in the affairs of the sept.

Gifts Available: Basic, Intermediate

Rites Available: Basic

Maximum Traits Per Category: 14

Maximum Willpower, Gnosis and Rage: 7

Renown Requirements:

- **Ragabash**: Any 12 Renown
- **Theurge**: Seven Wisdom, Two Glory, One Honor
- **Philodox**: Seven Honor, Four Wisdom, Three Glory
- **Galliard**: Six Glory, Five Wisdom, One Honor
- **Ahroun**: Seven Glory, Five Honor, One Wisdom

Other Requirements: An adren must be in training to fill one of the positions at a sept. She must also challenge and defeat another adren in some sort of contest. Note that defeating this adren does not have any effect on her Glory, though being defeated may affect the challenger's Glory. This challenge may take whatever form the challenged adren desires, and may be made appropriately easy or difficult depending on whether the adren feels the challenger is worthy.

Duties: An adren must give service to the elder who is training her. This takes most of her (out-of-game) time. Adren are considered eligible to become minor sept leaders and hold positions like Keeper of the Land, Gatekeeper, Guardian and Den Mother — positions that do not require a lot of actual authority. She is required to train fostern, and often must spend more time at the caern than she would like. This is one of the toughest Ranks to perform properly, because adren often have the responsibilities of an elder, but do not always have the authority to carry out those duties.

Privileges: Adren must be addressed with a term of respect by fostern and cliath. If an adren knows the *Rite of Binding*, she is allowed to create talens for herself and others. Her name is known outside her sept, usually within her tribe. She is allowed to learn and perform Intermediate Rites on her own. She can demand that the sept provide a place for her to live, even if it is just communal living quarters. (Demanding living space of a sept is seen as somewhat *déclassé*, and this privilege is usually invoked only by Garou with very low *Finances*.)

Note: Adren are usually in line for one or more sept positions. Everyone watches what an adren does, and Ragabash in particular will try to catch her doing something scandalous. An adren is expected to set a good example, making a Garou's adren years stressful ones indeed.

Athro - Rank Four

Athro have respect and authority within the Garou Nation. Others come to an athro for advice, and his word is respected at moots.

Gifts Available: Basic, Intermediate

Rite Available: Basic, Intermediate

Maximum Traits Per Category: 16

Maximum Willpower, Gnosis and Rage: 8

Systems

Renown Requirements:
- **Ragabash**: Any 17 Renown
- **Theurge**: Nine Wisdom, Four Glory, Two Honor
- **Philodox**: Nine Honor, Seven Wisdom, Three Glory
- **Galliard**: Eight Glory, Six Wisdom, Two Honor
- **Ahroun**: Nine Glory, Seven Honor, Two Wisdom

Other Requirements: An athro may fill one of the elder positions in a sept. These are: elder of an auspice, elder of a tribe, elder of a breed, sept leader, Warder, Master of the Rite and Master of the Challenge. One can be the elder of a tribe, auspice or breed and also be sept leader or Master of the Rite — these duties can overlap. He cannot advance to elder Rank if one of these positions is not available. He must either challenge the current elder for the position and defeat her, or wait until a position becomes vacant. In the latter case, he may have to contend for the position.

Duties: Athro are typically the leaders of the packs and the ones who receive quests and assignments to fulfill from a sept's elders. The most dangerous missions are assigned and the greatest chances to gain Renown exist at this level.

Privileges: An athro can be judged only by a sept's council of elders. He gets the best assignments, and is considered a teacher by all other Garou.

Elder - Rank Five

An elder is at the peak of her achievement as a Garou. Others look up to her as a paragon. She commands respect and obedience from those around her.

Gifts Available: Basic, Intermediate, Advanced

Rites Available: Basic, Intermediate

Maximum Traits Per Category: 18

Maximum Willpower, Gnosis and Rage: 9

Renown Requirements:
- **Ragabash**: Any 24 Renown
- **Theurge**: 10 Wisdom, Five Glory, Three Honor
- **Philodox**: 10 Honor, Nine Wisdom, Four Glory
- **Galliard**: 10 Glory, Eight Wisdom, Three Honor
- **Ahroun**: 10 Glory, Eight Honor, Three Wisdom

Other Requirements: Not surprisingly, an elder is expected to fill one of the elder positions in a sept. These are: elder of an auspice, elder of a tribe, elder of a breed, sept leader, Warder, Master of the Rite and Master of the Challenge. One can be both the elder of a tribe, auspice or breed and also be sept leader or Master of the Rite or Master of the Challenge — these duties can overlap.

Duties: As the elder of an auspice, tribe or breed, you are required to watch out for the interests of your auspice, tribe or breed within the sept. As an elder of an auspice, you have the power to veto Renown nominations. As an elder of a tribe, you have the ability to accept new members into the tribe and to ban certain Garou from the tribe. As an elder of a breed, you are responsible for all external liaisons with others of your breed — the metis elder is a position that is rarely filled, but if it is, the metis elder must watch over and give aid to all metis characters in the sept. Other positions are described in the section on the sept, pp. 18-20.

Privileges: Elders can only be judged by a council of other elders. An elder is free to do pretty much whatever she pleases as long as she fulfills her duties. Furthermore, an elder automatically commands respect and obedience from everyone around her.

Storyteller Note: If you don't have many players, it's best if elders are Narrator characters. Too many elders in a game may disrupt it, or make things extremely difficult for cubs and cliath.

Legend - Rank Six

Only one out of every thousand Garou ever attains the status and Rank of a living legend. A legend is no longer an individual. He belongs to the Garou Nation as a whole.

Gifts and Rites Available: All

Maximum Traits Per Category: 20

Maximum Willpower, Gnosis and Rage: 10

Renown Requirements:

- **Ragabash**: Any 31 Renown
- **Theurge**: 13 Wisdom, Seven Glory, Five Honor
- **Philodox**: 14 Honor, 12 Wisdom, Six Glory
- **Galliard**: 13 Glory, 11 Wisdom, Four Honor
- **Ahroun**: 14 Glory, 10 Honor, Four Wisdom

Other Requirements: A legend no longer fills any official position in a sept, but is known throughout the world of the Garou. Many might even consider a legend to be just that: just a myth, or perhaps someone who has died already. A Garou who earns enough Renown does not contend for the Rank of legend. Rather, it just sort of happens. Over the course of time he outgrows the daily rational world of sept politics and stable packmates, while they start treating him more like a totem avatar than a flesh-and-blood elder. His responsibilities are now to Gaia and the Garou Nation in general. He goes where he is needed, and triumphs over those threats that all others have failed to defeat.

Privileges: Gaia rewards legends with Renown, while the Galliards just seem to know which tales to sing. Gaia also knows when a legend falters (which should never happen), and directly punishes transgressions against Her or Her children.

Storyteller Note: It is recommended that once a character reaches legend status, she should be retired or made into a Storyteller character. Otherwise, there is incredible potential for disruption of the game for less-powerful characters; the threats that challenge a legend simply overwhelm most other characters.

Legends tend to be met to further a story along or to assist wayward Garou in times of dire need. They should not serve as player characters.

Facedown

A facedown is an honored tradition in Garou society. It occurs when two characters lock eyes in a test of wills for the purpose of intimidating each other. The idea is to force one's rival to back down before a conflict actually comes to blows. Garou commonly employ facedowns, primarily to settle minor disputes, scold pups and show discontent with a pack's leaders.

Success in a facedown is determined in one of two ways. First, if one of the players relents while roleplaying this action, his opponent is considered to be the winner, and is allowed to gloat over his victory as he pleases. If one of the players does not relent during a facedown, a Social Challenge is necessary to determine the victor. The Social Challenge proceeds as normal, with the loser breaking eye contact and losing the contest.

Frenzy

Frenzy is an uncontrollably violent state suffered by all Garou. Some claim it is the taint of the Wyrm within them that causes Garou to go mad, destroying and ravaging everything within their reach. Others disagree, believing that frenzy is the release of the animal within them all. Frenzy can happen at any time and can be provoked by anything. When it happens, it is sudden, bloody and often fatal. Not even the Stargazers are calm enough to forsake this horrible curse of the Changing Breed.

The trigger for a frenzy can be almost anything, depending on the character in question. For a Fianna Galliard, it could be a member of his audience mocking him as he performs; for a Wendigo Ahroun, it could be an ignorant, prejudiced white man making racist comments about Native Americans; for a Get of Fenris, it could be a bad moot. What triggers frenzy is entirely up to the personality of the character and the discretion of the Narrator. However, discretion is advised; a character in constant frenzy is no fun to be around, and will likely be "put down" by his fellow sept members.

To see if a character enters frenzy, the player performs a Static Willpower Challenge (current Willpower versus current Rage, no Traits risked).

A character can also try to instill frenzy in another character by taunting him and calling for a Social Challenge. If the attacker (the taunting character) wins the challenge, the defender must then test to resist frenzy. If the defender wins the challenge, nothing happens and the story continues as usual.

Once in the state of frenzy, a character attacks all those around him violently and without discretion. A frenzied character does not suffer penalties from wounds (simulating the blind, uncontrollable anger of a frenzied Garou). Frenzies usually last only about 10 minutes, or until the object or person that triggered the frenzy is removed from the character's vicinity.

A character may also enter frenzy voluntarily by spending a Rage Trait. Such an action can prove useful in a combat situation in which frenzy might be necessary to achieve victory — or even just surviving. It has its uses, but it is a dark gift.

A Garou in a fear-spawned frenzy asumes Lupus form. A Garou in an anger-inspired frenzy takes on Crinos.

Note: Be cautious when roleplaying frenzy. Do not jump about screaming at people, frothing at the mouth and clawing at the furniture. Remember, although frenzy is a violent state of mind, *you absolutely cannot strike other players, even in jest.* Just because your character is in an uncontrollable rage does not mean that you can forget the rules and become reckless. Use your own discretion, but act out only as much frenzy as the environment allows without upsetting your fellow players.

The Many Forms

The Garou have five forms that they may assume: Homid (pure human), Glabro (bestial human), Crinos (towering man-wolf creature), Hispo (dire wolf) and Lupus (pure wolf). Each of these forms gives a Garou a different set of advantages and disadvantages.

Changing forms requires a Simple Test and one turn for each form assumed. It therefore takes one turn and one Simple Test to change from Homid to Glabro, but a total of four Simple Tests and four turns to go from Homid to Lupus. Any test lost along the way marks the point where the Garou stops shifting until another turn has passed and the shifting process can begin again. *Primal Urge* allows retests.

Alternatively, a Garou may elect to spend a Rage Trait to make the change instantaneous, regardless of initial and final form. The player should be certain to alert those within sight that the change is taking place so that other characters can make an appropriate reaction.

A Garou can always shift into Breed Form instantly and at no cost. Furthermore, while in the Umbra Garou can change into any form, instantly and at no cost.

Although Garou can have difficulty communicating with humans and wolves, they can always communicate with one another freely. The language of the Garou is a combination of human phonetics and lupine snarls, and thus is pronounceable in all forms.

Homid: The Human

Trait Adjustments: None

Change Description: This is the normal state for characters who wish to interact with human society. This form is identical to human form in all ways. A Garou in Homid form does not regenerate damage, but may carry silver items without harm.

Glabro: The Bestial Human

Trait Adjustments: The character gains the following additional Physical Traits: *Ferocious*, *Brawny* and *Quick*. These Traits may be bid just like normal Traits. Once lost, they are gone for the duration of the session. A Garou also gains the following Negative Traits while in this form: *Tactless* and *Bestial*.

Change Description: A Garou in this form is still recognizably human, but differences from average humans are apparent. The Garou gains about six inches in height and may nearly double her body weight in muscle mass. Teeth and nails grow longer and body hair becomes profuse. While Glabro form can pass for human (barely), it will be remembered as strange and scary (as this form resembles the stereotype of a Neanderthal linebacker). In Glabro, the Garou's thick fingernails cause aggravated damage, but she can still handle most delicate manipulations.

Roleplaying: Full human speech is possible, but Glabro usually speak only one or two short sentences at a time, delivered in a guttural snarl.

Crinos: The Wolf-Man

Trait Adjustments: The character gains the following additional Physical Traits: *Ferocious* x 2, *Robust* x 2, *Relentless*, *Brawny* x 2 and *Quick*. These Traits may be bid just like normal Traits. Once lost, they are gone for the duration of the session. A Garou also suffers the following Negative Traits while in this form: *Bestial* x 2 and *Tactless*. A Garou can initiate no Social Challenges that are not meant to intimidate while in Crinos form.

As a Garou gains Rank, his Crinos form gains strength-related powers. At Rank 2, he may call for one free retest of any challenge that involves raw physical strength. At Rank 3, he gains the use of a fourth hand signal, the Bomb (which is thrown as a "Rock" but with the thumb pointing out, like a fuse). The Bomb beats Rock and Paper, and is only defeated by Scissors. At Rank 4, he gains one extra Health Level while in this form. At Rank 5, he wins all ties in Physical Challenges involving strength. At rank 6, he inflicts an additional level of damage with every success in hand-to-hand combat.

Change Description: Garou in this form often grow to a towering nine feet or more in height. The Garou's body is covered in thick fur, and her head becomes that of a snarling canine. Claws and fangs become pronounced and ready for combat. This form is most often assumed when a Garou is preparing to face great danger. Both the claws and teeth cause aggravated damage. When a character frenzies, this is the form she adopts as soon as she can (without spending Rage).

Roleplaying: When in Crinos form, the character takes on an appearance that evokes horrific racial memories in humans; any human seeing the Garou in this form is affected by the Delirium. Saying anything more complex than a few human words while in Crinos requires a Simple Mental Test.

Hispo: The Dire Wolf

Trait Adjustments: While in this form, the character gains the following bonus Traits: *Ferocious* x 2, *Tireless* x 2 and *Quick* x 2. He is also afflicted with the following penalties: *Bestial* x 2 and *Shortsighted*.

Change Description: This form is a huge, hulking, wolflike beast resembling the prehistoric dire wolf. The Hispo's head and jaws are massive, and his bite causes a second level of damage if a Simple Test is won after the initial combat challenge (this is not cumulative with any other damage enhancements). The Hispo can stand on his hind legs in emergencies, but he mostly stays on all fours. He weighs almost as much as the Crinos, but his wolflike legs enable him to run at one and one-half times normal wolf speeds. A Garou has paws instead of hands in Hispo, so he cannot hold objects except with his jaws.

Roleplaying: The Hispo form is a hunting machine and gains three extra Traits for comparison and overbids on any perception-related challenge. No human speech is possible in this form, unless a Simple Mental Test is won.

Lupus: The Wolf

Trait Adjustments: While in Lupus form, the character gains the following bonus Traits: *Tireless* and *Quick* x 2. He also incurs the following Negative Trait: *Bestial*.

Change Description: In this form, the Garou assumes the form of a wolf, usually a near-perfect specimen. The exact type of wolf is usually determined by the character's tribe. A character in Lupus form may not cause aggravated wounds with his claws, but may still do so with his teeth. In addition, a Garou in Lupus has exceptional senses. He may attempt to perform sensory feats that would be nearly impossible for a human: seeing in near-darkness, tracking by scent, hearing sounds too faint for the human ear, noticing beings hiding through Gifts or Disciplines, and suchlike.

Roleplaying: While in Lupus form, a character is driven mostly by instinct. A Lupus usually prefers to flee rather than fight a battle. Lupus cannot speak to humans, but may speak freely to wolves.

Note: It is highly advisable to use cards pinned to shirts or colored ribbons around the wrist to designate which form characters are presently in. This way everyone knows what is going on and can remain (and react) in character. Some troupes prefer to use hand-signals to indicate forms (hands over head for Crinos, hands held out front for Lupus, etc.). See page 249 for a complete listing of hand signals used in **Mind's Eye Theatre**.

Beyond the Velvet Shadow

Spirits and the Umbra in Apocalypse

The spirit world plays an instrumental role in the life of the Garou. A Garou can travel from the physical world to the spirit world (also called the Umbra), allowing him to interact with the spiritual landscape. As a member of a pack, a Garou shares a mystic connection to the spirit world through his relationship to his pack totem; this totem also binds the pack together. Spirituality is an integral part of anything a Garou does. Even the most cynical Glass Walker living in the heart of the most blighted city in the world can see spirits everywhere she looks. To the Garou, the entire world is alive with the spirits of Gaia.

It is the Storyteller's job to bring out the spiritual side of werewolves when playing **Apocalypse**. The spiritual aspect of the Garou is a rich and rewarding aspect of the game, but one that can be impractical to play and that can seriously damage the whole mood of the game if it is not handled well — and with consideration toward character development.

The Spirit Keeper

If spirits play more than a minor role in your game, there should be a Narrator whose job is to adjudicate and administer all spirit-related Gifts and rites, Umbral travel, totems and spirit combat. This Narrator, called the "Spirit Keeper," is also in charge of all the spirit plotlines and anything having to do with the spirit world. The Spirit Keeper should prepare for any **Apocalypse** session by defining any pre-existing spirits in the area and by creating some spirits in advance (just in case any are summoned). The Spirit Keeper also needs to know what the Umbra is like in all of the playing areas, and should be the final authority on all matters spiritual in gameplay.

The Umbra

There is a spirit world outside the perceptions of normal humanity. It lies alongside this world, separated from us by a wall of static reality called the Gauntlet. One must pass through the Gauntlet to reach the Umbra or return back to Earth. The Gauntlet is said to be a membrane woven by the Weaver to separate physical reality from the Umbra, but its origins are less important than its effects.

Stepping Sideways

Any Garou has the power to step sideways into the Umbra. In order to do this, the Garou must focus his eyes on a reflective or shiny surface, then perform a Static Gnosis Challenge against half the local Gauntlet rating (*Primal Urge*, *Enigmas*, etc. allow retests). If the Garou wins, she enters the Umbra at the end of the present turn. (A Storyteller may modify the difficulty if the reflective surface is something less or more difficult to focus ones eyes on; a full-length

mirror is very easy to work with, while a reflection in someone's eyes is incredibly difficult.) A loss indicates that the Garou cannot get through at this point and must move at least 20 steps from the area or wait five minutes in order to try again. A tie indicates that the Garou is only partially through. She must test again on the next turn; a success gets her through; a tie leaves her still trying, and a loss means she is stuck in the Gauntlet.

A Garou who is stuck in the Gauntlet is in trouble. She may try once per hour to get free by spending a Gnosis Trait and succeeding in a Simple Test. While stuck in the Gauntlet, the character may be attacked by Weaver Spiders, have horrible visions of places like Malfeas (the Wyrm's home realm), and/or experience other particularly unnerving events. While caught between worlds, a Garou cannot recover Gnosis. However, it is possible for a "stuck" Garou to be rescued by another werewolf, who makes a Static Gnosis Test (against 7 Traits) to free the prisoner.

Two or more Garou going into the Umbra at the same time may designate a leader. Only that leader tests against the Gauntlet, and her result affects everyone. If she gets stuck, the whole group gets stuck, and no one else can become leader and attempt to pull the group free until the present leader runs out of Gnosis. Garou with the Gift: *Grasp the Beyond* can take non-Garou with them into the Umbra.

The Spirit Keeper should keep a record of the general Gauntlet level of any given place in the play area, and may wish to put up signs indicating the local Gauntlet rating.

If a Garou is attacked while stepping sideways, she must win a Static Mental Challenge against a difficulty dictated by a Narrator before she can vanish into the Umbra (use 7 as a default difficulty) or that attempt to step sideways is canceled.

A Garou enters the Umbra holistically, but only the clothes she is wearing and the stuff in her pockets goes along with her unless she has dedicated a tool or weapon with the *Rite of Talisman Dedication* (see p. 132). Regardless of whether or not her Umbral travels are "real," a Garou's body is a real, physical thing in the Umbra, and not an astral form.

Gauntlet Ratings

Area	Gauntlet
Science lab	9
Inner city	8
Most places	7
Rural countryside	6
Deep wilderness	5
Typical active caern	4
Powerful caern	3
Greatest caerns	2

A Garou in the Umbra can, by standing still and focusing, peer back through the Gauntlet and see things in the physical world. This action, called "Peeking," requires a Static Gnosis Challenge against half the local Gauntlet rating (rounded up).

In order to exit the Umbra, a character must first Peek through the Gauntlet and focus her eyes on a highly reflective or shiny surface. She then must succeed at a Static Gnosis Challenge against half the local Gauntlet (rounded up). If there is no reflective or shiny surface to be seen, the character must perform a Static Gnosis Challenge against the full local Gauntlet rating before she can return to the physical world.

A character in the Umbra may not interact with people who are not in the Umbra unless some special Gift or fetish is used. The Spirit Keeper will probably want to be kept informed as to who is in the Umbra, as those characters will be available for special plot developments such as Umbral storms, Bane attacks and spirit visitations.

One of the advantages of the Umbra is that Garou can do battle in it without endangering the Veil. The Umbra also makes an excellent "escape route," although the Umbra can sometimes be more dangerous than the physical world. There are locations in the Umbra that correspond to places on Earth, although exact distances can become confusing in the spirit world.

As a Storytelling device, the Umbra is without equal. It is a metaphoric reflection of our world. Where there is pollution on Earth, there are seething masses of Wyrm-tainted power, called Hellholes, in the Umbra. Where there are great monuments to the Weaver, such as skyscrapers, bridges and sprawling cities in the real world, in the Umbra there are webs everywhere and Pattern Spiders busily weaving to maintain them. Outside the cities, the Umbral wilderness glows with an internal light, and the power of Mother Gaia is shown in all its glory.

During the day, the Umbral sky is dark; at night, it is illuminated by the light of Luna. If one were to travel far enough, one would soon pass through the areas of the Near Umbra (Penumbra) and approach the boundary that separates the Near Umbra from the Deep Umbra. The Deep Umbra is a strange and wild place, the position of which corresponds to deep space in the realm of the physical world.

There are two other Umbral planes accessible from Earth: a realm of rational spirits sometimes called the "High Umbra," and a realm of dark spirits and wraiths, called the "Dark Umbra."

The Umbra in Play

The Spirit Keeper may wish to create a separate area that's set up to evoke the atmosphere of the Umbra. Many dramatic and important scenes can be played in a place where it actually appears as though the players are no longer in this world. Narrators can create the appropriate ambiance for the area by using such elements as dry ice fog, special lighting, mood music and other decorations. However, this area should be kept separate from the rest of the game, and the Spirit Keeper should prevent anyone who is not "in the Umbra" from entering the area.

It is also possible that players will try to abuse their advantage by constantly entering the Umbra to escape potential danger. This is unwise, as the Umbra contains dangers unlike anything found on the Earth. A Spirit Keeper has free reign to throw Banes and other hazards at Garou who abuse the Umbra for purely tactical "drops" and "extractions."

To indicate that he is in the Umbra, a Garou should bring his right hand across his chest. Making this gesture lets other players know that he is in the Umbra and not really "there" — which can prevent no end of confusion during gameplay.

Spirits

Spirits are entities born of the Umbra that dwell there most of the time. There is a tremendous diversity of spirits in the Umbra, as every single thing on Earth has a sleeping spirit associated with it. Some spirits aren't sleeping any longer, and many things have awakened spirits associated with them. For example, a particularly well-loved '57 Chevy might actually have a wakeful spirit of Affection attached to it.

The difference between a waking and sleeping spirit is that one has an active consciousness and the other does not. **Laws of the Wild** focuses on awake, active spirits only. Sleeping spirits are not dealt with, unless the special *Rite of Spirit Awakening* is used (see "Rites" in Chapter Two, p. 131).

Types of Spirits

Most often spirits appear as animals, or anthropomorphic representations of abstract ideas. Spirits rarely look human, but often appear to be humanish, that is, variations on the basic human form. Narrators are free to modify spirits' appearances to fit the needs of their games.

Gafflings and Jagglings

The Garou think of spirits in terms of their general level of power. The weakest and smallest spirits are called Gafflings. These are mere extensions of the power of larger spirits. Slightly more powerful spirits are called Jagglings. These are common, everyday spirits with which the Garou interact. One type of Jaggling, called an Engling, can provide Garou with Gnosis. Spirits that are commonly found as servants of the Wyrm are called Banes.

The Incarna

There are a number of spirits that have grown in power to the point where they command many Jagglings and have a great supply of personal energy. These spirits, called Incarna, tend to have their own realms in the Umbra, and are often incarnations of ancient deities, powerful forces and archetypes, and other mythic beings. Many of the Incarna are very ancient, and therefore have correspondingly vast knowledge and powers.

Totem Spirits

Some of the most ancient Incarna are the animal spirits that were allies of the Garou when the Changing Breeds were first born. These animal spirits pledged that they would forever lend their wisdom, power and spirit children to the aid of the Garou, Gaia's noble sons and daughters.

These animal Incarna are called totems, and they have left their lasting mark on the tribes and packs of Garou. Occasionally, a totem sends one of its avatars, an extension of its will, to serve the Garou directly. This always occurs as a result of a pack forming, as the totem avatar becomes bound to the pack as part of the *Rite of Passage* or the *Rite of the Totem*. Each tribe, caern and pack has a totem associated with it, and many Garou adopt personal totems that they quietly follow on an individual basis.

The Celestines

Above the level of the Incarna are the Celestines — powerful and eternal spirits that embody fundamental forces in the universe. Gaia Herself is a Celestine, as are Luna and Helios. Celestines are the least "normal" appearing of the spirits. They assume abstract forms and communicate in strange ways. These entities are so transcendent and distant that it is difficult to describe them in simple terms; it is highly unlikely that a Garou is going to interact with a Celestine during the course of a game of **Apocalypse**.

Spirit Creation

Although the Garou have not completely plumbed the depths of the mystery of spirits and spirit lore, Narrators must be prepared and know all of the Traits that make up each spirit they use.

Spirits have Rage, Willpower and Gnosis and a pool of Power Traits that they use to activate special magical abilities called Charms. (In **Apocalypse**, both Gnosis and Power can be used to empower Charms.)

In order to create a spirit for use in the game, the Spirit Keeper must first decide what affinity the spirit has. A spirit's affinity is the fundamental theme or mood for the spirit — it is indicative of the spirit's purpose, personality and powers. For example, a spirit of war might be particularly good at fighting, and have the Charm: *Materialize*, which allows it to affect enemies in the physical world. Virtually anything can describe a spirit's affinity. Spirits that have a totem or an Incarna as their affinity are considered servants of that totem or Incarna. For example, a spirit with Wolf affinity is considered to be allied with the Wolf totem.

A spirit's affinity can be discerned with certain Gifts, such as *Detect Spirit*. If a character has the *Enigmas* Ability, affinity can also be perceived with a Static Mental Challenge (Spirit Keeper discretion on difficulty). Optionally, a Garou may simply wish to ask a spirit its affinity — it might actually tell her.

Next, the Keeper must decide what type of spirit his subject is. Most of the spirits a Garou is familiar with are Gafflings, Jagglings and totem avatars.

Spirit Keepers should use the spirit creation rules to flesh out the rest of a spirit. Spirits may be assigned Negative Traits to increase the number of Traits assigned to them.

Spirit Creation Table

Note: The number of points each spirit type has is in the table below this one.

Cost	Power
1	Per two points to spend on Willpower, Rage, or Gnosis.
1	Per point of Power.
1	Per point of an Ability.
2	Per Charm possessed.
2	Spirit has one Renown among other spirits.

For Totem Spirits Only

1	Totem can speak with all members of group.
1	Totem can find all the members of the group.
2	Totem is nearly always with one member of the group.
4	Totem is with each member of a pack and allows them to communicate mentally.
5	Totem can materialize in time of need without cost.
5	Totem is feared by agents of the Wyrm.

For more information, see the Spirit Creation Table. To determine the number of points available for spirit creation, see the information on pp. 192-193.

Gaffling

These are the smallest and weakest of all spirits.

Creation Points: 7
Negative Traits: 5 maximum
Power Pool: 7 maximum
Charms: *Airt Sense* only and at no cost
Rage: 5 maximum
Willpower: 5 maximum
Gnosis: 5 maximum
Abilities: 5 Maximum

Jaggling

These are the most common spirits in the Umbra.

Creation Points: 25; 30 if connected to a tribal totem
Negative Traits: Maximum of 5
Power Pool: 10 maximum
Charms: Any up to 5
Rage: 7 maximum
Willpower: 7 maximum
Gnosis: 7 maximum
Abilities: 10 maximum; maximum of 5 Traits per Ability

Incarna

These are the more powerful servants of totem spirits.

Creation Points: 40
Negative Traits: Maximum of 5
Power Pool: 20 maximum
Charms: Any up to 7
Rage: 8 maximum
Willpower: 8 maximum
Gnosis: 8 maximum
Abilities: 15 maximum; maximum level 6

Totem Spirits

All totem avatars come from these very powerful spirits, which represent and act as avatars for each animal.

Creation Points: 50
Negative Traits: maximum of 5
Power Pool: 30 maximum
Charms: 10 maximum
Rage: 10 maximum
Willpower: 10 maximum
Gnosis: 10 maximum
Abilities: 20 maximum; maximum level 7

Celestines

These are the most powerful spirits; Gaia and Luna are Celestines.

Creation Points: Unlimited (minimum 50)
Negative Traits: No more than five
Power Pool: Unlimited
Charms: Any
Rage: No maximum
Willpower: No maximum
Gnosis: No maximum
Abilities: Whatever you think they need at whatever level.

Storyteller Note: Celestines are beings of deific power, and no character should be able to make a Celestine even work up a sweat. If your Garou are actually taking swings at a Celestine to the point where you need to look at the spirit's Traits, there is something seriously wrong.

Spirit Combat

When a spirit attacks in the Umbra, it does so by making a Willpower Challenge against the target's Physical Traits. If successful, a spirit can make a Rage Challenge against the target's Gnosis and do a second level of damage (aggravated this time) if it succeeds. Spirits defend themselves against Physical Challenges by using their Willpower. They use Gnosis against Mental or Social Challenges. Damage is marked off against a spirit's Power Pool; spirits do not bid with Trait disadvantages once injured.

When a spirit is reduced to zero Power, it dissipates into the Umbra for a number of hours equal to 20 minus its Gnosis (minimum of five hours), after which it reforms somewhere in the Umbra with one Power Trait. Optionally, a Garou who reduces a spirit's Power to zero may elect to siphon up to five Traits' worth of Gnosis from the spirit in order to recharge his own Gnosis. If the siphoning of Gnosis drains the spirit completely, it dies. A Garou who kills a spirit in this manner automatically gains one Notoriety Trait (see p. 199). It doesn't matter who else saw you; Gaia did, and that's enough.

Charms

Charms are spirit powers. They often require a challenge of some sort in order to be activated. Charms can be borrowed with certain Gifts, and a Theurge can command a spirit to use its Charms to aid a Garou. Any spirit can buy Charms during character creation. Unless stated otherwise, a Charm lasts for one scene.

Access Caern
Power Cost: 6
Same as *Rite of the Open Caern.*

Acquisition
Power Cost: Variable
This Charm allows a spirit to take an inanimate object into the Umbra. Once it is in the Umbra, the spirit can use the item, play with it and move it around until the end of the scene, when it returns to the real world. ("How did my keys get behind the refrigerator?") Items up to the size of a thick wallet cost one Power Trait, while ones up to hat sized cost two, and larger items up to the size of a suitcase cost three.

Affinity Attack
Power Cost: 2/attack
This is a catch-all attack ability. It is a one-Health-Level attack associated in some way with the spirit's affinity. For example, a fire spirit will have a fire-based attack, though it's up to the Narrator to work out the details (hurled fireballs or gouts of liquid flame are possible applications, etc.).

Affinity Defense
Power Cost: 1
This is a catch-all defense ability. The defense must be associated with the spirit's affinity. For example, an air spirit may cause a wall of swirling wind to protect it against an incoming attack. It is up to the Spirit Keeper to define the type of defense for each spirit. This Charm absorbs one level of damage each turn.

Affinity Sense

Power Cost: 2

This enables a spirit to sense things in both the Umbra and on Earth that are appropriate to its affinity. For example, the *Affinity Sense* of a Glade Child (the spirit of a tree) might be *Forest Sense*, which would enable it to detect the changes made to an area around a forest, or to sense intruders in a wooded region.

Affinity Ward

Power Cost: Variable, +1/challenge

This enables a spirit to designate an area of the Umbra that is protected from other spirits of the ward's specific affinity. The area is usually circular in shape, and is about the size of a single room (10-foot diameter). The initial Power cost of this Charm is the number of Power Traits the spirit wishes to invest in protection. These Traits are the difficulty against which a Static Rage Challenge must be made by any spirit attempting to enter the area. These invested Traits are lost when the Ward is abandoned.

Agony

Power Cost: 6

This Charm doubles all wound penalties on a single target for one combat. If this modifier drops a character's available Traits below zero, he must spend a Willpower Trait in order to take any action.

Airt Sense

Power Cost: 1

This Charm enables a spirit to determine the best path through the Umbra to a given destination, and can help the spirit find hidden places in the spirit realm.

Appear

Power Cost: 3, +1/minute

This Charm allows a spirit to be seen and heard in the real world, but not touched or harmed. Furthermore, it may not touch or harm anything on Earth.

Break Boundary

Power Cost: 1 (more can be added at Narrator discretion)

A Static Gnosis Challenge made against a lock or other security feature opens it without causing damage to the boundary. Difficulty is Narrator's discretion.

Break Reality

Power Cost: 2–10

The spirit can disrupt the reality of a substance, and thereby modify its Umbral form, through a Static Gnosis Challenge (difficulty is Narrator discretion). This can be anything from putting a door in a wall (in the Umbra), to turning a house upside down. The cost is determined by the extent of the attempted change and how clever the idea is. If the Static

Gnosis Challenge is lost, the spirit will lose one Gnosis, so most spirits with this Charm are restrained in its use. Some Spirits have the *Break Reality* Charm only for specific areas associated with their affinity. For example, a Pattern Spider might have *Break Reality*, but might only be able to affect items related to Weaver-tech.

Calcify

Power Cost: 2/target

This Charm is possessed only by Weaver-spirits. It allows a spirit to bind a target to the Pattern Web by making a Willpower Challenge against the target's Rage. Each successful attack subtracts one Physical Trait from the target until there are none left and the target is encased in the Web. To free the prisoner, others must do damage to the Web equal to the number of Physical Traits lost by the target.

Call for Aid

Power Cost: 5

This Charm allows the spirit to call for help from other spirits of the same affinity. The spirit must succeed in a Static Gnosis Challenge (against seven Traits); any other spirits in the vicinity must respond for at least one turn.

Cleanse the Blight

Power Cost: 10

This Charm is similar to *Rite of Cleansing*, but purges spiritual corruption in the spirit's vicinity instead.

Disorient

Power Cost: 2

This Charm is possessed only by Wyldings. The spirit may totally alter how others perceive the local landscape (up to and including obscuring the four cardinal directions) with a successful Gnosis Challenge against the local Gauntlet rating (minimum of 6). When affected by *Disorient* during gameplay, a character must succeed in a Mental Challenge against the spirit or head off in the direction the spirit wishes.

Dream Journey

Power Cost: 10/visit

This enables a spirit to enter a person's dream and use Gnosis Challenges against the target's Mental Traits so as to change the nature of the dream. This Charm can be used for comforting, communicating dark portents and dream omens, or just walking through someone else's dream. The target must succeed in a Simple Test when she awakens in order to remember the dream.

Healing

Power Cost: variable

This is the ability to heal beings in the Umbra. Normal wounds can be healed at a rate of one wound per Power Trait. Aggravated wounds can be healed at a rate of one wound per two Power Traits. Anything living (Garou, spirits, humans...) can be healed with this Charm.

Informational Link

Power Cost: 3

This power enables a spirit to connect into the "cosmic switchboard" and gain information about virtually any subject. A Static Gnosis Challenge, the difficulty of which is equal to the complexity or specialty of the information sought, determines the level of detail of the information gained.

Intangibility

Power Cost: 4, +1/minute

This Charm protects a spirit from all attacks. A spirit can be seen and heard, but not touched or harmed when *Intangibility* is active. While intangible, a spirit cannot be affected by mental attacks, but can be tricked by outside influences into lowering its guard. *Command* would not work on an intangible spirit, but *Staredown* would.

The spirit cannot simultaneously use the Charm: *Reform* with *Intangibility*.

Local Sense

Power Cost: 10

Same as *Rite of the Badger's Burrow*.

Materialize

Power Cost: Variable

A spirit with this Charm may materialize and affect the physical world, assuming its Gnosis equals or exceeds the Gauntlet in the area. When it materializes, the spirit must spend Power to create a physical shape and to give itself bodily Traits. However, a spirit still uses its Gnosis for all Social and Mental Challenges. Power costs for creating a physical form are as follows:

Power Cost	Trait
1	Per one Physical Trait.
1	For each level of an Ability that requires physical action.
1	For Basic Health Levels (as per human).
1	Per Health Level above Basic (each extra one also increases size).
1	For natural weaponry (teeth, claws, etc.) that will do aggravated damage.

Spirits are not limited in their potential Traits. A spirit may stay materialized as long as it desires, but may not enter an area with a Gauntlet higher than its Gnosis. Spirits may not regain Power while materialized (without the use of certain Charms). If a materialized spirit's Health Levels are reduced to zero, it dissipates into the Umbra as normal. Aggravated damage suffered by a materialized spirit is removed from both its Health and Power.

Spirits rarely escape a sojourn on Earth unscathed, and circumstances must be dire for a spirit to use this Charm.

Mindspeak

Power Cost: 1/scene

This enables a spirit to speak directly with the mind of someone nearby, even if he is not in the Umbra or cannot understand spirits.

Obscure

Power Cost: 1/scene

This surrounds a spirit in an obscuring cloud or fog that keeps it from being recognized or identified. This fog cannot be penetrated by eyesight alone.

Open Moon Bridge

Power Cost: 5

This creates a Moon Bridge to a desired location. A caern need not be present at either end for a Moon Bridge to be opened by the use of this Charm. The maximum distance that can be traveled on a bridge of this sort is 1000 miles.

Possess Animal

Power Cost: 3, +1/scene

This enables a spirit to possess an animal if it wins a Gnosis Challenge against the Gnosis of the animal's spirit. The animal is then controlled by the possessing spirit until the animal is slain, the spirit runs out of Power or someone banishes the spirit (as with *Rite of Cleansing*). This Charm is usually the first step in creating a Wyrm-infested animal.

Possession

Power Cost: 3, +2/command

The spirit engages in a Gnosis Challenge against the target's Mental Traits. After that, a Social Challenge is required every time the spirit tries to command the target's body to move or perform specific actions. During a *Possession*, the spirit can use some of its Charms and Abilities through the host (Storyteller discretion). The target can spend a Willpower Trait to repel any attempt to use *Possession*.

Possess Tech

Power Cost: 1

The spirit controls one item of technology and can operate it as a human might. Of course, Gnosis Challenges may be required for the spirit to figure the item out; very few spirits are computer literate or certified mechanics.

Reform

Power Cost: 10

This Charm allows a spirit to dissipate and reform somewhere else in the Umbra, usually far away from its enemies.

Shapeshift

Power Cost: 5

This enables a spirit to change its size, shape, color or appearance. A shapeshifting spirit may look like anything it desires, but does not gain the Abilities or Traits of the new shape.

Spirit Static

Power Cost: 10

This Charm increases the strength of the Gauntlet by one in a particular place until it is sidestepped through a number of times equal to the enhanced level. The local Gauntlet rating then returns to normal.

Steal Gnosis/Rage/Willpower

Power Cost: 1/attempt

This enables a spirit to attempt to drain Gnosis (which can be converted to Power on a one-for-one basis), Rage or Willpower. The attacking spirit must win a Gnosis Challenge against the Garou (who bids Social or Mental Traits) or spirit that is the target of this Charm. If the attack is successful, the target loses a point of Gnosis, Rage or Willpower at the attacker's discretion. The spirit must announce beforehand which of the three Traits it is attempting to steal.

Garou and spirits can also submit to this Charm voluntarily in order to replenish a spirit.

Umbraquake

Power Cost: 5/10-foot area, 10/level of damage

The spirit can shake the Umbra in a confined area. Those standing are thrown to the ground and everyone in the affected area automatically takes a Health Level of damage.

Notoriety

Notoriety represents the reputation that a Garou has among spirits. For each Notoriety Trait that a Garou has, he receives a 1-Trait penalty when summoning spirits. The Spirit Keeper assigns or takes away Notoriety Traits based on her estimation of the way spirits perceive the character; Notoriety comes and goes depending on the character's actions. If a Garou gets enough Notoriety Traits, Wyrm-spirits might show up to offer him power, or an Incarna might send avatars to see why an offending Garou is messing with her children.

A good rule of thumb about Notoriety is that a character receives a Notoriety Trait every time he damages or otherwise negatively alters a spirit, summons a spirit for no good reason, treats a spirit disrespectfully or exhibits abusive behavior. Of course, this is not always applicable; if a Bane attacks you and you strike back, it's not likely that you'll gain Notoriety for that. If an Owl-spirit is set to watch a caern boundary, and you intimidate it out of your way without cause, you may receive Notoriety.

The only good thing about Notoriety is that it can be used in a Social Challenge if a Garou is attempting to intimidate a spirit into obeying him. Of course, doing so may very well earn the Garou another Notoriety Trait.

Bans

Sometimes a spirit may request that a Garou take on a Ban, that is, a restriction or requirement that serves the spirit's needs. This can be done as part of a bargaining process to get the spirit to do something, or as a potential means to erase Notoriety (the spirit will help erase the Garou's Notoriety if the Garou in question submits to a Ban). More often, a Garou voluntarily offers a Ban as a way of performing chiminage to repay the spirit for a favor. This often explains why so many Theurges adopt strange "superstitions" and customs.

If a Garou breaks a Ban, she automatically receives two Notoriety Traits in addition to regaining any Notoriety (if any) that was removed by the offended spirit. In addition, no spirit will trust the offending Garou for weeks, possibly longer. She may even lose Honor or Wisdom Renown, which is revoked by the members of her sept, whom the spirits will surely inform of her indiscretion.

Minor Bans include: never entering a door of a particular color, always wearing a specific token, never eating a particular kind of meat, never speaking a spirit's name aloud or always wearing a particular color.

Major Bans include: performing a sacrifice of some sort (not human!), getting a tattoo or brand, swearing an oath, agreeing to a quest or sacred journey, agreeing to adopt a new name (thereby "giving up" your old name) or freeing another captive spirit.

Totem spirits almost always require a Ban of some sort in payment for their assistance.

Delirium

Delirium is a state of mind that afflicts humans who see a Garou in Crinos form. Reactions vary greatly. Some humans run in sheer terror, while others cower on the ground in front of the Garou. A few completely disbelieve the incident ever happened. There are also those who become quite curious about the event and attempt to gain more information. It is therefore important that characters be careful when changing forms or running about as something other than a human or wolf. The integrity of the Veil must be preserved.

Delirium Chart

Willpower	% of the Traits of Human Population	Reaction Of Observer
1	10%	**Catatonic Fear**: This unfortunate just got a whopping dose of ancestral memory. He collapses into a fetal ball and whimpers, remembering nothing of the encounter later.
2	20%	**Panic**: The person runs as fast and as far as her feet can take her, running over anything that tries to stop her, often ignoring obstacles like plate-glass windows. The person remembers that *something* scared her.
3	18%	**Disbelief**: The person thinks he is hallucinating, attributing the Garou to stress, a trick of the light, drugs or the like. "This ain't happening! You're not real! I gotta quit drinking!"
4	15%	**Berserk**: Blind, frenzied fear goads her to action — any kind of action, even leaping on the Garou and pounding on him. She remembers seeing something big and hairy.
5	13%	**Terror**: Not as bad as Panic, but the human still moves away from the Garou as fast as he can. Even while running, he remembers to lock the door behind him, look for hiding places or get into his car and peel rubber. He will remember seeing something monstrous, big, hairy and mean.

| 6 | 10% | **Conciliatory**: Although on |

the verge of collapse, she does her best to calm and placate the beast, and remembers about half of the general stuff. ("It was big, and brown, and like a big dog—no, a wolf!") She may agree to anything to avoid getting hurt.

| 7 | 7% | **Controlled Fear**: Maybe |

he's a war veteran or a cop in the inner city. He keeps his cool (although terrified), and fights or flees as appropriate. Furthermore, he remembers most of the details of the situation. "I'm telling you, this...thing walked out of that mirror, sniffed around, and went back in when it saw me!"

| 8 | 5% | **Curiosity**: Instead of be- |

ing afraid, she's fascinated with the sight. Maybe she's a researcher of the paranormal, or just a loon who thinks the Garou is Bigfoot's cousin (in which case she might spill the story to a tabloid show or rag). She might start looking for the Garou to study him (from a safe distance). However, she is more likely to rationalize it away.

| 9 | 1.5% | **Bloodlust**: His reaction is |

anger rather than fear, and he remembers the encounter quite well. He'll run for his gun rather than a video camera or the door. "Hoo-whee, look at that! I'm gonna have me one of those for my livin' room!"

| 10 | 0.5% | **No Reaction/Blasé**: She |

displays no reaction to the Garou's appearance whatsoever. If spoken to, she responds politely and casually. This person either has nerves of steel or a brain of Jell-O. Needless to say, she remembers *everything* in perfect detail. "Oh, yeah, the big furry guy asked for directions, then took a left at the pizza joint."

The Curse

Whenever a Garou's Rage exceeds the Willpower of a nearby human or wolf, that human or wolf feels uneasy and nervous around the Garou. This is considered a curse by the Garou, for it prevents stable relationships, marriages and the like. Only among their own are Garou ever able to form lasting friendships.

All characters attempting to live normal human lives (marriages, businesses, hanging out with normal friends, playing roleplaying games, etc.) make a Willpower Test against their Rage (no Traits risked) once per cycle of the moon. A loss indicates that something has happened to ruin or hinder the character's relationship with those among whom he has been living. The Beast has emerged, the Delirium has engaged, and the character will never be completely trusted again.

Howls

Werewolves' howls are their most powerful and evocative means of expression. By howling, Garou may condense enormous amounts of information into a few notes. Mastering the myriad howls is the life's work of a Moon Dancer.

Howls are usually begun by one Garou, but often joined by others. Regardless of which howl is employed, harmony is disdained and cacophony is actively sought. When two Garou hit the same note, one instinctively alters pitch, thereby retaining the sought-after discord. The pack uses such tactics to make it seem larger than it is, and foes are thereby intimidated.

There are many types of howls; here are a few of the more common ones:

Anthem of War — To summon or rally the troops (proud energetic howls).

Call for Succor — To get aid (bark of a lost puppy).

Call to Hunt — To alert others to the position of prey (low ululation).

Chant of Challenge — To incite a fight, used by initiator of a challenge (barks and growls of self-praise, and aimed insults).

Curse of Ignominy — To mock those who have fallen from favor (snarling whine).

Howl of Introduction — Used when entering the area of another Garou, pack or sept; to let others know that you wish for permission to enter and intend no harm (warbling howl mixed with barks).

Dirge for the Fallen — A requiem for the honored dead (somber, low-pitched, drawn-out howl).

Snarl of Precedence — To claim an opponent for one-on-one combat (closed-teeth howl).

Song of Mockery — The Garou version of the "finger," added to any other howl (particularly annoying pitch parody).

Symphony of the Abyss — Used by Black Spiral Dancers when hunting to terrify foes (reverberating, mad whine).

Wail of Foreboding — General danger signal, often used to warn of natural disasters (wailing, rolling howl).

Warning of the Wyrm's Approach — (very sharply pitched howl, emitted in a series of brief staccato bursts).

Each area tends to have something akin to a local dialect in its howls, with particular tones and phrases equating to familiar sights, names and sounds. A great deal of information can be transmitted in this way.

As it's highly unlikely that all of the players in a game of **Apocalypse** are going to be able to master these howls, it is perfectly acceptable to call out the name of the Howl you are performing instead of actually howling.

Experience

Experience in **Laws of the Wild** is represented by giving each character one to three experience points at the end of each session. The number of points awarded is based on how well a character performed during the course of the story and how active a player was in the game. The Narrator decides how many points each player receives upon completion of the session. All players receive one point — this is standard. Exceptional roleplayers, those who played an exceptionally memorable part, should receive two. Three points should be awarded to those characters who performed acts of incredible insight and courage, making the game more memorable for everyone involved. On a normal night, each player will receive one experience point.

If you are a Narrator, you should be consistent and fair in awarding experience. Do it in the open, and be prepared to explain the rationale for your decisions. If the players disagree, hear them out and make sure you know the whole story, then award experience to those who have earned it.

Be careful, as awarding too many experience points can make characters too powerful too quickly. On the other hand, awarding too few disheartens the players and seriously damages their sense of achievement. Awarding experience points, therefore, requires a delicate balance between satisfying players and maintaining the integrity of the game.

• **Automatic** — Each character receives one Experience point per game. This represents the acquisition of common, everyday knowledge.

• **Roleplaying** — Narrators should encourage roleplaying. The best way to do this is to reward it tangibly with Experience.

• **Leadership** — You should award one point to each of those few players who had starring parts in a story. Someone who got involved, and by her efforts propelled the plot, deserves a third point. It should be noted that if more than one of the players were integral to the progression of the story, each of the players who showed such leadership should be awarded a point.

Using Experience

Experience points may be spent to purchase new Abilities, Traits and Gifts, improving a character and giving the player a sense of satisfaction as he watches his character grow more potent. The following chart lists the costs for improving Traits, Abilities and Gifts.

New Attribute Trait — One experience per Trait.

New Ability — One experience per Ability Trait.

New Gift — Three experience points for Basic Gifts, six for Intermediate Gifts and nine for Advanced Gifts. (**Note:** You must have enough Renown and be of the appropriate Rank to take a Gift. If you are of the appropriate Rank but don't have a Renown Trait that's not "spoken for," you cannot learn a new Gift. On the other hand, you can have all the Renown in the world but cannot learn Gifts past your Rank limits.) It costs an additional point to learn a Gift outside of your breed, auspice or tribe.

New Rite/Ritual — Two experience points for Basic, four for Intermediate, and six for Advanced Rites. (Note: Rites and rituals only cost experience points to buy if they are not available to be learned during game play. In that case, they cost only time.)

New Gnosis — Three experience per Trait.

New Rage — Three experience per Trait.

New Willpower — Three experience per Trait.

Buy off Negative Trait — Two experience per Trait.

Buy off a Notoriety Trait — Two experience per Trait.

Chapter Five: Extras, Extras

The wolf sniffed noses with him, and soon
they played about in the nervous, half-coy way
with which fierce beasts belie their fierceness.
— Jack London, *The Call of the Wild*

The Litany and The Silver Record

The Litany

Will you teach your children what we have taught our children? That the earth is our mother? What befalls the earth befalls all the sons of the earth.
— Chief Seattle

This is the great song of the ages, containing the traditions, codes and laws of the Garou. All Philodox are required to learn it by heart, and most Moon Dancers learn a significant portion of it. The Litany is a complex and often convoluted thing, but its intricacies serve the purpose of poetry more so than pontification. Practical application of the Litany is much simpler than the hours-long chants would seem to indicate.

The following are some of the basic tenets of the Litany; there are many others, often varying by sept or tribe.

Garou Shall Not Mate with Garou

If you produce a metis, it is sterile, cannot reproduce and therefore, is of no help in continuing the Garou line. Choose a mate who can help the Garou survive into future generations.

Combat the Wyrm Wherever It Dwells and Wherever It Breeds

Garou exist to fight the excesses of the Wyrm. If you allow yourself to be drawn away from that mission, you are aiding the Wyrm and weakening us all. If you blindly attack any Wyrm-creature you encounter, you will end up dead, quick. The idea is not to die for Gaia, but rather to make those poor fools die for the Wyrm.

Respect the Territory of Another

You do not take what is not yours. You do not claim protection or ownership of land that is already guarded by another Garou. This causes conflicts between Garou, which is bad for Gaia because it weakens us in our battle against the Wyrm.

Accept an Honorable Surrender

We are too few in number to go about killing each other every time someone gets offended. Duels to the death aid only the Wyrm. When a fellow Garou surrenders, accept your victory graciously and go back to fighting the Wyrm.

Submission to Those of Higher Station

Accept any reasonable request from someone who has been around long enough to have earned more Renown than you. You want to be respected for your deeds, so respect others for theirs.

Respect for Those Beneath Ye - All Are of Gaia

Lead by example. Teach through your actions. You will not always be strong, and those you help as you climb upward will be met again on your way down.

Do Not Suffer Thy People to Tend Thy Sickness

We no longer live in a time when the old and enfeebled must go into the wood to die. Instead, they can remain active members of the tribe, and their wisdom benefits the young. However, do not make yourself a burden to your people by expecting them to take care of you. Do not fight to remain in a position you are no longer best suited to hold.

The First Share of the Kill for the Greatest in Station

When you are leader, it will be your right and responsibility to make the decisions concerning the spoils of war. Until then, give your leaders the rights due to them from their station and demand responsibility for their actions, or challenge them. If you serve as the leader, remember that the spoils of war should go to the Garou who can best use them to aid the whole group.

The Leader May Be Challenged at Any Time During Peace

If you feel you would make a better leader, prove it. Take the position from the current leader — but only when the pack is not endangered by the challenge.

The Leader May Not Be Challenged During Wartime

Do not fight amongst yourselves while trying to fight the Wyrm. Do your internal fighting in private, and always show a united face to our enemies.

Circumstances must be most dire before you move against a leader while a threat to the group exists. If you are right in this desperate challenge, you will not be punished. If you are wrong, however, the Nation will know of your punishment, and the Galliards will sing of it for lifetimes to come.

Ye Shall Not Eat the Flesh of Humans

Regardless of the original reason for this part of the Litany, it has become a clear health issue. What humans eat and do in their Wyrm-tainted cities has made their meat bitter. Devouring it has made more than one Garou ill — and there is always the threat of creeping Wyrm-taint.

The Veil Shall Not Be Lifted

The very few times that Garou have allowed humans to know of their existence, it brought tragedy and death to many involved. We are hunted, and we serve Gaia best by turning hunters against the Wyrm rather than toward ourselves and our children.

Ye Shall Take No Action That Causes a Caern to Be Violated

If your choice of actions causes the Garou to lose one of their few remaining places of power and Gaia's strength, you will die.

Breaking the letter of the law of the Litany is not necessarily punishable by death. Major, tragic events must result from a violation of the Litany for Garou to order one of their own slain. In fact, the notion of the "letter" of the Litany is somewhat misleading, as the Litany does not exist in written form *per se*. While there are pictograms that depict each basic idea of the Litany, and oral lore, which takes many days to recite, there is no strict published version of the Litany annotated with footnotes. There can never be one, for each tribe, auspice and breed has given its own "interpretations" to the Litany — making the notion of a definitive version highly unlikely. However, the spirit of the Litany is preserved from version to version; among all Garou, the Litany is used to keep the peace and resolve conflicts.

The Silver Record

A myth is a metaphor for a mystery beyond human comprehension. It is a comparison that helps us understand, by analogy, some aspect of our mysterious selves. A myth, in this way of thinking, is not an untruth but a way of reaching profound truth.

— Joseph Campbell

The Silver Record is the only complete record of the Garou. It exists as pictograms, each one a reminder of one tale in the history of the Garou. All the great, Glorious, Honorable and Wise achievements of the Garou heroes are recorded in the Silver Record. All the Inglorious, Unwise and Dishonorable failures of those same Garou and others are also in the Record. If something happens that is important to the Garou as a whole, its tale is incorporated into the Silver Record, no matter what.

The Record begins with Phoenix, the first of Gaia, and continues down to the present day. It tells of the forming of the Triat, the First Times, the coming of the Gurahl, the Imbalance, the coming of the Garou, the One Tribe, the War of Rage, the splitting of the tribes, the Impergium, the forming of the Litany, the coming of the Black Spiral Dancers, the loss of the Croatan, the murder of the Bunyip and other events that have impacted the Garou.

No one Garou claims to know the entire Silver Record, but it is believed that if all Garou who know parts of it were to come together, none of it would be missing. All tribes must agree as to what is worthy of mention in the Silver Record; it is one of the bonds that unite all Garou.

Caerns

Places of Power

In certain areas where the Gauntlet is weak, wondrous things happen and the planet somehow seems more *alive*. The Garou know of these places and hold them dear; these holy places are called caerns. Garou defend their caerns fiercely and protect them from mages (who would drain them), vampires (who would control or destroy them) marauding spirits (who would eat away their energy) and the minions of the Wyrm (who would corrupt and destroy them).

Each caern has a rating from one to five, and is dedicated to a general purpose, like war or healing. A caern draws spirits of like nature to itself, and all rites performed at the caern have a slight tendency toward the direction of the caern's affinity.

Storytellers are advised to work with the players in designing the caern(s) with which the characters are going to be interacting. Caerns are rare things, and the more powerful the caern, the greater the characters' numbers and abilities must be in order to protect it from being found and overrun by the Wyrm's minions.

Access to a caern is something that is necessary for Garou to advance and learn new Gifts. Moreover, caerns can serve as neutral ground where characters can talk, as a place where spirits can set them on quests, and as other vital locations within your stories. On the other hand, your Garou storylines will die if the characters do not have access to a caern that has the properties instrumental to the characters' plotlines and goals.

Caern Chart

Caern Level	Gauntlet	Moon Bridge Distances*
1	4	1,000 miles
2	4	2,000 miles
3	3	3,000 miles
4	3	6,000 miles
5	2	10,000 miles

*The distance that can be traveled via Moon Bridge is determined by the rating of the caern being traveled from. Without a caern, Moon Bridges allow travel only up to 1,000 miles.

Be very careful in allowing your players to open Moon Bridges. Limitations of logistics and space can make it very difficult to run successful games when one pack is at the "home" caern, another is in the Amazon rainforest and a third is cavorting around the Schwarzwald.

Caern Types

Type	Power**	Spirits Encountered***
All	Open Moon Bridge†	Nature-spirit, Ancestor-spirit
Enigmas	*Enigmas* Ability	Illusion, Shadow, Chameleon-spirit
Gnosis	Gnosis Traits	Engling, wraith
Healing	Health Levels	Peace, Calm, Water elemental
Leadership	*Leadership, Intimidation*	War, Bird-spirit, Ancestor-spirit
Rage	Rage Traits	War, Pain, Glory-spirit
Stamina	Damage Resistance	Protection, Guardian
Strength	Physical Traits	War
Urban	*Streetwise*	City elemental
Visions	Oracular Visions	Bird-spirit
Will	Willpower	War, Honor-spirit
Wisdom	*Ritual, Expression*	Owl-spirit, Wisdom-spirit
Wyld	Anything, Any	Wyldling

**One Trait/level/effect is gained (see *Rite of the Open Caern*).

***These are the spirits most often encountered near caerns of that type.

†See *Rite of the Opened Bridge*.

Gathering at the Fires

Moots

Always remember; other council fires have been here before ours.

— Anonymous; from opening speech at a native council

Garou enjoy fellowship with one another, primarily because the only individuals who can truly understand their ways are other Garou. Only other Garou can truly share their dreams and their needs. The Garou are a lonely people, a dying breed. Their culture and their community are the last refuges that keep them sane in a world gone mad, and remind them of all that they are fighting for.

Despite their intense devotion and sense of obligation to Mother Gaia, the Garou cannot be Her soldiers all of the time. They must take time to gather, speak to one another, decide on new paths for the future, and, for what it's worth, have fun. These are the Last Times and the future is bleak, but no Garou will survive if the spirits of all are broken.

Harano, the dark depression that comes of fighting the good fight and losing, is an ever-present danger for the Garou. Although it is chiefly the job of the Galliards to watch their kin for signs of this blackness, sometimes even their perceptive eyes cannot see it coming. Therefore, it's important for a Garou to interact with other Garou and receive the spiritual and emotional support such contact provides.

The Moot

Moots are assemblies of Garou that combine social, religious and political functions, and thus, are tremendously important. Moots provide a lifeline of spirituality, strength, culture, law, tradition, honor and history that stretches into the deepest primeval times, back to the First Pack.

A general moot structure is given below for the sept moot. This is the most common type of moot that the characters will likely attend. Such moots are generally held monthly at any given sept's caern. Any Garou can attend, but Garou not of the sept are often viewed with suspicion.

Narrator's Note: The moot structure below is a general guideline. Each tribe has its own way of doing things. Alter or add to it as you see fit.

The Fool

It is tradition among the Garou that a Fool should be appointed for any moot. What the Fool does and says is never held against him. He can caper and dance, make fun of the Litany and dispute the word of anyone without retribution. Many of the more traditional septs always have a Fool, who provides a counterpoint so that the other Garou can show their feelings. In return, the Garou are supposed to affirm their heritage by

refuting the claims of the Fool. Of course, when a Fool agrees with a sept, that is also an insult; after all, he is a Fool.

After the moot, the Fool's privileges are suspended, and his words in the moot are supposed to be forgotten and/or forgiven. This is often hard for Garou to do, which is why many Fools don't go completely overboard — a wise Fool nettles where he can do the most good. The Master of the Rite appoints the Fool for a moot; the position is usually held by a Ragabash, although not always.

The Opening Howl

All moots start with the howl. From among the Galliards, a Master of the Howl is chosen. The Master of the Howl is honored for his participation, and it is his voice which starts the sometimes-booming opening howl. After the last strains of the howl die down, the Master of the Rite recites the Litany. The Fool reacts vehemently to the Litany, offering wild suggestions at every point.

Lately, among septs where there are more than one or two lupus, there is a second howl, a single mournful song that is supposed to remind everyone of the dwindling number of wolf kin. It echoes the fact that these are the Last Times. A lupus may take offense at a moot if the Mournful Howl is not sung.

The Inner Sky

This part of the moot starts in silence, and a Theurge who is named the Caller of the Wyld steps forward and, sometimes with four other helpers, addresses the five directions (North, South, East, West and Within), asking for their aid in the moot. The Caller then calls up the totem or totems of the caern, and asks for their presence.

Traditionally, some Garou take the part of the totems of the sept, dressing in masks and costumes to reflect the totem's nature. These performers are called the Shining Ones, and they symbolize the totem for the moot.

The Inner Sky is meant to be a method by which the Garou renew ties of community and respect with their totem and the spirits around them. If this thanking of the spirits is neglected at a caern for more than nine months, the power of the caern dwindles. A weakened caern can be revitalized at a moot through the normal expenditure of Gnosis by anyone present who is at the Wyrm Foe stage. This is done by spending a temporary Gnosis Trait to feed the caern forces. Once a caern is allowed to lapse into total dormancy, it must be reawakened with a moot at which one permanent Gnosis must be spent for every level of power of the caern.

Narrator's Notes: This is a good time to honor and thank your Spirit Keeper for the work he does at the caern. Have him play the totem and receive thanks from the Garou in this fashion. Every job should have its little perks.

Calling the Winds

One important aspect of the Inner Sky portion of the moot is that it renews the connection that the Garou have with their related spirits. Below is a sample "script" for use during the Inner Sky:

Caller of the Wyld: We have gathered in this sacred place of Gaia, having called our brothers and sisters of Gaia, and we now call our brothers and sisters of Luna.

(She faces East)

East wind! Bringer of the dawn of clear air! East wind! You who showed us the mirror side, the other side of the Velvet Curtain, come to us! We thank you for your clear thought and bright light!

(She turns to her right, to the South)

South wind! Bringer of the eternal fire! South wind! You who gave us the fire of rage within, that we may strike swiftly against our enemies, come to us! We thank you for your fiery anger and your guardian protection!

(She turns to her right, to the West)

West wind! Bringer of the rain! West wind! You who gave us the Changing Ways, come to us! We thank you for the many shapes you've shared with us!

(She turns to her right, to the North)

North wind! Bringer of cold from the mountain! North wind! You who brought us the Gifts and the Sacred Ways, come to us! We thank you for your great wisdom and strength!

(She stands with her hands above her, her eyes to the sky in the spring or summer, or with her hands pointing palms-down, her eyes to the ground in fall or winter.)

Inner wind! Bringer of blessings from Gaia, from within us! You who hold our Mother's power within us, come to us all! We thank you for your spirit and your inner peace!

Cracking the Bone

As the moon rises toward its zenith in the night sky, the Master of the Howl signals for the stage of the moot known as Cracking the Bone. This is done with a high keening howl that ends in a jagged, shattering note, much like the splintering of a tough, dry bone. This is the traditional time when those at the moot may make their grievances known, petition their peers for judgment on some matter, and propose or question sept policy.

Traditionally, a Philodox elder presides over Cracking the Bone, and in doing so, bears the coveted title of Truthcatcher. He alone recognizes those who would speak, and gives them permission to do so, at least among the more structured septs. The eldest among those gathered are generally allowed to bring any grievance forth first. Some septs have a "talking bone" that is passed about to remind those present of who currently has the right to speak.

Grievances can be almost anything — requests for arbitration between two Garou, accusations of violating the Litany, requests for approval in endeavors or simple requests for advice. In any case, all members of the sept are allowed to hear any part of Cracking the Bone, and in some tribes serve as a jury of one's peers. The Truthcatcher can interrupt at any time, asking questions or demanding clarification. Once all is said and done, it is he who hands down the final decision, the final ruling, and if appropriate, the punishment.

Different auspices show markedly different behaviors during Cracking the Bone. The Ahroun eagerly suggest trials by combat, while the Theurges remain a little distant. Philodox often become entranced by the quest for truth that they see as the core of this stage of the moot. The Ragabash shuffle, impatient at the seriousness of the whole affair, and the Galliards nearly burst as the Stories and Songs portion of the moot draws near.

Stories and Songs

Once again, the Master of the Howl assumes the mantle of authority and declares the beginning of the Time of Tales. At this signal, the Talesinger rises and leads the gathered Garou in a eloquent howl that runs the entire range of the wolf's scale, from the highest inaudible whine to a low bass rumbling that is felt more than heard.

This is the time when all Garou are reminded of what it means to be the Chosen Ones of Gaia. In story and song, parable and poem, the antics, heroics and sacrifices of those who came before this generation are retold with an energy and pride that imbues the listener with the strong sense of belonging that is at the core of Garou society. The Time of Tales is not just a time to remember the past, however. New tales are told about Garou now sitting at this very gathering. Those among the sept who have excelled beyond (or lagged behind) their peers may hear their names brought up by the Talesinger and her assistants.

The Talesinger is the moot position coveted above all others by the Galliards. To them, it is the ultimate canvas, the primary stage. By reciting the ancient lore of her kind and adding her own verses, a Talesinger can achieve a sort of immortality in the annals of the Garou's oral legacy.

Few hopeful Garou of any auspice miss this part of the moot, however, because being included in the evening's tales (which is complimentary, at the very least) can mean gifts of Renown for the recipient. In some septs, any Garou may petition the Talesinger for the chance to tell a tale to the collected Garou. In other septs, this would be considered brash and boastful, and another Garou, preferably a Galliard, must be convinced or asked to speak on behalf of the petitioner.

Regardless of the niceties, those gathered listen to each and every tale told, and once they are done, the Talesinger asks if anyone present would speak against the supplicant. Offering opposition is a very serious insult, akin to calling the Renown supplicant a liar, but it is an insult that must be borne

out. The challenger may tell her own tale. Once it is finished, the Talesinger appeals to the collected Garou for a decision. Those who support the claim to Renown call out first, and when their howls die down, those who dissent raise their voices. From this, the Talesinger judges whether to award the Renown or not (and if so, she suggests which Traits should be bestowed).

This process is repeated for as many petitions as the Talesinger will grant. If the "stage" is crowded, some may have to wait until the next moot.

Note: This is the roleplaying side of the Renown system. Characters must still receive the approval of auspice elders, etc. in order to gain Renown. On the other hand, if the entire sept feels that a character deserves a little extra Renown, a Storyteller can certainly use her discretion.

The Revel

While the members of the sept are still heady from the inspiring stories of the Talesinger, the Master of the Howl lets her gaze pass silently over the masses of Garou until she locks eyes with the Garou who might be this moot's Wyrm Foe. This Garou, who leads the Revel, represents the consummate warrior.

It is no surprise that many eager Ahroun desperately try to catch the Master of the Howl's gaze. Once eyes meet, the would-be Wyrm Foe rises and closes with the Master of the Howl. The two circle each other in an intense staredown that the challenger must win before assuming the role of Wyrm Foe. In most septs, the Wyrm Foe is chosen beforehand, and the staredown is merely for show. In a few septs, however, the Wyrm Foe has no such warning and the staredown is very real. If she is unable to defeat the Master of the Howl, another is chosen.

Once the Wyrm Foe has secured her position, most of her fellows erupt into a cacophony of howls and yelps; she is expected to quiet them with a howl that rises above the din and demands submission.

At this time, the primal passions of the Garou approach their climax, and the Wyrm Foe is the only measure of control present. She calls for mock battles, ritual hunts, displays of strength and wild dances that channel the vibrant energy of the gathered Garou.

As the energy level reaches its zenith, the Garou channel their Gnosis into the caern to maintain its connection to the Umbra. A caern requires two Gnosis Traits for each power level, in addition to one Gnosis Trait from each Garou present. Those Garou present can be issued cards to represent their Gnosis Traits. They may tear up or otherwise destroy these cards to represent the fueling process.

Narrator's Notes: Preparing for a Moot

You may wish to hold your moots outdoors on private property, especially if the moon is going to be full and bright. If you can't do that, you should create an indoor moot area instead. Decorate the area appropriately, and you may get across the primeval, ritualistic feel of a moot.

Organize the people in charge of each segment of the moot. If you've never done this before, you may feel the need for a rehearsal before the whole sept gathers.

The important thing about the moot is that you keep it moving. If, for some reason, you skip a section of the moot, just go on to the next — it's not going to be a disaster. If you stop to correct too many problems or redo sections, you'll never achieve the roleplaying mood that you're supposed to evoke: that of being a Garou among other Garou.

Other Types of Gatherings

Aside from the moot, there are many other gatherings that occur in and around the sept. Indeed, there are almost always Garou around a caern. They come for a sense of community. They come to share concerns, report to their elders and simply to rest on Gaia's sacred ground. Here are some of the lesser gatherings that the Garou hold around their caerns' fires.

Moon Circles

Each auspice elder of a sept holds a gathering once during her phase of the moon. The Ragabash play jokes on one another, discuss dark trouble, play games and go on scouting missions. The Theurges exchange notes on spirit summoning, local spiritual happenings, occult lore and other bits of knowledge while they cast their divinations and tell prophecies. The Philodox engage in monthly verbal dueling, discuss various points of the Litany and go over the politics of the caern. The Galliards hold a bardic circle in which all present must contribute a story, song or at least a poem. The Ahroun stage contests and informal challenges, tease and insult each other, and test their strength and endurance. A favorite contest is moon-leaping, which involves jumping as high as one can toward the moon.

Pack Tourney

Garou often get together in packs that serve as teams for a tourney, which is actually a party/contest/festival. Packs stick together, competing for status, prized fetishes and talens. A tourney is usually held after a particularly important victory against the Wyrm, or in salute to an honored visitor. A great feast of fresh game is prepared. Mead, cider, wine and the purest spring water are all served. Tourneys are good ways to win Honor, Glory and even Wisdom Renown without endangering oneself unduly. Tragically, however, tourneys are often thought wasteful in these Last Days. Still, even the stern Shadow Lords and miserly Bone Gnawers call a tourney from time to time.

Turning the Sun

In order to "turn" the sun, Helios, the Garou stage four special holidays at the solstices and equinoxes. Each holiday has a different meaning based on the time of year. In the spring, there is a wild bacchanal to which many Kinfolk and wolf-friends are invited (and at which many Kinfolk are conceived). In summer, the Garou dress in their greatest finery to honor Gaia on Her day, and many Baptisms of Fire are performed. Fetishes are blessed and

hidden in the Earth in Her honor. In fall, the quieting land is honored, and the dead of the past year are remembered. In the winter, the Garou believe that the Wyrm's power grows until the solstice, at which point Gaia begins to gain strength and power again. Winter solstice is celebrated with a huge bonfire, and many Garou are invested with their new Ranks at this time. Many of the fetishes blessed and created on the summer solstice are produced and given as presents to the cubs of the sept at this time.

Tribal Moots

In addition to the sept moot, the various tribes at a sept may hold moots from time to time to discuss tribal business. These moots are called by the tribe's elder. It is unwise to miss one of these moots, for they provide the elder a chance to guide a Garou's path toward higher Rank, and serve as means of spreading news across the whole sept. Tribal moots tend be less formal than sept moots.

The Council of Elders

From time to time, all the elders of the sept are called together by the sept leader to cloister themselves in a clearing, cave or some similar area. The Garou elders meet and discuss problems pertaining to the sept, and they emerge only when they are all in agreement. A rattle, staff or some similar symbol is passed from hand to hand as a representation of the right to speak at such a council; none in attendance may speak unless he holds the symbol. These meetings go on into the late hours, and hard-headed elders often keep others from leaving until their points have been won.

Harano

Harano is an inexplicable gloom and inexpressible longing for unnamable things; some say it is caused by contemplation of Gaia's suffering. Garou who suffer from Harano are prone to depression, lassitude and sudden mood swings. They may not act at all, or may explode into intense but ill-advised activity; one never knows. What is certain is that a Garou suffering from Harano is certainly not at his best, and may well be a liability to his pack, his sept and the fight for Gaia.

It is not common for a Garou to plunge into Harano, but it happens often enough for it to be a concern. Any Garou who has suffered some sort of crushing defeat recently (losing in combat, failure of a plan, loss of a loved one, extended humiliation) must make a Mental Challenge against 10 Traits. If he fails, he slips into Harano. While this condition is not permanent, the gloom of Harano is hard to lift.

A player whose character suffers from Harano must make a Willpower Test against 7 Traits each scene. If he fails, the Garou plunges into either:

• Frantic, desperate activity — The Garou must succeed on a Simple Test to avoid acting immediately on any impulse that comes to mind. Furthermore, he is down three Traits on all Mental and Social Challenges, and loses all ties;

• Deep gloom and depression — The Garou must succeed on a Simple Test to act at all. Otherwise he simply curls up and hopes the world goes away. In addition, he is down three Traits on all Mental and Social Challenges and loses all ties.

These effects last for the duration of a scene. A new test must be made at the beginning of the next scene.

Furthermore, the senses of any Garou in Harano are inevitably distorted by his intense inner torment; all Garou in Harano are down one Trait in any challenges involving sight, smell or hearing.

Those who suffer from Harano may have moments of lucidity with the expenditure of a Willpower Trait. This lifts the gloom for as many hours as a character has permanent Willpower Traits. Harano is not necessarily permanent — extraordinary Garou may free themselves from its grip after exceptional travails (at Storyteller discretion).

Fetishes

Sometimes a spirit is bound to an item, infusing the item with part of the spirit's power. A Garou may begin a game with a fetish if her player has bought levels of the Fetish Background, although fetishes are usually acquired or even made during the course of a story. When a fetish is acquired by a Garou, the werewolf must attune it to himself by spending a number of temporary Gnosis Traits equal to the Gnosis of the item. After he successfully attunes a fetish, the Garou may attempt to activate its powers. This is done by succeeding in a Gnosis Challenge against half (rounded up) of the fetish's Gnosis Rating, or by spending a Gnosis to activate the powers automatically. The Garou must win this challenge every time she attempts to use the fetish.

Note: While prop fetishes might be fun to create and add to the mood of your game, it is often easier to create item cards for fetishes. These cards can detail the Traits and powers of a given fetish, making it easier to use the fetish when no Narrators are around.

Fang Dagger

Fetish Trait Cost: 3

Gnosis: 6

Spirit Affinity: War, Wolf or Snake

Melee Bonus Traits: 3

Negative Traits: Short

A Fang Dagger is a blade carved from the tooth of some great beast. It is easily concealed.

After a character wielding a Fang Dagger has won a combat challenge, he may then activate the dagger. If the activation is successful, the damage inflicted is doubled (no more than four Health Levels of damage in one blow), as the fang "bites" deeper into the wound.

Spirit Tracer
Fetish Trait Cost: 2
Gnosis 5
Spirit Affinity: Hunting, Predator-spirits

This fetish consists of an iron ingot suspended by a single human hair. When the wielder concentrates on a specific spirit, the ingot pulls in the direction of the spirit until the Garou puts the fetish away.

Phoebe's Veil
Fetish Trait Cost: 3
Gnosis: 7
Spirit Affinity: Illusion, Shadow, Hiding, Chameleon

A small golden pendant in the shape of a half moon, Phoebe's Veil is attached to a leather thong, and is meant to be worn around the neck. When the fetish is activated, the wearer becomes invisible to both mundane creatures and spirits. This magic works against all senses but touch. (Use the Gift: *Blissful Ignorance* for particulars.) The character wearing the fetish can touch things without becoming visible only if he succeeds in a Static Mental Challenge against seven Traits.

Sanctuary Chime
Fetish Trait Cost: 3
Gnosis: 6
Spirit Affinity: Protection, Guardian, Turtle

This fetish is a miniature tubular bell that, when activated, sounds chimes into the wind. All spirits, unless specifically invited to do so, may not *Materialize* within 100 feet of the spot where the chime hangs free in the open air.

Monkey Puzzle
Fetish Trait Cost: 4
Gnosis: 6
Spirit Affinity: Ghost, Illusion, Trickster

The Monkey Puzzle is a talisman of amber containing a single human hair. When activated, it causes all humans viewing the Garou to believe him to be a normal human, regardless of current form. There are no tests associated with this effect. However, the fetish doesn't mask the actions of a Garou who wields it; maneuvers such as tearing out an enemy's throat will be seen as the act of a psychotic. Kindred, mages and humans with Numina may perform a Mental Challenge against 6 Traits to see through the Puzzle's effects if there is reason for such people to suspect something is amiss. This fetish stays active for one scene.

Spirit Whistle
Fetish Trait Cost: 4
Gnosis: 8
Spirit Affinity: Madness, Discord, Screech Owl

The Spirit Whistle is a small, ivory whistle that makes no sound when blown unless it has been activated. When activated, it emits a wailing scream causing immense pain to all spirits within the wielder's line of sight. Any spirit present when the activated Whistle is blown must win a Static Mental Challenge against eight Traits or flee from the scream's source for the rest of the scene.

Blanket of Peaceful Dreams

Fetish Trait Cost: 2

Gnosis: 7

Spirit Affinity: Bird-spirits

This handmade blanket protects the sleeper from bad dreams and invasion of his dreams. Any creature attempting to influence or harm a sleeper ensconced within the Blanket must win a Static Challenge against the blanket's Gnosis of seven as if it were a Gauntlet. A failure means that the attacker cannot affect the sleeper. The blanket also lulls nightmares into submission, allowing peaceful sleep.

Stone of Wealth

Fetish Trait Cost: 3

Gnosis: 8

Spirit Affinity: Any Totem-spirit

This fetish appears to be nothing more than a very old "worry" stone. When rubbed (activated), it brings the user wealth. Wealth does not always mean money, which is Wyrm-tainted, nor does the summoned wealth necessarily come instantly. Instead, the stone provides the resources a Garou needs to complete her tasks. These resources usually appear in the form of funds or marketable items. The Storyteller is the final arbitrator as to how the fetish's power manifests. Each time the stone is used in a single session, the next test using the Stone during that session is against an additional 2 Traits.

Gaia's Poultice

Fetish Trait Cost: 2

Gnosis: 8

Spirit Affinity: Healing, East Wind, Unicorn-spirits

Gaia's Poultice is an herb-filled bandage. This wrapping, when activated, automatically heals one level of damage from an open wound on which it is placed. This fetish takes one hour to recharge between uses.

Gnostic Bag

Fetish Trait Cost: 4

Gnosis: 9

Spirit Affinity: Engling, Ancestor-spirits

The Gnostic Bag appears as nothing more than a small leather pouch with fringes, odd paintings and Garou pictograms on it. The pouch literally holds Gnosis. To activate it, the user reaches into the bag, "grabs" a Gnosis and eats it. The bag holds nine Gnosis Traits. These can be recharged if the owner expends temporary Gnosis from her pool into the bag.

Heart of the Spirit

Fetish Trait Cost: 5

Gnosis: 10

Spirit Affinity: Any Totem-spirits

This fetish is a small, heart-shaped piece of rose quartz. The Heart of the Spirit allows the character attuned to it to store up to 10 Traits worth of Rage, Willpower or Gnosis in it (one type only; they cannot be mixed).

Storage of these Traits is accomplished by activating the fetish and spending the Traits the character wants stored. These Traits may be called upon with another activation test at any rate per turn.

Key to the Umbra

Fetish Trait Cost: 2

Gnosis: 5

Spirit Affinity: Weaver-spirits

This small key, when activated, reduces the difficulty of passing through the Gauntlet by two, and allows the passage even without a reflective surface. If a character spends three Gnosis, she can take one other willing character with her when using the Key, though she must be touching them skin to skin for the fetish to work.

If a character attempts to use the Key to trick someone into the Umbra for the purpose of causing her harm, the fetish will refuse to function.

Kinship Doll

Fetish Trait Cost: 2

Gnosis 8

Spirit: Any Totem-spirits

This fetish appears to be nothing more than a crude handmade doll. However, when a Garou holds and activates it, the doll announces the location and condition of any one Kinfolk whose name is spoken by the user.

Loon's Refund

Fetish Trait Cost: 3

Gnosis: 8

Spirit Affinity: Cockroach, Spider, Weaver-spirits

This fetish is an ATM card with mystic Garou symbols covering both sides. It is a universal card that can be used in any ATM machine to get $500. In order to use it, the fetish's owner simply needs to succeed in activating it (and has to remember to get the receipt!). If the wielder of the Refund uses it more than once per session, he must make a Simple Test or the fetish is destroyed by Weaver-spirits.

Moon Watch

Fetish Trait Cost: 1

Gnosis: 4

Spirit Affinity: Lunes, North Wind, Owl

The Moon Watch acts like a normal wristwatch that also shows accurately the phase of the moon, except that it never needs to be set or wound. Furthermore, when it is activated, the Watch displays the auspice of any one Garou in the vicinity.

Wise Bag

Fetish Trait Cost: 3

Gnosis: 4

Spirit Affinity: Wisdom, Owl, North Wind, Wolf

A Wise Bag is a bag of tokens, bones and other small items. When the fetish is activated, the owner can reach inside and gain one small "fact" about people in his surrounding area (e.g., breed, tribe, species, vampire, mage, ghoul, Kinfolk, etc.). This bag cannot detect the Wyrm, but can relate knowledge of someone's Negative Traits if the fetish's owner can defeat the target in a Mental Challenge. If any of the pieces inside the Wise Bag ever goes missing for more than 24 hours, the bag becomes spiritually dead and no longer functions.

Rat's Tooth Necklace

Fetish Trait Cost: 1

Gnosis: 4

Spirit Affinity: Rat

When activated, the Rat's Tooth Necklace gives the user the temporary Physical Trait: *Nimble*, the temporary Mental Trait: *Cunning* and the temporary Negative Mental Trait: *Impatient*. Whoever wears the Necklace gains the respect and admiration of all the Bone Gnawers in the area, who constantly try to barter for it, if not steal it outright.

Sands of Sleep

Fetish Trait Cost: 1

Gnosis: 3

Spirit Affinity: Desert, Dream, West Wind

When the fetish is activated and the sand is scattered in an area, all those in the area must spend a Willpower Trait immediately or fall asleep. Even if a character spends a Willpower Trait, she gains the Negative Physical Trait: *Lethargic* for the duration of the scene. Those in frenzy either fall asleep (if they don't spend a Willpower Trait) or come out of frenzy (although they will not be Lethargic at that point). The sleep lasts until some loud noise or other outside stimulus wakes the sleepers, or until they have gotten a good eight hours' sleep.

Baneskin

Fetish Trait Cost: 3

Gnosis: 7

Spirit Affinity: Bane, Wyrm or Chameleon

This tiny piece of spirit, carefully wrapped in leather, causes all malevolent spirits, especially Banes, to react to the wearer as if she were a Wyrm-creature and a trusted soul. Baneskin does not need to be activated, but its effects can be seen through with close scrutiny by suspicious spirits who win a Gnosis Challenge against the fetish's Gnosis.

Tear of Renewal

Fetish Trait Cost: 3

Gnosis: 6

Spirit Affinity: Wolf, North Wind, Engling

These milky-white, tear-shaped stones grant a Garou Gnosis. By spending a Gnosis Trait to activate a Tear, the Garou gains three Gnosis Traits, up to his maximum. The fetish can be used this way seven times before the spirit within it dies and the fetish becomes useless.

Elk Tooth Necklace

Fetish Trait Cost: 2

Gnosis: 5

Spirit Affinity: Elk

This necklace of teeth allows its wearer to run and jump twice as far and twice as fast as normal. When activated in combat, its bonuses are not cumulative with those of other Garou Gifts.

Klaives

A klaive is a sacred weapon of the Garou. There are many kinds of klaives, ranging from simple klaives to the special and powerful Great Klaives, of which only seven are known to exist. Each klaive has a spiritual affinity with War, Thunder, Falcon or Stag, and is considered attuned to whomever is carrying it (at no cost). A Garou must have a number of Honor Traits equal to the level of the klaive she carries in order to be considered its "rightful owner." If not, other Garou will constantly attempt to wrest the klaive from its current owner, either through formal challenges or outright theft.

Simple Klaive

Fetish Trait Cost: 3

Gnosis: 6

Melee Bonus Traits: 3

Klaives, the ritual daggers of the Garou, are rare weapons. A klaive's bite is deep and always causes aggravated wounds. A klaive is always dedicated to its wielder and is usually tied to its owner's wrist to prevent its loss during battle. Loss of a simple klaive results in the immediate loss of one Honor Trait.

Grand Klaive

Fetish Traits Cost: 5

Gnosis: 7

Melee Bonus Traits: 4

Negative Traits: Heavy (for Homid form only)

A Grand Klaive is large, usually as long as a broadsword. Not only is a Grand Klaive usually made of silver, but it is also correspondingly deadly. In addition to its obvious uses, a Grand Klaive typically has two unique powers that its wielder can activate. The first is *Luna's Fire*, which causes the blade to burst into flame. This adds two bonus Traits during combat Challenges and also causes an additional wound on all successful attacks.

A Grand Klaive's second power can be anything, but in most cases it is *Summoning*, which calls the blade to the wielder's hand through the Gauntlet. The weapon must be "stashed" nearby in the Umbra for this power to work; not even a Grand Klaive can be summoned from far away.

Usually a Grand Klaive has a second spirit imbued in it. This second spirit gives the weapon a Charm, which can also be activated by the wielder (substituting her Gnosis for Power).

Great Klaive

Characters cannot purchase a Great Klaive; one has to be discovered or awarded. The powers of each Great Klaive are legendary and dangerous in the extreme. Each Great Klaive has a specific personality and is usually attached to one of the few Garou heroes in the world. A Great Klaive can give the wielder 6 additional Traits in combat, has all the powers of a Grand Klaive and all the spirit Charms of an average totem spirit Incarna.

Talens

Talens are like fetishes, but with one exception: They are strictly single-use items. One Fetish Trait provides a Garou with a number of talens comparable in power to a single fetish, depending on the Spirit Keeper's decision. Talens can be used by anyone who has them. If the possessor of a talen is not Garou, Willpower must be substituted for Gnosis or Rage in order to utilize the item.

Clear Water

Gnosis: 4

Spirit Affinity: Water, Purity, East Wind

This talen contains a purifying spirit in a flask of water. When the spirit is poured into a polluted body of water, up to and including bodies as large as rivers and lakes, the water is instantly cleansed of Wyrm-taint. When consumed, the talen acts like the Gift: *Resist Toxin*.

Pine Dagger

Gnosis: 6

Spirit Affinity: Pine Tree, North Wind

This talen destroys the Materialized form of a spirit upon contact. When struck, the spirit must win a Willpower Challenge against 6 Traits or be banished back to the Umbra. This dagger is made from the heartwood of a downed pine tree.

Bane Arrow

Gnosis: 4

Spirit Affinity: War, Air, Pain

These act as normal arrows but do not require a bow to use. Instead, they launch themselves. When activated and released, these obsidian-headed shafts fly immediately to the targeted Bane (either in the Umbra or materialized on Earth). Bane Arrows automatically hit and inflict two levels of aggravated damage.

Moon Sign

Gnosis: 5

Spirit Affinity: Wolf, Luna, Wyld

When this small waxen seal of a full moon is thrown down before a Garou, he must succeed in a Willpower challenge against 5 Traits or change immediately into Lupus form. This involuntary transformation costs the subject a Rage Trait.

Death Dust

Gnosis: 6

Spirit Affinity: Bear, Wisdom, North Wind

This small jar of dust, when broken open, activated and sprinkled over the body of a recently (within a day) dead creature, allows the wielder to communicate with the spirit of the corpse for five minutes.

Note: Death Dust does not summon wraiths; rather, it brings up the spiritual "echoes" of a dead soul. Wraiths can be summoned through use of this talen if they agree to appear. For more information on wraiths, see **Oblivion**.

Wyrm Sign

Gnosis: 6

Spirit Affinity: Chimera, Uktena, South Wind

This piece of unfired pottery is painted with a sigil of the Wyrm. It causes all creatures of the Wyrm in the area to be outlined in green fire, and thus be immediately revealed for what they are. Furthermore, the Wyrm Sign causes fomori to scream in terror; other Wyrm creatures react less violently. If the sigil painted on the fragment is tampered with, the talen will not function properly. This fact is generally known by Skindancers, who hate Wyrm Signs.

Moon Glow

Gnosis: 8

Spirit Affinity: Lune

This is a single moonbeam caught in glass. When activated before travel in the Umbra, it ensures that the trip is safe (in other words, free of random encounters; concerted enemy action can still disrupt such a journey). Once the user arrives at her destination, the glass containing the moonbeam shatters.

Nightshade

Gnosis: 5

Spirit Affinity: Night, Darkness, Uktena

This talen is distilled from the very essence of night. One fluid ounce of this liquid, when quaffed, turns the imbiber's body into shadow for the next two scenes, rendering him virtually invisible in dark areas and allowing him access through the smallest of openings. Many forms of heightened senses reveal the shadow if it is out of place, but it is otherwise not detectable.

Basket of Bones

Gnosis: 8

Spirit Affinity: Fire

This basket is woven from plant fibers and the bones of fallen agents of the Wyrm. Decorated with beads, it has a handle carved from ash wood. Any one item of the Wyrm, be it a gob of toxic waste or an evil fetish, instantly burns to powder when placed in the Basket. The Basket itself turns to ash after three uses.

The item must fit completely within the basket for the Basket of Bones to work. You cannot, for example, jam this talen on a fomor's head and hope for the best.

Pack Totems

These totems are powerful spirits who are intimately involved with the Garou and interact with them on a personal level. When a pack is formed, it is traditional for one of the totem spirits to take a particular interest in the pack. During character creation, each character has a chance to buy levels of the Totem Background which can be used to strengthen a pack's totem.

Before you play your first game as a member of a pack, you must help your pack choose a totem by the fairest means available. First, total all the Pack Totem Traits that are available to your group, then decide what kind of totem your pack should have.

As long as you are a member of the pack, you gain benefits based on the affinity of your pack totem, and your pack totem is bound to both you and your packmates. If you leave the pack (which is accomplished not by physically leaving, but by formally declaring yourself no longer a member of the pack), then you take your Pack Totem Traits with you, and the pack totem suffers accordingly. If you gain more pack members who have Pack Totem Traits, you may purchase new powers for your totem or upgrade its power level (Gaffling to Jaggling, or Jaggling to totem avatar). Anyone in the pack may choose to spend experience points to give the pack totem more Traits.

Pack totems usually require a minor or major geas in exchange for their patronage, depending on their unique personalities and the power they offer in return. A character can only benefit from the advantages of one pack totem and one sept totem at a time. Personal totems are connected to an individual, but do not grant the advantages of a pack totem, regardless of affiliation.

Pack totems are divided into three categories: Respect, War and Wisdom

Buying a Pack Totem - The Cost

Purchasing a totem avatar costs a base of five Background Traits. Alternatively, a pack formed without a totem avatar can spend five experience points and adopt a totem later during its travels. A totem avatar is an actual spirit who serves the pack's Incarna totem. The spirit is dependent on the pack for its power. In other words, a spirit will never be more potent than the Traits the pack has invested in it. In effect, the pack invests a bit of itself in the Incarna totem and, in return, that Incarna sends a totem avatar spirit of appropriate might to aid and watch over the pack.

Five Background Traits (or experience points) provide the pack with a basic totem avatar to watch over it. The more Background Traits and experience the pack puts into the totem avatar, the more potent it will be, and thus, the more helpful it will be to the entire pack. No more than five Traits may be dedicated to a totem per character (unless, on very rare occasions, the Storyteller gives her approval).

Basic Totem Avatar

When a pack gets a basic totem avatar, the avatar is initially quite weak. It possesses power roughly equivalent to that of a Jaggling. However, unlike a Jaggling, a totem avatar can increase in power through contributions made directly by the characters in the pack. Additionally, the characters can purchase a special affinity for their totem. If they do so, the totem, drawing upon its affinity, endows all members of that pack with certain advantages. Each avatar has its own unique contributions to make to its pack. The bigger the contribution, the costlier the affinity.

A pack's totem avatar begins with the following basic statistics:

Negative Traits: May buy up to 3 maximum

Power Pool: 5

Charms: 3

Willpower: 5

Rage: 5

Gnosis: 5

Abilities: 10 levels

See Spirit Creation Table, p. 192.

Totem Affiliation

The pack must decide who its totem avatar serves. Directing a totem avatar's affiliation can be costly to the pack, but can also provide strength. The different options and their costs are listed below. These costs are in addition to the five Background Traits (or experience points) that the pack initially spends on its totem.

Each totem makes a contribution (or contributions) to the pack. In return for being chosen and choosing the affiliation of the totem avatar, the totem "adopts" the pack and refers to its members as her children. There are two types of contributions: general and exclusive. A general contribution, such as one that grants each pack member an additional Trait or Traits, can be used by the entire pack. An exclusive contribution is used by only one member of the pack. The entire pack must decide who will benefit from this sort of contribution, and can use any means agreeable to come to a decision. If the pack cannot decide who should gain the benefit of the exclusive contribution, then the totem avatar withholds the benefit until the pack can come to a unanimous decision. In other words, the pack must cooperate or lose the use of a potent advantage. Once a pack member has the benefit of an exclusive contribution, it is hers until she either relinquishes it or is no longer a member of the pack.

Totems of Respect

Pegasus

Cost: 4

The Pegasus is a noble winged horse who embodies the pure rage of the Wyld and the spirit of the Wyld flying free. Pegasus is concerned chiefly with sacred places, ever seeking to protect them.

Pegasus gives all of her children an extra Willpower Trait. Pegasus shares her knowledge of the Wyld by giving the Ability: *Animal Ken* x 2 to her children.

Ban: You must always aid females of all species who are in need, especially young ones.

Stag

Cost: 4

Stag symbolizes life, death and rebirth to the Fianna, and they heed his grand wisdom. Stag leads the Wild Hunt and is the representation of the masculine power of nature. Stag gives all his children an extra Willpower Trait and shares with them his knowledge of the woods, giving each pack member the Ability: *Survival* x 2.

Ban: You must always aid faeries or their kin.

Grandfather Thunder

Cost: 5

This totem does not allow itself to be chosen as a pack totem; instead, it chooses which packs to adopt. Thunder then sends one of his stormcrows to watch over a pack instead of a relegating a totem avatar. He never travels himself, nor does he choose a pack that has not requested him. Thunder grants all of his adopted children two Willpower Traits and two Social Traits: *Commanding* and *Intimidating*, plus the Ability: *Etiquette* x 2. All children of Thunder also gain the Negative Social Trait: *Untrustworthy*.

Ban: You should never tell the truth to those you do not respect. You must not respect those you can dominate.

Falcon

Cost: 4

Great Falcon, the raptor, watches over honor and justice in the Garou world. Those who dare to ascend his high aeries come away with stories of glory and honor to match those of the greatest legends. Falcon sends his children to watch over the most promising packs, particularly those in which Silver Fangs are prevalent. The Silver Fangs are served by Falcon, who helps them maintain communication and thus, unity.

Falcon gives all his children two Willpower Traits and the Ability: *Leadership* x 2. Falcon's children gain the Social Traits: *Charismatic* and *Dignified*.

Ban: All children of Falcon must have at least one Honor Trait. Falcon does not lend his aid to packs that are not sufficiently honorable. If any member of the pack ever loses all of his Honor, he must immediately perform the *Rite of Contrition* and do something, *anything*, to regain his lost Honor. Until then, Falcon will not aid the pack.

City Father/Mother

Cost: 3

Each city forms its own spirit, but great cities form City Father/Mother — the city embodied and personified. For example, New York's spirit is a husky Italian man, while Atlanta's is a slightly worse-for-wear (but still beautiful) Southern belle.

The City Father grants all of his children one Influence Trait having to do with his city: *Bureaucracy, High Society, Finance, Health, Industry, Legal, Media, Police, Politics, Street, Transportation* or *Underworld*. In addition, the City Father shares his secrets by giving his children the Ability *Streetwise* x 2.

Ban: The City Father occasionally asks for "favors." Do them, and do them quickly.

Totems of War

Rat

Cost: 5

Cunning and vicious, Rat is a totem of survival but can be fierce in a fight if cornered. Rat provides all of his children with two extra Willpower Traits and an extra Physical Trait: *Brutal* when biting and *Graceful* when hiding or sneaking.

Ban: You must never kill vermin.

Fenris

Cost: 5

Also known as Grandfather Wolf, Fenris is the warrior-wolf. He expects no quarter and gives none. He provides all of his children with one Rage Trait and the extra Physical Traits: *Ferocious, Wiry* and *Tough*.

Ban: You must never turn down an opportunity for a fight.

Griffin

Cost: 4

A symbol of great rage, Griffin is the expression of all lupus' anger and their hunger for blood. Griffin guards wilderness areas and represents the most primal and animalistic powers. Griffin gives all of his children the ability to communicate with all birds of prey and the Physical Traits: *Ferocious, Quick* and *Tenacious*.

Ban: You must not associate with humans, and homids are not usually accepted by Griffin.

Wendigo
Cost: 5

Wendigo is the cannibal spirit of the frozen north who devours the hearts of his foes. He teaches the Garou the wild tactics of the storm in battle. Wendigo gives all of his children two extra Rage Traits and the Ability *Survival* x 2.

Ban: You must aid native peoples whenever they are in trouble.

Bear
Cost: 5

The Great Bear is a fierce warrior but also very wise in peacetime. Children of the Bear are all given the Ability *Medicine* x 2 and gain the Physical Trait: *Stalwart* (this Trait can never be lost, but can only be bid as the last Physical Trait), as well as the Gift: *Mother's Touch*, usable once per session.

Bear is a totem that has fallen out of favor ever since the War of Rage, when the Gurahl (the werebears) fought the Garou. Therefore, it is harder for any pack of the Bear to gain Honor Renown (they lose one every time they gain three), and both the Narrator and the Philodox of a sept should keep track of this.

Ban: Bear lays no Ban on his children, knowing that they are burdened enough.

Coyote
Cost: 5

The ultimate Trickster and the shadow in the woods, that is Coyote. Coyote, the tree root that trips the mighty hero, grants to each member of his packs three more Physical Traits in any challenge related to stealth, the Abilities: *Survival*, *Subterfuge*, and *Streetwise* x 2.

Coyote accepts any old ragtag collection that calls itself a pack, even ones comprised of creatures besides Garou. He literally accepts anyone who will have him. However, all children of Coyote soon discover that they are often used as scapegoats when bad things happen, as Coyote is considered by some to be bad luck. Packs that follow Coyote are not considered to be especially wise (they lose one Wisdom Trait for every three they earn).

Ban: Coyote makes no demands on his children.

Totems of Wisdom
Owl
Cost: 5

Stealthy and silent, Owl is the predator who flies mostly at night. He sees many things and knows many secrets, but keeps his silence. Owl grants all of his children two extra Physical Traits in any challenge dealing with stealth, silence or quiet. Each member of the pack also receives wings in the Umbra that effectively allow flight and double movement rate (it is twice as hard to find your way in the Umbra if you are not following the paths, so packs with Owl as totem tend to buy a lot of *Enigma* Ability). At the Storyteller's discretion, Owl also grants one use of *Omen of Doom* (see Silent Strider Tribal Advantage) at the cost of one permanent Willpower Trait.

Ban: Owl asks that his children leave animal sacrifices to him in the forest, tied in place or caged.

Unicorn

Cost: 5

Proud and powerful, this totem is the symbol of unity and mystical strength among the Garou. Although some think her gentle nature implies weakness, that is a foolish assumption. Unicorn's strength lies in her purity of purpose and the sharpness of her horn. Unicorn gives all of her children the ability to move through the Umbra at twice normal speed, the Social Trait: *Diplomatic* and the Mental Trait: *Calm* in all challenges dealing with healing or trying to resolve disagreements peacefully.

Unicorn balances this by making all of her children down one Trait in all challenges that involve trying to injure or harm another Garou (who is not Wyrm-tainted). Unicorn's children gain one free retest when performing any Gifts involving peace — healing, protection, etc.

Ban: Unicorn asks that her Garou aid and protect the weak, the helpless, the abused and the exploited, but never to the extent of furthering or aiding the Wyrm.

Cockroach

Cost: 5

Hardy, quick and adaptable, Cockroach has been around for a long time, and will be around after the Apocalypse is but a memory. It provides all of its children with the ability, while in the Umbra, to peek into data streams and onto computer disks, "reading" the information that is there by succeeding in a Gnosis Challenge against the level of electronic security. Followers of Cockroach gain the following Abilities: *Computer* and *Science*, and one free retest with any Gift that affects technology.

Ban: Cockroach asks that none of its brethren be slain by the pack.

Chimera

Cost: 5

She of Many Faces, the Lady of Mirrors, the Ever-changing — Chimera is the totem of enigmas and a puzzle herself, all at the same time. She appears in many forms, a different one each time she shows herself. She gives each pack member the ability to change what he looks like in the Umbra with a successful Gnosis Challenge (against seven Traits), the Ability: *Enigmas* x 2 and the Mental Trait: *Insightful*.

Ban: Chimera will not aid the pack if the members do not seek enlightenment.

Uktena

Cost: 5

This dark, powerful and ancient water spirit has the features of both a serpent and a cougar. Uktena watches over and protects his children when they are in the Umbra by giving each member of the pack one level of protection (see the Gift: *Luna's Armor*). Once this Trait is used, it can be renewed only if the character who used it stays in the Umbra for one week.

Also, each time a pack member gains three experience points, he gains one more that can only be put toward learning *Enigmas*, *Occult*, rituals, Gifts or other mystical knowledge. Children of Uktena are down one Trait in all Social Challenges with Garou of other tribes.

Ban: Uktena asks that his children recover, hold and protect (not use) lost artifacts and fetishes from the Wyrm's minions (who sometimes include mages, but always include Tremere vampires).

Antagonists

In **Mind's Eye Theatre**, people who work against the players' characters are called antagonists. Occasionally, players assume the roles of antagonists and face off against other players. For the most part, though, antagonists are played by Narrators.

Fomori

Fomori are humans who have been become servants of the Wyrm. As such, they have been granted special powers and abilities. These abilities come with a price, though, as each fomor is twisted in some foul and perverse manner. Though this perversion is not always readily apparent to the eye, all fomori reek of Wyrm-stench to any who are able to detect it.

Most fomori have Attributes and Abilities similar to Garou, though many may have boosted Attributes in one or more areas (usually Physical). Each fomor possesses some strange ability or power that it may use against opponents. Fomori are not known for subtlety, beauty or intelligence. They are the foot soldiers of the Wyrm.

Some Random Fomori Powers

Extra Arms	Extra attacks (must bid one additional Trait for every extra attack).
Fat Armor	The first level of damage the fomor receives per attack is always absorbed by layers of unnatural fat.
Shark Teeth	Fomor's bite does aggravated damage.
Berserker	Five Rage Traits that work just like those of Garou.
Claws	The fomor does aggravated damage in *Brawl* challenges.
Poison Tumors	Any time the fomor is hit, poison spatters all over the attacker (effects decided by a Narrator).

Or, take a Merit and match it in a particularly nasty way with a Flaw. See "Merits and Flaws," pp. 141-153.

Skindancers

Hail, hail, hail elect of all the devilish, hail! A boon I ask thee, unparalleled Phantom of Darkness, Within this circle I have made, Make me a werewolf strong and bold, The terror alike of young and old…Make me a man-eater. Make me a woman-eater. Make me a child-eater. Make me a werewolf.

— from a medieval incantation attributed to a Wyrm-tainted mage

Werewolves by artifice, not genetics, the Skindancers are known as the Forbidden Tribe. These disaffected Kinfolk have, through a dark ritual, found a way to transform themselves into werewolves. Skindancers have allegiances only with spirits who normally have no truck with Garou. Wyld-spirits will have nothing to do with Skindancers and will not teach them any Gifts. Weaver-spirits avoid them to the point that they will not acknowledge the mockeries' existence. It is rumored that even the Wyrm does not work with these false Garou, for Black Spiral Dancers fight Skindancers at any opportunity.

The Skindancers' totem is Minotaur, a creature like them, made from the magics and science of legend. It and its underling spirits of dark myth are the only spirits known to associate with the Skindancers. The Skindancers have been seen in Arizona, searching for an Enigma Caern that once belonged to the Nuwisha, and in the Pine Barrens of New Jersey. Rumors also have surfaced that one or more Skindancers underwent a conversion, but that upon entering the silver waters of Erebus, they died quite painfully. Most Skindancers have Attributes and Abilities similar to those of standard Garou. They do not, however, possess any Gifts unless they have allied themselves with a particular totem or received instruction from Banes. Those Skindancers taught by Banes bear the taint of the Wyrm. (Further information on Skindancers is contained in **Chaos Factor** and **World of Darkness: Outcasts**.)

Note: All Storytellers should be aware that the process of becoming a Skindancer causes Wyrm-taint, but the taint is not complete. Rough estimates indicate that the conversion to Skindancer brings a Kinfolk about 70 percent over to the side of the Wyrm, but rarely more. Skindancers are not designed to be allies of Gaia's warriors; they are a nightmare reflection of inhumanity, and an object lesson in the perils of trying to become what one is not.

Rituals and Gifts

Ritual of Sacred Rebirth (level 5 Mystical)

Taught by Wyrm-spirit

This heavily guarded secret rite involves the collection and preservation of five Garou pelts (not just the hair; the skin is needed as well). The skins must be from Garou born under the same auspice and may be collected over time (if preserved in the proper ointments and minerals). Then, during the auspice of the skins' former owners, the ritualist sews the skins together and performs the hour-long ritual, after which he performs a Mental Challenge against 10 Traits. Success means the skins fuse with the ritualist forever, and he becomes (for all practical game purposes) a werewolf. Failure, on the other hand, indicates that the transformation did not occur, and that the gathered skins are now useless for the would-be Garou's purposes.

Even if the skins were given willingly (and it's hard to imagine the circumstances leading to *that*), the Skindancer is still only a frenzy or two away from full-blown Wyrm-taint. A successful Mental Challenge, performed by another Garou, will reveal the stitches where the skins were sewn together on a Skindancer's pelt. Once revealed as a false Garou, a Skindancer can rarely expect kind treatment from true werewolves.

Bane Spirits

Banes are created just as spirits loyal to Gaia are, except Banes are servants of the Wyrm. They assume countless forms in order to destroy and corrupt what they can. Some Banes are the avatars or personifications of such principles as Hate and Disease; others are less archetypal but just as deadly. Banes are the most common and direct enemy the Garou have. See "Spirits," p. 190.

Sample Bane Charms

Blighted Touch
Power Cost: 2

If the spirit succeeds in an attack on a Garou, the target must win a Willpower Test or be forced to bid two Traits in any challenge for the rest of the evening.

Corruption
Power Cost: 1

The spirit whispers an evil suggestion into a target's ear. The target must succeed in a Mental Challenge against the spirit's total Gnosis or be forced to act upon that thought somehow.

Incite Frenzy
Power Cost: 3

The spirit can cause frenzy in others. If the spirit wins a Rage Challenge against the target's Willpower (no Willpower Trait bid), the target enters frenzy instantly. The frenzy lasts one scene.

Possession
Power Cost: 5

The Bane may possess a living being or inanimate object. The spirit tests its Willpower against the target. If successful in the challenge, the spirit begins the process of taking possession of the victim. *Possession* is gradual; only after six hours will the spirit be in full possession of the body and able to manifest certain characteristics and abilities through it.

During the six hours spent taking possession, the spirit must remain undisturbed. If it is found and attacked during this time, the link between spirit and host is broken. Otherwise, the spirit takes possession of the target, now called a fomor, and can be attacked without injuring the host only in the Umbra. Attacks in the Realm will damage the Bane's host as surely as they damage the Bane itself.

Black Spiral Dancers

The Lost Tribe was once known as the White Howlers, noble and powerful Garou who were Kin to the Picts of ancient Scotland. They entered the Wyrm's den with the thought of combating it on its home territory…and were swallowed utterly by it instead, then vomited back to Earth as the Black Spiral Dancers. Corrupted in both body and mind, Black Spiral Dancers are fearsome opponents; they usually attack Garou on sight.

When in Crinos, Black Spiral Dancers are monstrosities, with slaver-jawed, misshapen heads and glowing eyes. They often have patchy fur, batlike ears, jagged teeth and other deformities. In Homid form, Dancers are usually physically or mentally twisted, and their features are often describable only as "inhuman."

The totem of the Black Spiral Dancers is Whippoorwill, whose mad call they mimic during their hunts. Black Spiral Dancers are generated like other Garou, but most are metis. Their "Gifts" often resemble mutations, but the exact nature of each Gift is up to the Storyteller. Here are some suggestions:

Level One   **Sense Wyrm** — Same as the Metis Gift.

Level Two   **Bat Ears** — Same as the Gift: *Heightened Senses*.

Level Three   **Patagia** — Flaps of skin, like those possessed by a flying squirrel. When the Black Spiral Dancer leaps from a height, these flaps allow him to glide rather than plummet. The skin flaps exist in all of the Dancer's forms.

Level Four   **Crawling Poison** — The Black Spiral Dancer's claws and bite transmit a slow poison that prevents regenerative powers for the rest of the session. The Dancer must win a Gnosis Challenge against the target's Physical Traits in order to use this Gift.

Level Five   **Balefire** — The Black Spiral Dancer can hurl spheres of sickly green flame. If they hit, the target must win a Physical Challenge (against Eight Traits) or mutate in some harmful way (Storyteller discretion).

Hunters and Humans

Humans present an interesting challenge to players of **Apocalypse**. Garou characters encounter humans on a regular basis, and they can be valuable contacts or deadly adversaries.

Some humans, known as Kinfolk, have close ties to the Garou. These humans have Garou ancestry, but did not inherit the gene that allows werewolves to shapechange. Although most Kinfolk are wonderful allies of the Garou, there are a few who have become jealous of their brethren's power and seek to steal it for themselves. These Kinfolk are among the most insidious of the Garou's many enemies. Some have even become Skindancers (see above).

Another source of great danger to the Garou is Pentex, a massive mega-corporation controlled by the Wyrm. Although some aspects of Pentex are not of the Wyrm — most of the low-level employees are quite ordinary people, and many branches are run entirely by mortals engaged in legitimate business activities — many of its upper-level agents are controlled or possessed by Banes. Pentex Strike Teams and security agents are well-armed and better-equipped to deal with the threat of encroaching Garou. In fact, there are quite a few fomori (see p. 231) numbered among these teams' ranks.

When Worlds Collide

Vampires

Known as "Leeches" by the Garou, these undead beings live primarily in the Wyrm-corrupted cities. They are traditional enemies of the Garou, although not all of them bear the taint of the Wyrm. In fact, some of them have been known to ally with Garou in short- or long-term pacts, and alliances between the two groups are built and collapse all the time. Kindred with low Humanity (more than two Beast Traits) will register as Wyrm-tainted to Garou sensitive to such things. All members of the sect called the Sabbat are Wyrm-tainted, as they have no Humanity at all.

The youngest members of this race have Attributes and Abilities similar to those of Garou characters, although their elders are creatures of incredible power. Vampires have their own powers, called Disciplines, which are similar to Garou Gifts. For further information on vampires in live action, see **Laws of the Night**.

Note About Blood Traits: Garou have 12 Blood Traits. If a vampire drinks even one Trait's worth of Garou blood, she gains the active Beast Trait: *Furious*. The second Trait's worth of Garou blood (or the first, if the vampire already has *Furious*) throws her into frenzy until the blood is purged from her system. Storytellers are advised that the last blood in is usually the last blood out.

Mages

Mages are practitioners of ancient arcane lore, also known as magick. They are humans of great power, and most Garou avoid them whenever possible. However, a few Garou have been known to ally with mages, and occasionally form friendships. Mages practice their own form of the Veil, keeping themselves out of sight of mortals and most Garou.

Mages can add new depth to a story, but should be used only as Narrator characters. A mage can be a useful contact should a character seek an item of a mystical nature. It is possible that a mage could request a service of some sort in exchange for the item. Such contact with mages can lead to a whole series of new stories. A mage could even be a Garou's patron, offering rituals or enchanted objects in exchange for things that the Garou has access to, such as the names of spirits. Some mages seek to steal power from Garou caerns by tapping caerns to fuel their magicks; thus, they can serve as antagonists.

Mages have the usual Attributes and Abilities of the average Garou, with Mental Attributes being primary. Mages always have at least three Willpower Traits, as one must be strong-willed to work magick. A mage may use his magick to warp reality around himself in whatever way the Storyteller sees fit, depending on the mages' level of power.

Mummies

Mummies all have one thing in common: They have received the gift of the Spell of Life, an ancient Egyptian ritual that renders the recipient immortal. Of all the individuals inhabiting this dark world, mummies are the only ones who experience a continuous cycle of life, death and rebirth. They are therefore true immortals and, as such, are rarely — if ever — extinguished.

Mummies almost never involve themselves in the affairs of others, although there is a faction among them that works against a clan of vampires called the Followers of Set. On those occasions when a mummy does involve herself in Garou affairs, it is often for personal reasons — an old friendship, perhaps, or an enmity from a previous life.

Most mummies are aware of the existence of Garou, whom they call Lupines, and are aware of their various strengths and weaknesses. A mummy's typical role is manipulative rather than confrontational. However, mummies' knowledge of Garou weaknesses and their centuries-old skills make them deadly adversaries. Luckily, mummies are exceedingly rare.

Mummies have access to various potions and amulets (many of which can grant them additional traits). A mummy begins with eight primary, six secondary and four tertiary Attribute Traits. Bear in mind that, because of their immortality, it is entirely possible for mummies to have considerably more Traits than listed here. Mummies have literally millennia of life experience, and therefore can vary widely in Abilities. However, each mummy has at least eight different Ability Traits. Some mummies even have magical powers at their disposal.

For more information on mummies, see **World of Darkness: Mummy, Second Edition**

Wraiths

The Restless Dead are rarely encountered by the Garou, as each race has a healthy respect for the others' abilities. The Silent Striders seem to know the most about these driven souls, as members of this tribe are often haunted by the Restless Dead.

More information for use of wraiths in **Mind's Eye Theatre** games can be found in **Oblivion**. Otherwise, use spirit Charms to simulate the powers of wraiths.

Wraiths cannot be bound into fetishes unless they agree to the arrangement.

The Other Shapeshifters

The Garou are not the only children of Gaia with the knowledge of the Changing Ways. There are a few others who can shift into animal forms. In ancient times, the Garou made their bid for clear dominance over the other shapeshifters in a war that began between the Gurahl and the European Garou. The so-called War of Rage quickly escalated to include all of the Changing Breeds. It ended when the Silver Fangs declared it over, halting hostilities before the other races were totally wiped out. The other Bête have never recovered their number, and many have never forgiven the Garou.

The other skinchangers live on the periphery of the World of Darkness, existing as fringe-dwellers in remote places. They tend to be confrontational with the Garou, but more recently, the youngest generations of each kind seem to understand each other better.

These breeds are the ones that the Garou know to exist and are most likely to encounter. Other skinchangers are said to have survived the War of Rage, but this information is regarded as rumor only.

Ananasi (Werespiders)

Totem: Any

In the Beginning Times the Ananasi served the Weaver, but then the Weaver went mad. The queen of the Ananasi went to the Weaver to cure it, but the Weaver encased her in a dark opal and turned her over to the Wyrm. The Wyrm then used her as a hostage to get the Ananasi to serve its corruptive ways. Then the queen commanded her subjects to leave the Wyrm and serve the Wyld to free her. Most did, but in the end, the Wyld's forces could not fully trust the Ananasi. Today, the werespiders protect Gaia and work toward freeing their queen. The Ananasi can survive only by drinking blood (human or animal), have Blood Pools like vampires (instead of Rage), are nocturnal and basically are living vampires. Their forms are Homid, Lilian (eight-appendaged, spiderlike humanoid form), Pithus (giant spider) and Crawlerlings (an army of very small spiders). If Ananasi are needed as Storyteller characters, they should be designed with access to Weaver, Wyrm and Wyld Gifts.

Bastet (Werecats)

Totem: Bastet have their own totems, ranging from Butterfly to Hatii the Thunderer and King-of-Beasts. Garou know little about these totem spirits, save that they are powerful.

The "Eyes of Gaia" have the grudging respect and eternal distrust of the Garou. The watchfulness, curiosity and graceful arrogance of the Bastet throw them into sharp contrast with the Garou, whom they see as crude, uncouth, dirty and stupid. The Bastet regard themselves as the guardians of humanity, so the Impergium drove a tremendous wedge between the two Changing Breeds. In the last century, this animosity has cooled, however, as more Bastet recognize the damage that unchecked human growth has wrought on Gaia. Bastet have access to Silver Fang Gifts, as well as any other Gifts related to social interactions, grace, cunning and combat.

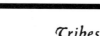

Tribes

There are nine distinct Bastet tribes:

Tribe	Duty	Cat Type
Bagheera	the sages	Panthers
Balam	the defenders	Jaguars
Bubasti	the mages	Egyptian Abyssinians
Ceilican	the mad ones	Housecats
Khan	the berserkers	Tigers
Pumonca	the guardians	Cougars
Simba	the warrior kings	Lions
Swara	the messengers	Cheetahs
Qualmi	the shamans	Lynxes

Storytellers should adjust a character's access to Gifts in order to reflect a Bastet's tribe accurately.

Corax (Wereravens)

Totem: Raven or Helios

The Corax have looked to the sun and wisdom since ancient times. Their alliance with the Garou is almost as old and strong as Raven's brood; the wereravens have closer ties to the Garou than any others. Corax spend their time gathering shiny things and information from hidden corners of the world. Moreover, Corax have often served as messengers between the spirit world and the mundane, for they have learned to travel through the Umbra swiftly. Corax have access to spirit Charms as Gifts, Silent Strider Gifts and any other Gifts having to do with travel or information gathering.

Gurahl (Werebears)

Totem: Bear and Ursa Major (the Great She-Bear)

The Gurahl are pacifiers, purifiers, protectors and healers. They claim mastery of death as well as life, and can step through the Dark Veil into the lands of the Lower Umbra. The bear cults spread throughout the world are testament to Gurahl influences and interaction.

It was a failure of the Gurahl, allowing the Wyrm to gain a foothold in the world in ancient times, which led directly to the creation of the Garou. Conversely, the Gurahl decision not to teach the Garou how to defeat death was one of the causes of the War of Rage. Gurahl can spend Rage at a one-to-one ratio to increase the number of Health Levels they inflict in Physical Challenges. Gurahl have access to Philodox and Children of Gaia Gifts, and any other Gifts or Rites related to healing or peace.

Mokole (Werelizards)

Totem: Dragon

The Mokole call themselves the "Memory of Gaia," and can recall tales from the time of the Dinosaur Kings and beyond. They have fought the Garou since those first times, and since they were wiped out in every region but the Congo and Amazon Basin, they still hate the Garou about as much as they hate humans.

The Mokole still gleefully practice the Impergium to this day. If needed as Storyteller characters, they should be designed with access to Ahroun, Black Fury and Get of Fenris Gifts. A Mokole's full animal form can be of any one reptile type (alligator, snake, komodo dragon). Their monstrous form is always a 20-foot dinosaur of one sort or another.

Nuwisha (Werecoyotes)

Totem: The Trickster, Coyote, the Changing Man

The Nuwisha were once also blessed by Luna, but they took one of their practical jokes too far and now are all cursed to be No–Moons. They see themselves as protectors of the Umbra and teachers of life's lessons through humiliation. The Nuwisha's decision to defend the Umbra before the Earth led to a rift between them and the Garou. Nuwisha have access to any Ragabash Gifts related to stealth, trickery and deceit.

Ratkin (Wererats)

Totem: Rat, City Father/Mother, Thunder (rare)

Ratkin have always been the skulkers in the shadows, the outcasts and the unwanted. Originally, it was their job to keep the human population in check, but when their ways of subtlety and natural selection did not work, the Garou stepped in and began the Impergium. The Ratkin and the Garou fought, and nearly all the Ratkin were destroyed. Those who remained retreated to the sewers, where they breed with the rats that dwell in the dark.

Ratkin are the ugliest of Gaia's children, and they seethe with Rage against those who vanquished them. On the other hand, in recent years they have been known to work with Garou who do not bear them ill will; some claim they have formed a bond with the Bone Gnawers. Unsurprisingly, Ratkin and Bastet *hate* each other. Ratkin have access to some Shadow Lord, Ragabash and Bone Gnawer Gifts, specifically those dealing with information, movement and survival.

Rokea (Weresharks)

Totem: Unknown

If the Garou are considered the most deadly predators on the land, the Rokea hold that title for the waters of the planet. Little is known about the Rokea; they have little connection to Gaia, cannot travel into the Umbra, and do not have any vulnerability to silver. They are mystically connected to the sea and have dealt with recent pollution problems by "removing" the offenders on the open ocean. Rokea have access to Ahroun and Lupus Breed Gifts (adjusted for underwater use).

Kinfolk

O Great spirit, who made all races, look kindly upon the whole human family, and take away the arrogance and hatred which separates us from our brothers.
— Cherokee prayer

Those who are born of Garou ancestry but who do not become Garou themselves are called Kinfolk, and they occupy a unique niche in Garou society (if they become involved with it at all). The most direct definition of the role that Kinfolk take among the Garou is that of second-class citizens; Kinfolk cannot earn rank as Garou can, cannot change forms, are noticeably less efficient in combat and cannot sidestep into the Umbra. As such, full Garou often look down upon their less able cousins.

On the other hand, Kinfolk, both human and lupine, bear Garou children and rear them until their First Change. They also act as go-betweens, couriers, spies and sometimes cannon fodder for the embattled Garou. Werewolves regard Kinfolk as gifted, precious and valuable, but not as equals. They may be friends, but they are rarely partners.

Kinfolk are the buffers between Garou and human society. The vast majority are content with not having "bred true." They revere their secret pedigree, and will do almost anything to aid the Garou fight to save Gaia. Only a few actually grow to resent not being Garou. However, the Wyrm finds its way into the hearts of such Kinfolk and uses them to devastating affect against the Garou.

There are certain advantages to being Kinfolk. While Kinfolk are not Garou, they do draw certain gifts from their heritage. Kinfolk can have Numina (see **Antagonists** for **Mind's Eye Theatre**): True Faith, Hedge Magic and Psychic Abilities. They can learn minor Gifts and rites, and some even awaken their Avatars enough to become mages. Kinfolk are immune to the effects of silver and the Delirium, and they do not panic animals by their presence. Garou law still applies to Kinfolk, but they can get away with a lot more than Garou can because, after all, they're only Kinfolk.

The Tribal Roles of Kinfolk

• **Black Furies**: Their Kinfolk work in politics, business and property ownership, setting up wildlife preserves and fighting for civil rights. In general, the women run the show, but in male-dominated cultures, male Kinfolk are more visible (out of necessity). One European network, the Sisterhood, dates back to the days of medieval witch-hunters, and still works to protect and aid the oppressed, gather occult artifacts and guide worthy Garou through the group's homelands. Many of these Kinfolk wield political power and magical abilities. American Kinfolk often run domestic violence shelters and vigilante teams. Lupine Kinfolk guard the Furies' preserve areas, caerns and shelters.

• **Bone Gnawers**: Members of this tribe have perhaps the closest relationship with their Kinfolk. They form close adoptive families and help each other to survive. Bone Gnawers don't look down on their Kinfolk nearly as much as other Garou do, possibly because of the way the other Garou look down on them.

The Barking Chain is an important gossip network of Bone Gnawer Kinfolk. Members bark and yelp information across cities, and find jobs doing the "distasteful" chores of the rich and powerful, where they often have opportunities to scrounge up useful gossip and information.

- **Children of Gaia**: These Kinfolk often reflect what is best in both wolf and man. Humans work endlessly for peace and understanding through social change, and lupines stand sentinel over caerns and wilderness retreats. Both display greater tolerance than many "normal" members of their species.

- **Fianna**: Boon companions, drinking partners and links in the mystic chain that spans centuries, these Kinfolk tend to be the bards, artists and rabble-rousers of their towns or packs. Unfortunately, the fighting that divides Ireland also divides the Fianna and their Kinfolk.

- **Get of Fenris**: Inspired by their cousins' ruthless nobility, the Get's Kinfolk strive for greatness in all things. The savage Get are as harsh on their Kinfolk as they are on themselves, producing strong warrior lines and some of the most powerful wolves and greatest warrior-heroes of history. Few tribes foster such fierce loyalty — or such rabid hatred — among their Kinfolk.

- **Glass Walkers**: From the safehouses of the Mafia, to the boardrooms of Wall Street, to the Tong strongholds of the Far East, the Glass Walkers have Kinfolk in high places. Such a combination of pressures usually makes these Kinfolk into extremes, either loyal to the tribe unto death or utterly self-serving. They are seeded into executive boards and street gangs. The Glass Walkers tend to keep closer tabs on their Kinfolk than do the other tribes. The few lupine Kinfolk are either zoo wolves or pets.

- **Red Talons**: Red Talon Kinfolk are wolves. Period. They protect and are in turn fiercely protected by their Garou cousins. Red Talon Kinfolk watch and report to the Talons but rarely play a direct role in their cousins' affairs.

- **Shadow Lords**: This tribe exacts the highest toll from its Kinfolk. It is beaten into their heads that in this Wyrm-ridden world they must think like the Wyrm, fight like the Wyrm and sometimes act like the Wyrm. Nothing less than total ruthlessness is respected, and nothing less than perfection is accepted. The constant trials, threats and discipline imposed by these Garou have made their loyal Kinfolk something to be reckoned with, but have also driven many into the coils of the Wyrm.

- **Silent Striders**: All too few of these Kinfolk ever learn of their heritage, but those who do become the most welcome of allies: ready with a warm bed, cash and a safe refuge. Most are also wanderers — Gypsies, drifters, wolves. Few other tribes inspire such loyalty and friendship in their Kinfolk. In return, the Striders respect and cherish their Kinfolk, and never willingly place them in danger.

- **Silver Fangs**: The Kinfolk of the First Tribe are the movers and the shakers of human society, the nobility, gentry and old money. The Fangs' lupine Kinfolk range across huge protectorates, lording over vast tracts of land. Throughout history, the Silver Fangs have wielded power through their human cousins. While the days of hereditary nobility are gone, Kinfolk of the Fangs have risen to the challenge of a new world and excelled in business and politics — fields where ability is often more important than breeding.

• **Stargazers:** The mentor-student relationship that is the norm among the Stargazers extends to the way they treat their Kinfolk. It is said that their lupine Kinfolk think more abstractly than humans do, and are far more wise. Some Kinfolk guard and maintain the monasteries of their cousins, while all tend to reach for the mystical paths and spiritual awakenings that they believe will save the world.

• **Uktena:** These Kinfolk come from native peoples of all lands. They are brought together and given purpose through their kinship. Uktena Kinfolk scour the globe to learn new secrets to bring to their Garou cousins and walk the places that most never even dream exist.

• **Wendigo:** These Kinfolk cultivate the old ways of their ancestors and work toward new beginnings. Ordered by the Wendigo to avoid all contact with the Wyrmcomers, they have an attitude that has given rise to extreme isolationism among their communities. Lupine Kinfolk of the Wendigo roam the deep northwest forests.

• **Black Spiral Dancers:** These Kinfolk make up a sorry and dangerous lot, taught to accept their place or die slowly. They are the stalkers, the serial killers and the other scum that continuously bubbles to the top of the human gene pool. Lupine Dancer Kinfolk are clearly both mentally and physically sick, and they pass their illnesses on to those whom they attack.

Creating Kinfolk

Kinfolk can be created as player characters by using the rules for humans in the **Antagonists** book, or by following the same basic steps as Garou characters, with these exceptions:

Instead of Gifts, a Kinfolk character gets nine points that he can spend in the following ways:

Basic Homid Gift that does not require Gnosis or Rage to activate — 3 Traits
Basic Rite that does not require Gnosis or Rage to activate — 3 Traits
Numina (as per **Antagonists**) — Varies
Merits and/or Flaws — Varies

See also "Kinfolk Background," pp. 49-50.

Obviously, Kinfolk don't get Rage, Gnosis, or the ability to change shape, and certain Backgrounds are inappropriate for Kinfolk characters.

Do's and Don'ts

Apocalypse will put you in contact with a lot of different people, some of whom are likely to be wired on adrenaline and consumed by the danger and mystery of the story. Under such circumstances, intensity can lead to disagreement and arguments, and neither is conducive to having a good time. Listed below are some important guidelines to help keep tempers in check and the story flowing smoothly. Do your part to make everything work.

• **Don't go wild** — The idea here is not to get carried away and hurt yourself. You should never pretend to attack anyone physically, and you should never do anything remotely dangerous. Describe and mimic any action that could be considered even slightly dangerous.

• **Be a teacher** — Achieving victory by taking advantage of someone's lack of knowledge is completely without class. Teach the sucker every trick and nuance beforehand, and then beat him anyway. Now *that's* a triumph worth bragging about.

• **Don't use weapons** — We've said it before, we'll say it again. Don't even carry representations of weapons.

• **Protect the Veil** — Don't perform illegal-seeming activities in public places, and make sure you use prop cards for any unusual items that your character possesses.

• **Don't overact** — Don't act out strong emotions unless everyone present is aware of what's going on.

• **Stay in character** — Step out of character only if you must. Respect others' need to step out of character. Never abuse this courtesy by saying you are out of character just to avoid an encounter.

Experienced players learn to weave the system of challenges into their conversations, and can be rather sly about it; they can avoid alerting the "mundanes" that anything is happening. This is the linchpin of **Mind's Eye Theatre**. Real people try to solve things calmly and collectively, not by slamming each other into walls. Characters should follow their example.

• **Don't debate the rules** — Don't start rules arguments during the game. Call for a Narrator. If you have a problem with a Narrator's call, wait until after the game to argue your case. In the meantime, don't hold up the rest of the plot.

• **Foster intrigue** — Don't ever limit yourself to the goals and motivations that a Narrator gives you at the start of a session — take control. Get involved! After all, it's your story.

• **Create your own plots** — Create your own story and work other characters into it one by one. Characters are made to act, not to react.

• **Watch out for other players** — Keep an eye out for players who look bored; a bored player is the perfect assistant Narrator. Remember that some players who get really bored tend to have their characters start killing other characters for no reason other than to have something to do.

• **Respect the Narrators** — Remember that the Narrators have gone to a huge effort to create the story. Be nice to them. Request their help only when you really need it, and thank them whenever they do come to the rescue.

• **Roleplay, roleplay, roleplay** — Not everything has to come down to a challenge. Avoid "rulesmongering" and roleplay things out instead. A challenge should be a last resort, when players cannot agree upon what should happen. It's much easier and more fun to agree and storytell than it is to play Rock-Paper-Scissors. If you use the rules only as a contingency to fall back on, you emphasize storytelling.

• **Enjoy the surprises** — Be ready for surprises and learn to enjoy them. The world your character occupies is full of mysteries; you shouldn't know how everything works. Treat each situation as a puzzle, and attempt to deduce a solution. That's what your Narrator hopes you will do.

Don't bring out-of-game knowledge to your character. Just because you've read every **Werewolf** supplement cover to cover doesn't mean that your new cub character has any idea of what's happening to her. Bringing outside knowledge in game is called "metagaming," which is a polite name for "cheating."

• **Be patient with changes** — Be patient when things change in midstream. Tell the Narrator about your plot ideas before the game starts, so she has time to prepare for your plot's effects. If your ideas are good, the Narrator will probably thank you and write your plot into the next story.

FAQ

Which vampiric Disciplines work against Garou in the Umbra?

None.

Can Garou Gifts that heighten senses or reveal truth, such as Truth of Gaia, Sense Wyrm and Scent of True Form, be used against vampires who employ Disciplines such as Mask of 1000 Faces, Illusion or Soul Mask?

Yep. These Gifts allow a Mental Challenge against the vampire. A success sees through the Discipline, while a tie or loss still indicates that something is amiss — sort of that anxious feeling animals often exhibit before a big storm.

This sort of power is rife with possibilities for abuse (*"Well, I failed the test but I still know something's wrong so I blast the entire area with my shotgun and then jump on the bits."*), so Storytellers need to watch its application carefully.

Can a Garou be sensed and/or attacked when she "peeks" from the Umbra?

No, nor can Disciplines be used against the Garou, as long as he remains in the Umbra.

How big does a reflective surface have to be for a Garou to use to step sideways, and can it be in the Umbra?

The "mirror" must be shiny enough for light to glint off it; pools of quicksilver, actual mirrors and chrome bumpers all work, and the surface can be in either the Realm (physical reality) or the Umbra. The size of the object used as a mirror does not matter, but small objects are more difficult for Garou to concentrate on.

What is the highest possible level of the Gauntlet?

Nine.

Does a Garou have the breed of his father or mother?

A Garou takes the breed of his mother.

Don't Black Furies have to help female Black Spiral Dancers?

No, a Fury can kill any female who is "of the Wyrm."

Tribal Advantages or Drawbacks never require a character to do anything obviously stupid or suicidal. They are meant to enhance roleplaying, not to provide cheap ways to kill off characters. On the other hand, players should be held to their Advantages and Drawbacks as much as possible. Use some common sense.

Can a Garou's tribe, breed or auspice modifiers allow him to have more Traits than might normally be allowed for his Rank?

Yes.

When does a vampire become Wyrm-tainted and when does he become a Servant of the Wyrm?

A vampire is designated as being Wyrm-tainted when he has three or more Beast Traits. A vampire becomes a Servant of the Wyrm when he has five Beast Traits. All Sabbat vampires are, by definition, Wyrm-tainted, and a Sabbat vampire becomes a Servant of the Wyrm when she acquires her third Path Trait.

Can a Garou attempt to track someone using Unseen Presence?

Yes, but only when in Lupus form or while using some form of heightened senses.

Can two Garou with the Gift: Spirit Speech use the spirits' language to speak to each other?

Yes. Just make certain that any characters eavesdropping on the conversation are aware that the discussion is taking place in *Spirit Speech*.

What is the maximum number of times a character can have a particular Influence?

Vampires, Garou, ghouls, and so on can have Influences only up to the number listed in **Laws of the Night** (pp. 29-37). What those specific Traits are is irrelevant.

How often can a Garou burn a Rage Trait to move from Mortally Wounded to Incapacitated?

She can do so until she runs out of Rage Traits.

Does every Garou have a Tribal Advantage and Drawback?

Tribal Advantages and Drawbacks are optional, but a character cannot have one without the other. The character must take both or neither.

*In **MET: Masquerade** and **Laws of the Night** it says that Gangrel vampires do not show a taint of the Wyrm when dealing with the Garou. Only Gangrel with three or more Beast Traits bear the scent of the Wyrm. Is this true?*

Gangrel are the exception to the rule of *Sense Wyrm/Beast Traits*. They "smell" different to Garou because of their "beastly" nature between them, and thus don't hold to the standard rules vis-à-vis Wyrmitude. Use the ruling from **Laws of the Night**.

Incidentally, there is only one other exception: vampires who have achieved Golconda. These Leeches never show any Wyrm Taint.

How do vampires appear to a Garou "peeking" from the Umbra?

A vampire appears as a swirling mass of roiling blackness to a Garou "peeking" from the Umbra. The more Beast or Path Traits the vampire possesses, the thicker and more vicious the cloud appears.

The use of Disciplines cannot hide this effect. Even Obfuscate won't disguise the true nature of a vampire from a "peeking" Garou.

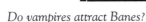

Do vampires attract Banes?

Like flies. Banes are drawn to hate and other negative emotions, which means that vampires and their actions are the Bane equivalent of an all-night smorgasbord. This is not to say that a vampire is likely to be aware of the swirling mob of Banes following him around, and it's not as if vampires actively encourage Banes to follow them around. For their part, Banes don't like vampires at all. It's just that Kindred provide good feeding, and no Bane will pass up the sort of meal that a vampire's night-to-night existence usually offers.

What happens if a vampire travels into the Umbra?

Simply put, a vampire in the Penumbra is in trouble. Banes who spot the unfortunate bloodsucker will gravitate to his position and either attempt to kill him or maneuver him into a situation where he will be killed.

Fortunately, the Penumbra is lit by Luna, whose light is not harmful to vampires. Even daytime in the Penumbra doesn't have a Sun *per se*; the face of Helios is always hidden by thick clouds that prevent a vampire from taking damage from sunlight. On the other hand, there are places in the Umbra where the sun does shine brightly, and wandering vampires must beware wandering into one of these freakish zones at the risk of going up in flames.

Can a Garou see through Obfuscate powers?

When in Hispo or Lupus form, a Garou has the equivalent of Heightened Senses for peering through the effects of most Obfuscate powers. With a successful Mental Challenge(and the usual warning against metagaming), the character can detect an Obfuscated vampire. It takes two successful tests of this sort to pierce *Soul Mask*, however.

What about Abominations?

In a word, no. No no no no no no no. If your Storyteller insists on inserting an Abomination character into his chronicle, the character should remain in Stoyteller hands only, and should be onstage for as little time as possible. Under no circumstances should players be allowed to create and play Abomination characters. They simply unbalance the game too much.

And if anyone in your game has a problem with this, remind him: They're called *Abominations* for a reason. Gaia doesn't like them. Vampires don't like them. Other Garou don't like them either. In fact, the vast majority of Garou would rather end their existences than become a Wyrm-tainted mockery of what they once were. As far as **Werewolf** cosmology goes, any right-thinking Garou would rather do the macarena along the Black Spiral than become an Abomination.

So, in other words, no.

PS-And no long-lost Bunyips, White Howlers or Croatan, either. Extinct is forever. After all, that's part of what **Werewolf** is all about.

Do lupus characters need to invest in Linguistics to indicate that they've learned to speak the dominant local human tongue?

Nope. You get that one for free.

There are a lot of places in this book where a Simple Test is mentioned. Do I need to win these Simple Tests in order to succeed, or is a tie good enough?

Unless the Gift or other power in question specifically states that a win is needed, a win or a tie both work.

What if I want to create a character who's not a cliath?

Talk to your Storyteller about adding (or subtracting) the appropriate number of Traits for a different Rank character. Remember, playing a different rank affects your starting Renown, Trait maximums and so forth. Default Rank is cliath, however.

What happens if I exceed a Trait Maximum after changing form?

Trait maximums are for Breed Form only. Transformations, Gifts, and other sundry functions can raise a character over her Trait maximums.

There seem to be a lot of systems for getting Renown in here. Whioh one is right?

Yes.

In all seriousness, they're all effective ways of doling out Renown.

I've noticed that not all of the Basic Gifts are available to beginning characters. Is this correct?

Absolutely. Some things are worth waiting for.

Mental Traits

Social Traits

Physical Traits

Fetishes/Talens

Influences

Merits/Flaws

Backgrounds

Abilities

Gifts

Gnosis
○ ○ ○ ○ ○ ○ ○ ○ ○ ○
□ □ □ □ □ □ □ □ □ □

Willpower
○ ○ ○ ○ ○ ○ ○ ○ ○ ○
□ □ □ □ □ □ □ □ □ □

Rage
○ ○ ○ ○ ○ ○ ○ ○ ○ ○
□ □ □ □ □ □ □ □ □ □

Rites

Laws of the Wild

Player_____

Character_____

Chronicle_____

Nature_____

Demeanor_____

Breed_____

Auspice_____

Tribe_____

Rank_____

Renown

Honor_____

Glory_____

Wisdom_____

Rock

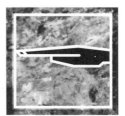

Paper

Bomb

Scissors

You can't
see me

I have majesty

Traveling in
Umbra

Stuck in
Gauntlet

Crinos

I'm in
disguise

Index

THE LONG NIGHT

Live action

roleplaying

for Vampire:

The Dark Ages

December 1997

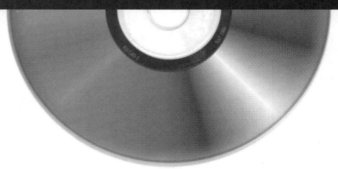